The Breakdown
of Democratic Regimes
LATIN AMERICA

BE

The Breakdown
of Democratic Regimes

LATIN
AMERICA

Edited by
Juan J. Linz and Alfred Stepan

The Johns Hopkins University Press
Baltimore and London

Originally published, 1978
Fourth printing, 1987

The Johns Hopkins University Press, 701 West 40th Street,
Baltimore, Maryland 21211
The Johns Hopkins Press Ltd., London

Library of Congress Cataloging in Publication Data

Main entry under title:

The Breakdown of democratic regimes, Latin America.

Includes index.
1. Latin America—Politics and government—Addresses,
essays, lectures.   I. Linz Storch de Gracia, Juan
José, 1926–   II. Stephan, Alfred C.
JL952.B7   320.98'003   78-594
ISBN 0-8018-2023-5 pbk.

Contents

Editors' Preface
and Acknowledgments

How and why democratic regimes break down are the central questions addressed by the contributors to this volume.[1] Such breakdowns have long preoccupied social scientists. However, much of the existing literature on the subject has focused attention on the emergence of nondemocratic political forces or the underlying structural strains that lead to the collapse of democratic institutions.[2] Implicitly if not explicitly, the impression often given by such works is that of the virtual inevitability of the breakdown of the democratic regimes under discussion. While recognizing the scholarly legitimacy and analytic utility of studying antidemocratic movements and structural strains, we have addressed a somewhat different aspect of the breakdown of democratic regimes.

Given the tragic consequences of the breakdown of democracy in countries such as Germany, Spain, and Chile, we believed it intellectually and politically worthwhile to direct systematic attention to the dynamics of the political process of breakdown. In particular, we felt it important to analyze the behavior of those committed to democracy, especially the behavior of the incumbent democratic leaders, and to ask in what ways the actions or nonactions of the incumbents contributed to the breakdown under analysis. Did the prodemocratic forces have available to them other options that might have alleviated the crisis of democracy? Was the breakdown of democracy indeed inevitable? A closely related concern of the participants was the endeavor to abstract from the historical record recurrent patterns, sequences, and crises involved in the dynamic process of breakdown.

This publication has a long and complex history. Juan J. Linz's involvement with the question of the breakdown of democracy began with his concern with the fate of Spanish democracy, a fate that affected him as a child in Spain and as a citizen. Linz's reading of the monumental work on the breakdown of the Weimar Republic by Karl Dietrich Bracher led him to ask broad theoretical questions, which he explored with Daniel Bell at Columbia University in the mid-1960s. Linz and Alfred Stepan met at Columbia during this period, when Stepan was beginning to write a dissertation on the breakdown of democracy in Brazil, a process he had seen at first hand while writing articles in Latin America for the *Economist*. Other contributors who were at

Columbia University at the same time included Paolo Farneti, Peter Smith, Arturo Valenzuela, and Alexander Wilde.

In order to encourage scholarly exchange on the political aspects of the breakdown of democracy, a panel was organized under the auspices of the Committee on Political Sociology. This panel met at a number of sessions at the Seventh World Congress of Sociology, held at Varna, Bulgaria, in 1970. Before the congress, Linz circulated a short paper titled "The Breakdown of Competitive Democracies: Elements for a Model," which became the focus of discussion by the members of the panel engaged in studies of individual countries and attending the congress. Among the contributors to the complete hardcover edition of this volume presenting initial drafts of the papers at Varna were Erik Allardt on Finland, Paolo Farneti on Italy, Rainer Lepsius on Weimar Germany, Juan Linz on Spain, Walter Simon on Austria, Peter Smith on Argentina, Alfred Stepan on Brazil, and Alexander Wilde on Colombia. Arend Lijphart was a stimulating commentator.[3]

After fruitful exchanges at Varna, we dispersed, with the firm commitment to continue working on the project and to hold a conference in a few years focusing on the comparative and theoretical aspects of our work. In order to introduce other important cases and different perspectives, Stepan encouraged Guillermo O'Donnell to write on the crisis of democracy in Argentina in the decade after the fall of Perón, and Julio Cotler and Daniel Levine to discuss the Peruvian and Venezuelan cases. After the overthrow of Allende in Chile, the editors invited Arturo Valenzuela to analyze the tragic events leading to the end of democracy in Chile.

With the generous support of the Concilium of International and Area Studies of Yale University, and the Joint Committee on Latin America of the Social Science Research Council and the American Council of Learned Societies, the augmented group met at Yale University in December 1973, at a conference chaired by Linz and Stepan, by then both members of the Yale faculty. At this meeting the papers presented benefited from the able suggestions of Douglas Chalmers, Edward Malefakis, and Eric Nordlinger, who acted as discussants. At the end of the conference, the participants decided to revise their work in the light of one another's findings and the collective discussion of areas of similarity and dissimilarity. A year at the Institute for Advanced Study in Princeton allowed Linz to revise his introduction and maintain contact with the co-authors.

Despite the group's interest in underlying, recurrent patterns of breakdown, there has been no attempt to force individual contributors into the procrustean bed of the editors' own thinking. The reader will discover important differences in the authors' intellectual orientations, which grew in part out of the diversity of the democracies studied and reflect in part genuine differences of opinion on the relative weight to be attached to political forces, even after these forces had been given due consideration by all contributors.

It should be stressed that this volume is an initial social scientific effort at middle-level generalizations about complex historical reality. Such a work is, of course, never a substitute for fundamental historical studies of individual cases; rather, it builds upon such studies and, we hope, draws the attention of historians to more generalized propositions, propositions they can in turn pursue further in their own work. Although we are concerned with middle-level generalizations, it is the editors' view that the historicity of macro-political processes precludes the highly abstract generalizing of ahistorical social scientific models of the type susceptible to computer simulations and applicable to all past and any future cases. It is our hope, nevertheless, that scholars interested in developing more formal models may build on our work and incorporate into their models the complex realities here discussed. At this stage of the analysis our collective attention to the political dynamics of the breakdown of democracies has brought to light a number of recurring elements which are discussed at length in Linz's introductory essay. The independent contributions made to breakdowns by political incumbents is a theme that emerges in almost all the papers and has justified our attention to this aspect of the problem, an aspect all too often overlooked. Indeed, in reference to the democratic breakdown in many if not most of the cases analyzed, the editors concur with the remark made by the great German historian, Friedrich Meinecke, upon hearing of the appointment of Hitler to the chancellorship: "This was not necessary."

The individual studies shed new light on some of the most historically important cases of breakdown of democracy, such as Germany, Italy, Spain, and Chile. In addition, some of the less well-known cases forcefully illustrate hitherto neglected aspects of the question of the survival of democracy. Daniel Levine's study of Venezuela examines a fascinating case of political learning. Ten years after the breakdown in Venezuela in 1948, many of the institutional participants in the breakdown—the church, the army, the political parties—consciously and successfully devised strategies to avoid such a breakdown when a new attempt to forge democratic institutions began in 1958. Alexander Wilde's discussion of the reequilibration of Colombian democracy in the 1950s also shows how political learning was crucial for the construction of a consociational democracy. The chapter by Risto Alapuro and Erik Allard discusses the little-known case of Finland, in which, despite intense conflict, the process of breakdown described in other chapters was avoided. The analysis of nonoccurrence as well as of occurrence increased our understanding of the breakdown process.

With the publication of this project, many of the contributors are turning their attention to closely related issues that loom large on the scholarly agenda. High priority for further work along these lines should now be given to the analysis of the conditions that lead to the breakdown of authoritarian regimes, to the process of transition from authoritarian to democratic regimes, and especially to the political dynamics of the consolidation of postauthoritarian democracies.

The editors want to thank The Johns Hopkins University Press for its help in publishing a project of such large intellectual scope and sheer physical size as this one. We want to give special thanks to Henry Tom, the social sciences editor of the Press, for his great assistance. The project would not have arrived in the reader's hand without extensive copy editing. Jean Savage and Victoria Suddard also helped in the early stages of copy editing.

Yale University   JUAN J. LINZ
                                                                    ALFRED STEPAN

NOTES

1. An extensive discussion of the definition of democracy and the criteria for the selection of cases is found in Juan Linz's introductory essay, entitled *The Breakdown of Democratic Regimes: Crisis, Breakdown, and Reequilibration*. This essay is also available separately as a Johns Hopkins University Press paperback.
2. Much of this literature is discussed in the work by Linz just cited.
3. The crisis of democracy in Portugal in the 1920s, France in the 1950s, Peru and Greece in the 1960s, and the continuing conflict in Northern Ireland were also discussed in papers presented by Herminio Martins, Steven Cohn, David Chaplin, Charles Moskos, and Richard Rose, respectively. Conflicting obligations did not permit them to continue with the project. Richard Rose developed his paper in a somewhat different direction and published it separately as a book, *Governing without Consensus: An Irish Perspective* (Boston: Beacon Press, 1971).

The Breakdown
of Democratic Regimes
LATIN AMERICA

1.
The Breakdown of Democracy in Argentina, 1916-30

Peter H. Smith*

Democracies are not expected to break down. Most contemporary theoretical formulations depict democracy (however defined) as the *culmination* of political development (however defined). Studies of political change accordingly tend to focus on the presumed transition from some sort of traditional order through an intermediate phase, perhaps authoritarian, to the creation of a modern polity—that is, a democratic one. And here the analysis stops. The implicit assumption seems to be that democracy, once achieved, will be stable and self-sustaining. The notion is almost analogous to Walter Rostow's concept of an economic takeoff; when political systems lift off the ground, they commence their drive toward maturity.[1]

Like the other countries discussed in this volume, Argentina challenges and even contradicts this formulation. Between 1916 and 1930 Argentina had a political system which met the definition of democracy as a government that "supplies regular constitutional opportunities for peaceful competition for political power (and not just a share of it) to different groups without excluding any significant sector of the population by force."[2] As a result of electoral reform in 1912, instituting universal male suffrage for Argentine citizens and the secret ballot, voter turnout leaped from approximately 20 percent to more than 65 percent, thereafter oscillating between 50 and 80 percent.[3] While the popular base of authority broadened, parliamentary procedure and political parties acquired crucial roles in the articulation and aggregation of group interests. Civilians continued their domination of the political scene. In 1916 presidential power passed smoothly from long-entrenched Conservatives to Hipólito Yrigoyen, leader of the largely middle-class Radical party; another Radical, Marcelo T. de Alvear, won the election of 1922; in 1928 Yrigoyen, at the age of seventy-four, returned to office with a thumping 67 percent majority. But in 1930 the armed forces, in collaboration with civilian ele-

*The author would like to thank the Graduate School at the University of Wisconsin–Madison and the American Philosophical Society for helping to support this research.

ments and with the apparent support of the populace, pulled off a military coup.[4] Argentine democracy was overthrown.

What could have led to this result? Aside from its intrinsic interest, the question draws theoretical significance from the fact that Argentina would seem to have satisfied the commonly considered socioeconomic prerequisites for democratic development.[5] Economic growth was strong: spurred by massive immigration and the exportation of beef and wheat, the gross national product increased by roughly 4.5 percent a year from 1900 to 1930, while per capita income—despite the immigration—grew at an annual average rate of 1.2 percent. In 1914 the absolute level of per capita GNP came to approximately $480 in U.S. dollars (of 1950), a very impressive figure for that era (and I would guess that it was twice this high in the coastal regions and in Buenos Aires, then the center of national politics).[6] Social mobilization was pronounced: the census of 1914 showed that 65 percent of the adults were literate, 36 percent of the population lived in urban areas (20,000 or more inhabitants), and the rate of migration was high. Occupational data reveal that about one-third of the economically active population in 1914 belonged to the middle class—a category that would claim nearly 40 percent by 1947.[7] In short, Argentina presents a case of democratic breakdown in a relatively developed society.

A second characteristic of the situation, particularly important for comparative purposes, is the quality of Argentine democracy. My definition (borrowed from Juan Linz) suggests that democracy is a relative concept, susceptible to various refinements by degree. Robert A. Dahl has argued that pluralism partakes of two dimensions: participation, which is the extent to which people are entitled to take part in the political process; and competitiveness, or contestation, which refers to the extent of effective political opposition.[8] To establish a rough classification table 1 divides both dimensions into three-point scales: high, medium, and low. By these standards Argentina during 1916–30 would, in my judgment, rank high on competitiveness but

Table 1. Classifying Argentine Democracy

Degree of Participation	Degree of Competitiveness		
	Low	*Medium*	*High*
Low			
Medium			Argentina, 1916–30
High			

only medium on participation. Elections were hotly contested and winners rarely emerged with more than 60 percent of the vote; but for reasons spelled out below effective suffrage was extended to less than one-half of the adult male population—and women were excluded entirely (although they were not then seeking access either).

Our task, then, is to explain the breakdown of a functioning but limited democracy in a relatively prosperous society. In an effort to do so I shall first consider the possibility that the political system was overwhelmed by external forces, especially the economic depression that began in 1929 (Argentina was not involved in any wars or other cataclysmic events at this time). Then I shall explore the internal and structural characteristics of the political system which might account for its evident debilitation.

Short-Run Economic Causes

One of the standard explanations for the collapse of Argentine democracy maintains that the worldwide depression threw the country's vulnerable export-import economy into a downward spiral which, in turn, discredited the Yrigoyen regime. Governmental inaction—due partly to the aged president's infirmities—outraged a desperate populace and prompted the military to act in the name of efficiency and economic recovery. This same process seems to have occurred throughout Latin America, where governments tumbled like dominoes in 1930; Argentina furnished no exception to the rule.[9]

This argument finds partial support in a sudden decline in GNP per capita between 1929 and 1930. On the other hand, figure 1 also demonstrates that the drop in income only *began* in 1930. One wonders whether its effects would have been strong enough to produce a violent reaction by the early part of the year, when anti-Yrigoyenist plotting commenced; a revolt of 1931 or 1932 might be better explained by these data. Besides, according to this index World War I had plunged the country into an economic crisis of equal or greater severity, and Yrigoyen weathered that storm without major threats. Gross GNP data do not provide a conclusive case for the short-run economic argument.

We might learn more by trying to determine which groups suffered most from the 1929–30 decline. Figure 2 reveals that the crisis hit the export sector: the value of exports dropped sharply, and continued importation produced the most negative balance of trade in decades. But the fall in exports cannot be traced to the market for meat, where prices and values held firm up to September 1930 (figure 3). Since civilian participants in the coup were closely involved in the production of cattle and beef, this situation cannot account directly for their political action.[10]

The wheat market presents another picture, one in which export values

Figure 1.　Per Capita Gross National Product, 1914–32 (in 1950 dollars)

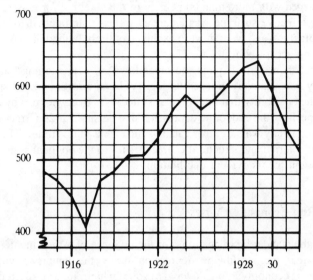

SOURCE: United Nations, Economic Commission for Latin America, *El desarrollo económico de la Argentina*, mimeographed (Santiago de Chile, 1958), E/CN.12/429, Add. 4, p. 4.

Figure 2.　Exports and Balance of Trade, 1914–32 (in millions of pesos)

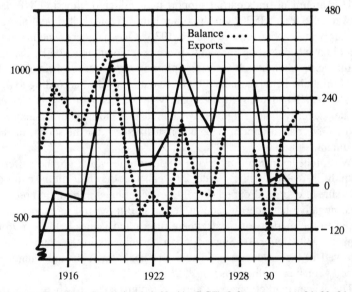

SOURCE: Dirección General de Estadística de la Nación (DGE), *Informes* nos. 11, 24, 33, 34, 40 (Buenos Aires: DGE, 1924–33). Data for 1928 are incomplete.

Figure 3.   Monthly Prices and Exports of Chilled Beef, 1927–31

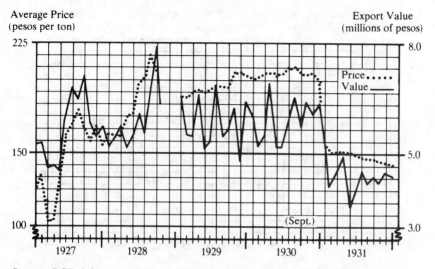

SOURCE: DGE, *Informes* nos. 33, 34, 40 (Buenos Aires: DGE, 1928–33). Data for 1928 are incomplete.

dropped steeply in 1930 (figure 4). Yet this does not explain the revolution. In the first place, this crisis was due mainly to reduction in supply because of drought, not because of Yrigoyen's policy (note how prices maintained their level up until the coup). Second, wheat farmers and other agriculturalists had very little political strength, partly because so many still retained foreign citizenship (about 70 percent in 1914); nor did they make many effective demands in 1930.[11] Undoubtedly there was economic hardship on the grain belt, and some politicians were deeply concerned. But the situation does not appear to have become really intolerable by 1930.[12]

Nor did the onset of the depression generate much pressure from the working class. After a steady rise from 1918 to 1928, a drop in real wages hurt middle- and lower-class consumers. But this reversal did not lead to labor agitation. According to both the number of strikes and the number of strikers, union activism dropped sharply after World War I and stayed fairly low throughout the late 1920s. During the period of democratic politics, real wages were at their lowest and strikes were at their highest from 1918 to 1920, when Yrigoyen crushed the labor movement with military force; by comparison, his second administration was tranquil indeed.[13] It is extremely unlikely that fear of a proletarian revolt or some sort of Red scare could have prompted revolutionaries to throw Yrigoyen out of office.

Generally speaking, the economic impact of the depression does not furnish a convincing causal explanation for the 1930 coup. To be sure, there were problems, particularly regarding foreign exchange and public finances,[14] but

Figure 4.   Monthly Prices and Exports of Wheat, 1927-31

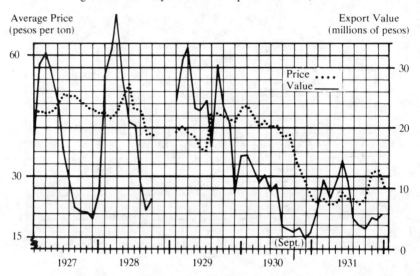

SOURCE: DGE, *Informes* nos. 33, 34, 40 (Buenos Aires: DGE, 1928-33). Data for 1928 are incomplete.

quantitative measures do not show truly startling dislocations or politically "unsolvable problems." And the most significant piece of qualitative evidence is negative. While some civilian members of the anti-Yrigoyen conspiracy referred to "economic crisis" as one reason for their action, most participants failed to mention it or gave it very low priority.[15]

In brief, the economic depression might have emphasized weaknesses within the political system and thus been necessary for the revolution, but it was not itself a sufficient cause. Dahl has neatly summarized the situation: "As it did for most other countries, the onset of the Great Depression in 1929 created serious problems for Argentina [though not in 1929]. But other polyarchies were also hit by economic crisis. Some that were also highly dependent on international trade, like Sweden, and even some that were heavy exporters of agricultural products, like Australia and New Zealand, nonetheless met the crisis with actions that retained, restored, perhaps even enhanced the confidence of their citizens in the effectiveness of their government. In Argentina, things went differently."[16] The question is why. In search of an answer, let us turn to the political arena.

A Crisis of Legitimacy

Political explanations for the downfall of Argentine democracy have frequently been partisan, *ad hominem,* and superficial. One argument stresses

Yrigoyen's age, illness, and possible senility; his government is viewed as leaderless, inept, and riddled with corruption. Another claims that a scheming alliance among all anti-Yrigoyen forces led to a partisan deadlock, denied the will of the people, and provided rationalization for a long-planned overthrow. Still another asserts that Yrigoyen's intention to nationalize petroleum deposits antagonized foreign oil companies, who retaliated by supporting the revolution. Without dismissing these possibilities—though they seem more symptomatic than fundamental—I would prefer to examine some basic structural features of Argentine politics. Democratic systems have withstood inept leadership, *empleomanía*, partisan bickering, and foreign pressure before. What made Argentine democracy so weak?

One way of dealing with this question is to employ the concept of "crisis" as formulated by the Committee on Comparative Politics of the Social Science Research Council. According to this view, political change can be understood as the sequential appearance and resolution (or nonresolution) of political crises in five separate problem areas: identity, legitimacy, participation, penetration, and distribution. Crisis occurs when problems in one or more of these areas require institutional change, and in this case two kinds of crisis are pertinent: crises of participation, which appear when sizable elements of the population, heretofore excluded from the system, demand effective participation in the political process; and crises of legitimacy, which appear when sizable portions of the politically relevant population challenge or deny the normative validity of claims to authority made by existing leadership.[17]

With regard to Argentina between 1916 and 1930, my proposition is this: the electoral reform of 1912 constituted an effective short-run response to a crisis of participation; but its unforeseen consequences created a crisis of legitimacy which ultimately prompted the 1930 coup.

Elaboration of this argument begins with an appreciation of the sequential relationship between economic and political development. In Argentina the formation of a landowning aristocracy *preceded* the establishment of constitutional rule in 1853–62. This was the elite which, while in the process of expansion and consolidation, founded and directed the country's parliamentary system. Throughout the late nineteenth and early twentieth centuries an exclusive circle of aristocrats, epitomized by the Generation of 1880, simultaneously held the keys to economic, social, and political power.[18] They gained control of the army; they openly rigged elections; they made the only major political party (Partido Autonomista Nacional, or PAN) a tool of the administration; and they restricted the decision-making process to their own circles. Congress was not widely used as a forum for the expression of interests, and most significant decisions were made by *acuerdo*—literally by informal "agreement" with members of the executive branch, not by presenting the issues and alternatives to the public.

As these aristocrats continued to consolidate their power, the centralization of authority gave paradoxical emphasis to the fundamentally passive relationship between politics and Argentine society at large. By the late nineteenth century, the distribution of political power had become essentially dependent upon, and derivative from, the distribution of social and economic power. Mobility was unidirectional: socioeconomic prominence was a necessary, and sometimes sufficient, precondition for the attainment of political influence. And though aristocrats built up the strength of the state and used it for promoting economic policies, the political system did not provide—nor was it intended to be—an autonomous power resource.

Expansion of the export-import economy eventually gave birth to middle-class groups which challenged the political supremacy of the landed elite. Allying these new social sectors with *nouveaux riches* landowners and some discontented aristocrats, the Civic Union launched an armed revolt against the government in 1890. After some supporters came to terms with authorities, the predominant wing—the "Radical" Civic Union, or Unión Cívica Radical (UCR)—boycotted elections in protest against fraud and led open rebellions in 1893 and 1905.

Thus emerged a crisis of participation. No doubt these events also raised some questions about the legitimacy of the system, but this does not (in my view) necessarily point to the existence of a "legitimacy crisis" as such. Most opponents of the regime, including the Radicals, seem to have believed in the propriety and desirability of popular elections and constitutional government. Their complaint concerned the faithless violation of the rules, not the substance of the rules themselves. Fundamentally, they wanted to take part.

In time, the Conservative leaders of the old elite found a strategy to meet the situation: in 1911–12 they put through an electoral reform designed to give Radicals a share of power, coopt them into the system, and maintain political stability. Despite the mountains of praise which have been heaped upon President Roque Sáenz Peña for this generous and "democratic" act, it was a calculated maneuver to salvage the prevailing system. Concerned about labor unrest and the apparent threat of violence, Sáenz Peña may have realized that the decision would yield power to the opposition, as it did when Hipólito Yrigoyen was elected president in 1916, but he seems to have understood the underlying commitment of the middle classes to the existing political and economic structure and did not regard their Radical leaders (many of whom were from the aristocracy) as a threat to it.[19]

Two aspects of the Sáenz Peña law underscore the limits of reform. First was the seemingly innocuous requirement that adult males must hold Argentine citizenship in order to vote. Given the large number of unnaturalized immigrants, however, the law actually offered voting rights to less than 50 percent of the adult male population; and since immigrants comprised about one-half of the expanding middle class and an even greater share of Argentina's working class (around 60 percent in urban areas), this meant that suffrage was effectively extended from the upper class to selected segments of the middle class, to the distinct disadvantage of the lower class, especially the urban working class. Second was the so-called "incomplete list," a rule which stipulated that parties could present candidates for only two-thirds of the available seats in the Chamber of Deputies and that individual voters could cast ballots for two-thirds of the vacancies. In practice this regulation usually meant that the first-place party in each provincial election won two-thirds of the province's places in the Chamber; the second-place party got the remaining third; and all other parties were shut out entirely. Thus the incomplete list discriminated sharply against small parties, discouraged the formation of new movements, favored the established interests, and set forth a paradoxical principle: the greater the degree of competition, particularly multiparty competition, the less representative the delegation.[20] In the meantime, national senators continued to be elected by the provincial legislatures rather than by direct vote. Despite the electoral reform, this was to be a limited democracy indeed.

The pattern of challenge and response in the appearance and resolution of this crisis of participation provides a basis for this paper's fundamental argument: that the electoral reform and consequent redistribution of political strength were meant—at least by Conservatives—to uphold and comply with longstanding rules of the Argentine political game.[21] Central to this code was the idea of a balance of power and government by consensus, or what Argentines called the *acuerdo*. Whereas power had previously been parceled out to competing factions *within* the landed aristocracy, it would now be shared *between* the aristocracy and rising middle-class groups (to the virtual exclusion of the lower class). As a result of this understanding, political conflict would retain several traditional features: (1) fluid party allegiance instead of intense partisan loyalty, (2) intraclass fighting instead of class struggle, and (3) continued dependence of the distribution of political power upon the distribution of economic power.[22]

Though it is doubtful that Radicals struck a conscious bargain of this sort, there is no sign that they determined to violate the code. They drew many of their leaders from the same social ranks as did Conservatives, and Radical rhetoric constantly emphasized "morality" in government rather than changes in structure, policy, or procedure.[23] These challengers were seeking power, not alteration of the social system.

More crucial to my argument is the importance which Conservatives attached to the rules of the game. Congressional debates on the 1912 electoral reform reveal discernible traces of these latent assumptions. Discussion of the provision for guaranteed minority representation in the Chamber of Deputies under the incomplete list, for instance, showed the constant conviction that Conservatives would have the majority and direct a kind of coalition government.[24] Thus the reform would guarantee and institutionalize the central tenet of the code: power would be shared among competing factions that would reach decisions by consensus.

Proponents of the reform also appeared to believe that the specific characteristics of traditional conflict would persist. Many looked forward to the reinvigoration of political parties, by this time in disarray, but not to clashes drawn inflexibly along party lines. Legislators should serve the nation, they said more than once, not the interests of party or region. There would be no class warfare: disagreements under the new system ought to be muted, controlled, undemagogic, settled gracefully by "gentlemen." And the retention of Conservative majorities, of course, would ensure that the socioeconomic elite would continue to run the political system. All the rules would stay intact.

Thus many aristocratic Conservatives regarded the maintenance of these norms as essential to the legitimacy of the cooptation strategy and electoral politics in general. To them, democracy would be acceptable only so long as the rules of the game were upheld.

I might point out that these prescriptions concerned the behavior of political leadership, not the actions of rank-and-file citizens. In stressing this code I am choosing to emphasize the role of elites, or leaders, in Argentina's political system. This is not to deny the importance of masses. It merely reflects my view of Argentine politics during this period as an interplay among elites in which the populace, through voting, could strengthen one side or the other. But the crisis of Argentine democracy eventually emerged on the elite level, not because of pressure from below.

While the electoral reform brought immediate changes in voting patterns of the electorate,[25] Radical and Conservative leaders seem to have complied with traditional forms of political practice until the mid-1920s—and then the rules collapsed. By the end of the decade the Radicals, whose consecutive victories at the polls stunned complacent Conservatives, were not sharing power with anybody; they held almost all of it. This was partly due to expansion of the electorate, which roughly doubled in size from 1916 to 1930 and gave the Radicals a mass constituency.[26] In the Chamber of Deputies they possessed a clear majority by 1920; after a split between the "Personalist" Yrigoyen wing and the "Antipersonalist" Alvear faction in 1924, the Yrigoyenist UCR held two-thirds of the seats by 1930. Though Conservatives managed to prolong their hegemony in the Senate, and thus maintain a power base, time was running out; by 1930 Yrigoyenists had a substantial delegation in the upper chamber and they threatened to gain a full majority in upcoming elections.

As these alterations took place within Congress, relationships were also changing between the executive and legislative branches. During the first two Radical administrations there were significant challenges to presidential power. Congressmen often subjected cabinet members to grueling interpellations, questioned government policies, ignored or scrapped executive proposals in favor of bills by senators or deputies. By the later twenties, though, this practice had declined. According to one indicator of legislative "resistance" or "compliance" with presidential demands, there was a sharp and cyclical

Figure 5.   Degrees of Party Voting in the Chamber of Deputies, 1904–30

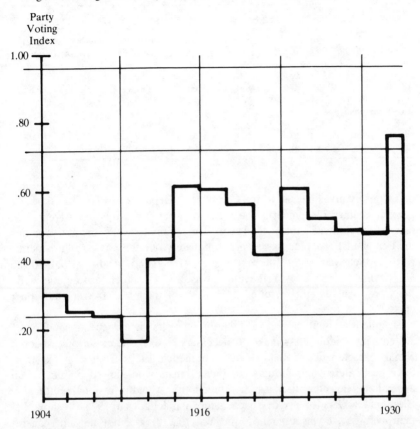

transition from compliance before 1916 to resistance in 1916–25 to almost total compliance in 1926–29.[27] Not only were the Conservatives losing out in Congress; parliamentary politics were giving way to centralized presidential power, now in the hands of Radicals.

Intense partisanship also came to replace the loose party affiliations of the early Yrigoyen years. Figure 5 shows how a Party Voting Index, based on roll-call voting in the Chamber of Deputies and ranging from 0 to 1.0, climbed from low levels in the period prior to electoral reform, oscillated between high and moderate levels after 1916, and reached a peak in 1930.[28] By 1928–30 the Yrigoyenist UCR and its opposition were almost always voting against one another. Deviations from the party line had nearly disappeared.

Moreover, party conflict acquired perceptible social overtones. Table 2 indicates that upper-class aristocrats figured prominently among both Radicals

Table 2. Aristocrats Elected to the Chamber of Deputies

Party Affiliation	1916–18		1922–24		1928–30	
	Number of Deputies	Percentage Aristocrats	Number of Deputies	Percentage Aristocrats	Number of Deputies	Percentage Aristocrats
Conservative bloc	39	77.0	33	57.6	28	57.2
All Radicals	75	48.0	100	27.0	111	19.8
(Personalists)			(49)	(14.3)	(100)	(19.0)
(Antipersonalists)			(29)	(41.4)		
(Unclassified)			(22)	(40.9)	(11)	(27.3)
Other or unknown	20	45.0	33	18.2	21	19.0
Entire Chamber	134	55.9	166	31.3	160	26.2

and Conservatives elected to the Chamber of Deputies in 1916–18 (about 48 percent against 77 percent). The break between Yrigoyen and Alvear then divided the Radicals along social as well as regional lines; in the mid-twenties the Personalist group contained proportionately one-third as many aristocrats as the Alvear faction (14 percent against 41 percent). And by 1928–30 the UCR, almost completely Yrigoyenist, was only 19 percent aristocratic while the Conservatives still recruited 57 percent of their leaders from the upper class.[29]

Despite the implications of this finding, the heterogeneous quality of Argentina's middle class makes it necessary to examine closely the specific social characteristics of Radical leaders in the late 1920s. They do not seem to have been merchants, farmers, or industrialists who viewed politics as an avocation. They comprised a special breed: they were professional politicians. Biographical data for Yrigoyenist senators and deputies in 1928–30 show that their average age was around 45, meaning that this was not the same generation which had guided the Radical movement prior to 1916; that they were usually university-trained lawyers; and that they had taken up politics while still in their twenties. There was very little lateral mobility from Argentina's socioeconomic elite into Yrigoyen's political elite during his second administration. As one observer recalled with disgust, "the Congress was full of rabble and unspeakable hoodlums. The parliamentary language used up to then had been replaced by the coarse language of the outskirts of the city and the Radicals' committees. . . ."[30] At least regarding leadership, it began to look as though the political system no longer reflected the distribution of power within the economic system.

While political authority passed into the hands of new social groups, the power of the central government expanded as well. As one expression of this trend, Radical presidents resorted to federal "intervention" in the provinces much more than did previous leaders (in effect, interventions meant federal takeovers of provincial governments). Of ninety-three such actions from 1862 to 1930, thirty-four took place during the fourteen year period of Radical rule, and during his own two terms Yrigoyen intervened at least once in every single province.[31] The economic impact of political decision-making also increased. In the decade from 1920 to 1929 federal expenditures climbed from 9 percent of GNP to nearly 19 percent.[32] This fact alone helps explain the intensification of political pressure as the decade wore on: by 1930 there was more at stake than in 1916.

The acceleration in the centralization of power underscores the importance of Argentina's constitutional structure, which gave great authority to the president and to the majority party. It was not quite a winner-take-all system, and the incomplete list made explicit provision for minority representation in the Chamber of Deputies. But winners took an awful lot: Yrigoyen had nearly total control over patronage; he (and his cabinet) could make many key decisions; and—to take an example—he was well within his legal rights when intervening in the provinces.

Finally, Yrigoyen and his followers made ambiguous use of their power. There is substantial evidence that his economic policies would have been acceptable and even favorable to rural landed interests.[33] This was not the issue. What mattered was the distribution of political power. Typical in this regard was Yrigoyen's excessive use of the power of intervention, which he appears to have employed in order to eliminate pockets of Conservative strength. Debates over the electoral credentials of deputies consumed an inordinate amount of time; in 1930—as a result of such bickering—the legislature passed no laws at all. Though Yrigoyen's physical infirmities and the bureaucracy's ineptness undoubtedly slowed down the decision-making process, concern with the allocation of political power brought the parliamentary machinery to a total halt. This stalemate and publicity about it no doubt engendered public frustration and may help account for popular approval of the September revolution.

In summary, all the traditional rules of Argentina's political game had been seriously violated, particularly after 1928. The Radicals' steady accretion of votes destroyed any balance of power. Intense partisan struggles replaced fluid party allegiances. Subtle social alignments on the elite level, and possibly among the voters too, threatened to end intraclass maneuvering.[34] The political system came to represent an autonomous threat to the socioeconomic system, both through Yrigoyen's recruitment of professional politicians and through the accumulation of independent political power. Understandably enough, in view of their initial expectations, Conservatives came to see democracy as dysfunctional and therefore illegitimate.[35]

Despite the depth of their discontent Conservatives could not oust Yrigoyen by themselves. They found some eager allies in another institution: the armed forces, some of whose members started planning a coup of their own as early as 1929.

The Military

Argentina's nineteenth-century liberals regarded a professional army as an essential part of national development. Only a well-trained military establishment, they reasoned, could crush provisional caudillos, maintain order, and thus provide conditions for the kind of economic growth they sought.[36]

Acting on this perception, Domingo Sarmiento began the trend toward professionalization by founding the Colegio Militar (1870) and the Escuela Naval (1872), still the basic training schools for officers in present-day Argentina. A few years later President Julio Roca, himself a general, greatly encouraged the trend. During the 1890s his colleague and protégé, General Pablo R. Riccheri, negotiated large-scale purchases of new German weaponry. In 1899 Roca and Riccheri engaged a German mission to train staff officers in modern methods and military technology, thereby inaugurating a forty-year period of service collaboration between the two nations. In 1900 the Escuela Superior de Guerra was created by the Ministry of War.

This emphasis on expertise precipitated fundamental alterations in the structure and outlook of Argentina's officer corps. By 1910 the criteria for promotion had changed from political favoritism to seniority and, more particularly, to the mastery of modern warfare. Related to this was a shift in control of promotions from the presidency to an all-military committee composed of commanders of army divisions and headed by the highest-ranking general. As the army developed a common esprit, based partly on a sense of its own efficiency, it also acquired substantial institutional autonomy.

Eventually the possibilities for advancement by merit opened careers to members of the middle class. Specifically, as various studies have revealed, many of the newly promoted generals were sons of immigrants, most notably from Italy.[37] For a considerable portion of Argentina's top-echelon officers, military careers provided avenues to upward social mobility. Gratified by such an opportunity, they forged a strong allegiance to the institution as a whole—and a jealous regard for its independence, honor, and professional reputation. Deeply resentful of intrusions by outsiders, especially "politicians," they often viewed civilian officials with a mixture of scorn and apprehension.

Throughout the twentieth century the Argentine armed forces, particularly the army, steadily gained in importance. By 1930 the armed forces consisted of around fifty thousand men; by 1943 this number had doubled, and by 1955 it had doubled again. In the meantime the military share of the national budget climbed from around 20 percent in the 1920s to approximately 50 percent in 1945.[38]

In short, the process of professionalization gradually turned the Argentine military, especially the army, into a formidable political force quite apart from, and sometimes antagonistic to, the country's constitutional apparatus.

To one degree or another, there was constant tension between military and civilian authorities. And as the legitimacy crisis developed in the 1920s, many officers came to look on politicians with outright contempt.

In this context Yrigoyen adopted the ultimately disastrous policy of turning the army into a source of patronage, promoting officers on the basis of partisan allegiance rather than seniority or merit (partly in order to repay accumulated debts among the military men who had supported his attempted coups in 1893 and 1905). Such maneuverings naturally angered many officers who were intensely proud of the army's professional autonomy and honor and who, largely for this reason, took part in or abetted the 1930 coup. But most striking is the sequence of events: Yrigoyen intervened in military affairs *before* the army intervened decisively in politics, and the officers responded in *reaction* to his interference.[39]

Responding to Yrigoyen's infringement upon the armed forces and to the general process of political decay, military leaders, like the Conservatives, came to view his rule as illegitimate. There were some fundamental disagreements, but Yrigoyen's opponents in the army concurred on one basic point: somehow the traditional rules of the game should be restored.

One group, led by General Agustín P. Justo—himself an Antipersonalist Radical—sought a return to pre-1916 politics. This faction thought the Yrigoyenists had grossly abused electoral and parliamentary procedures. With the Personalists out of the way, power would revert to the aristocrats, conflict would be restrained, the possibility of class struggle would disappear, *gente bien* would rule once again. Thus the democratic structure would reassume its normal, proper, and legitimate functions.[40]

Another group, led by General José F. Uriburu, had a more drastic solution: the creation of a semi-Fascist corporate state. The problem was not Yrigoyen but the system itself. Combining Catholic precepts with admiration of Mussolini's Italy, Uriburu sought to establish a hierarchical order based on social function. He thought the vote should be "qualified" so that the most cultivated members of society would have the predominating influence on elections, and he wanted to reorganize Congress in order to take power away from political professionals—"agents of political committees," as he disdainfully called them. In his "functional democracy" legislators would represent not parties but corporate interests—ranchers, farmers, workers, merchants, industrialists, and so on. A vertical structure of this sort would create a basis for rule by consensus, eliminate class conflict, and perhaps most important—in the Argentine case—reintegrate the political system with the economic system. Once more, and now by conscious design, the political arena would reflect the distribution of power within the economic arena; the pre-1916 rules of the political game would be restated and put into law.[41]

As time wore on, two important elements thus came to regard Argentine democracy as illegitimate: Conservative civilians and segments of the military (this latter group containing two main camps). Conditions for the coup were ripening.

The Coup

The pace of events rapidly quickened during 1930.[42] Signs of trouble appeared in the congressional elections early in the year, when the UCR lost its hold on the federal capital (Buenos Aires) for the first time in fourteen years. And Yrigoyenists did poorly in other major provinces: the great majorities of 1928 were reduced in Buenos Aires and Santa Fe, and reversed in Córdoba and Entre Ríos. As though to underscore the nature of the legitimacy crisis, Congress quarreled from May until August about the legality of key provincial elections. The UCR was flaunting its superiority, and the opposition, badly outnumbered despite the election results, could only boycott sessions in an effort to prevent quorums. As Yrigoyen's critics denounced his use of power, word spread that he would perpetrate another intervention, this time in Entre Ríos.

On 9 August legislators from the opposition parties published the "Manifesto of the Forty-four," protesting Yrigoyen's "arbitrary and despotic" rule and proclaiming the need to "save Argentina's democratic institutions and prevent the ruin of the country." Because of its explicit statement of political grievances, the manifesto merits extensive quotation. "Whereas," the signers proclaimed,

...the system of republican, representative, and federal government of our Constitution has been de facto annulled by the Executive Power, whose arbitrary and despotic will is today the only force which exerts control on public affairs.

The Executive Power has subverted and deformed the rule of provincial autonomy and has violated the law of primary education, the law of secondary education, the organic laws of the army and the navy ... [a series of other laws] and international agreements accepted by this country.

Public funds are squandered without any criteria other than the caprice of the President and the electoral needs of the *oficialista* party [the UCR], precisely at the time that government resources are declining and taxpayers are suffering the effects of a growing economic malaise.

While the country is experiencing greater and greater difficulty in selling its products abroad, the President ignores, with unconscionable negligence, the public outcry in behalf of agrarian interests.

Added to this institutional crisis is a serious economic crisis resulting from the devaluation of our currency, the lack of positive action by the government and the manifest lack of direction [*desorbitación*] in the acts of the Executive Power.

It is urgent to denounce and change this state of affairs by a united, energetic, and patriotic parliamentary and popular action by all men who wish to save Argentina's democratic institutions and prevent the ruin of the country, though this should not mean the pursuit of electoral ends, the abdication of partisan beliefs, or the creation of artificial political conglomerations.

We hereby resolve:

To coordinate parliamentary action in both chambers in order to require the Executive Power to comply with the national Constitution, to spend public funds properly and to faithfully execute fundamental organic laws.

To coordinate the opposition outside of Congress, to publicize . . .the illegal acts of the Executive Power and the ruling party [*oficialismo*] and to stimulate a civic spirit of resistance. . . .

To develop a plan of action conducive to the achievement of these goals and, if necessary, to solicit the support of all citizens who desire for this Republic a constitutional and democratic government. . . .[43]

The Manifesto of the Forty-four reflects the fundamentally political quality of Argentina's crisis on which I have based my argument. True, the legislators made some reference to economic problems, but these complaints were slightly wide of the mark: precisely in order to stimulate rural exports the Yrigoyen government had negotiated a bilateral trade agreement with Great Britain—the so-called D'Abernon Pact, not yet ratified by the paralyzed Congress (nor would it ever be). Even so, the general thrust of the statement was political. Yrigoyen was abusing his power, he was disregarding laws, he was spending money for partisan reasons, he was negating provincial autonomy—and something had to be done.

A few days later, on 13 August, military members of the Uriburu faction (which included some civilian collaborators) signed a pledge to overthrow the Yrigoyen government, in accordance with their "patriotic duty." Emphasizing the political character of the crisis, the officers solemnly observed:

The institutions of government have reached such a level of corruption that the country will soon be wallowing in misery and bankruptcy.

Parliament no longer exists: under the orders of the President, a disciplined and obedient majority has crushed the rights of the minorities . . . with the insolent insensitivity of preponderance.

The people already see, with indifference, the gradual process of social decomposition resulting from a system which must be brought to an end, cost what it may.

Ignorance and crime have replaced efficiency and respect for law, respect for tradition, and respect for all the moral values which we have received as a dear inheritance from our elders.

As Argentines who love our country, we pledge to save it from final ruin or die in the attempt.[44]

A series of public assemblies to rally support for the Manifesto of the Forty-four then took place in several of Buenos Aires' major theaters. On 20 August the Antipersonalist leaders—former members of the UCR—became outspoken in their opposition: "We must rise up, not only in alliance but also in solidarity with all the other organic forces of action and opinion, in order to save . . . our ideals, and cooperate in the defense of our embattled democracy.''[45] Antipersonalist leaders in Entre Ríos issued yet another declaration.[46]

As rumors of a coup began to circulate, Yrigoyen became ill and took to bed. His minister of war, General Luis Dellepiane, urged him to take decisive action by arresting suspected conspirators and shaking up his cabinet. Yrigoyen failed to respond—perhaps because of his illness—and Dellepiane quit in frustration on 2 September. Publication of his letter of resignation, alluding to corruption and irregularities within the government, encouraged the conspirators. Other military officers, seeking a way out of the crisis, urged the resignation of the president and his entire cabinet. Then came the final sequence of events.

3 September: Matías Sánchez Sorondo, a civilian member of the Uriburu clique and later Uriburu's minister of the interior, meets with political leaders of the anti-Yrigoyen parties.

4 September: Student demonstrations at the University of Buenos Aires lead to violence and casualties.

5 September: Because of his illness Yrigoyen delegates power to Vice-President Enrique Martínez. Members of the military conspiracy, which included both the Uriburu and Justo groups, meet with political party leaders to assure civilian presence at Buenos Aires military bases the following day.

6 September: Columns start advancing early in the morning. Vice-President Martínez, possibly anticipating his own elevation to the presidency, takes little action; within eight hours he resigns. A few hours later Yrigoyen, who had left his sickbed in an effort to secure support from the military garrison at La Plata, also resigns. Uriburu steps in as provisional president, and news of the coup prompts a jubilant celebration in downtown Buenos Aires.[47]

Thus the coup. "As a politico-military effort," Robert Potash has said, "this coup was the product of a prolonged period of exploratory talks, a three-month organizing effort, and a high degree of last-minute improvisation. Its success was attributable not to its physical strength—600 cadets and 900 other troops comprised the force that marched on the government—but to its psychological impact on the general public and the rest of the military, and to the paralysis of its opponents."[48]

Although Uriburu directed the provisional government, the Justo group eventually won out. Elected to the presidency in 1931, General Justo and his supporters concocted an elitist and fraudulent pseudo-democracy. While rigging elections and profiting from a Personalist boycott, he governed through a multiparty *Concordancia*. Conflict was limited, partisanship lax, tension fairly low. It seemed as though the rules of the game were again in effect, but the image proved to be illusory. During the 1930s industrial growth and internal migration led to the appearance of an articulate, mobile, aggressive, urban proletariat—which the Concordancia proceeded to ignore. In time the self-consciously elitist structure of parliamentary politics became increasingly obsolete, so the masses finally turned to an authoritarian solution: the populist dictatorship of Juan Perón. Democracy would not be tried again till 1973, and even then it would not last for long.[49]

Summary and Speculations

The breakdown of democracy in Argentina was the product of a crisis in legitimacy. The crisis was essentially due to the abandonment of longstanding political norms. There remain two fundamental questions: why were the norms abandoned? and could Yrigoyen have acted to avert the crisis?

Some critical factors defied manipulation or resolution by short-run political strategies. Insofar as they caused apprehension, for instance, impending economic difficulties came from outside the system. One-sided election results—which heightened Conservative fears—reflected the collective will of voters, and as a political competitor Yrigoyen could hardly have been expected to surrender electoral gains.

The decisive nature of the Radical triumphs, especially in 1928, points up one of the most fascinating aspects of Argentina's political scene: the utter inability of the Conservatives to cope with the realities of electoral politics. Having created the system, Conservatives promptly lost control of it, and the extent of their demise all but beggars belief. Prior to the Sáenz Peña law Conservatives had a near-monopoly on the vote; in 1916, after the reform, they won about 42 percent; in 1922 and 1928 they slipped to less than 25 percent.[50] This situation contrasts sharply with that in Sweden and Britain, for instance, where traditional elites continued to dominate systems after the extension of the suffrage. The understanding of the failure of Argentine conservatism will require intensive research,[51] but part of the explanation surely involves two related variables: first, the absence of a sedentary peasantry, which has furnished the base of Conservative strength in many other societies; and second, the high degree of urbanization, which placed a large proportion of the electorate beyond the reach of traditional landed elites.

Despite external restraints of this kind, however, it still appears that Yrigoyen might have alleviated the legitimacy crisis through one or more of the following actions:

(1) Yrigoyen might have taken the advice of his war minister and shuffled his cabinet. Specifically, he could have invited some distinguished Conservatives to take portfolios, perhaps three of the total of eight, and created a national government (as Ramsey MacDonald did in Britain). This measure might have done a great deal to ease the legitimacy crisis

because it would have reinstated, in part, the traditional rules of the game.[52]

(2) Yrigoyen could have tried to heal the intraparty split between the Personalists and the Antipersonalists, perhaps inviting one or two Antipersonalists into the cabinet as well. This cleavage helped precipitate the legitimacy crisis because it divided the party along social lines, as shown in table 2, and hastened the virtual expulsion of aristocrats from positions of political power.

(3) Yrigoyen could have stopped his practice of intervening in the provinces; in particular he could have announced his intention *not* to intervene in Entre Ríos, then an Antipersonalist stronghold, and to respect the integrity of senatorial elections in 1931.

(4) Similarly, he could have instructed Radical deputies to approve the credentials of recently elected members of the opposition.

(5) Finally, Yrigoyen might have announced his intention not to tamper with the military, as an institution, and to utilize purely professional criteria in the matter of promotions.

Even though these tactics might not have prevented the coup, especially if they had been implemented as late as August 1930, Yrigoyen's failure to adopt them calls for an explanation. His alleged near-senility and his illness might well have clouded his judgment, but the problem was much more basic than that; had Yrigoyen been in total command of his faculties, I suspect he would have done just what he did.[53] For it does not appear that Yrigoyen or the Radicals purposely betrayed a conscious agreement with Conservatives, or simply changed their minds along the way. What is most striking, in fact, is the very consistency of the Radicals' behavior, since they continued to act like an opposition party once they were in power. The attitudes and tactics which helped them *acquire* power before 1916 did not help them *solidify* power after 1916. Catering to military factions served the interests of an opposition, for instance, but undermined the authority of a president; disputes over congressional credentials could dramatize the plight of an opposition but obstruct the administrative need for policy output; intransigence might allow an opposition to bring attention to key issues but, in leading to the defection of the Antipersonalists, would weaken a government coalition. It is difficult to say why the UCR maintained this inflexible posture, but I might suggest that (1) for Yrigoyen's own generation, the twenty-six-year experience as an "out" group from 1890 to 1916 had created a firm and antagonistic "oppositionist" mentality;[54] and (2) for the new generation of Radical party professionals, political power represented upward social mobility, and they were unwilling to share such a precious commodity with other groups.

More important than the Radicals' unchanging stance, however, was the changing structure within which they operated. Almost by definition, democratic politics after 1916 were incompatible with the traditional rules of the game: quite naturally the exercise of universal suffrage gave great power to the mass party; public campaigning and conflict hardened party lines; the exigencies of electoral politics gave rise to nonaristocratic professional politicians; and popular focus on politics produced demands for an autonomous and powerful government. Moreover, the presidential structure of the Argentine system gave overwhelming power to the majority party and discouraged coalition politics. Conservatives wanted democracy to uphold the rules of the game; but the structure was unsuited to this function, and the pursuit of democratic practice led to the violation of those rules. For Conservatives and their military allies, in brief, democracy became dysfunctional and therefore illegitimate.

Such a process suggests two general conclusions about the breakdown of democracy. First, the inherent tendencies of democratic structures can lead to a crisis of legitimacy and eventual decay. In this case, the electoral and parliamentary apparatus stopped serving its originally intended purposes and created new functions of its own. For key sectors of society the unacceptability of these functions delegitimized the structure, which they promptly overturned. Economic problems may have intensified the urgency of the situation, but they did not bring about the 1930 revolution. The political system had already been gravely weakened by its dysfunctional abandonment of traditional rules. To present the argument in Juan J. Linz's terms: the inefficiency and ineffectiveness of the democratic structure in upholding tacit political norms led to a legitimacy crisis which prevented any efficient or effective response to an unsettling (but not recognizably unsolvable) economic situation, and this paralysis further compounded the legitimacy crisis.

Second, Argentine democracy did not break down despite the level of economic development. In a way, it broke down—or, more precisely, failed to increase its responsive capability—because of the *kind* of socioeconomic development which took place in Argentina and the *sequence* between socioeconomic and political change, since these factors conditioned both the shape of political crises and the nature of elite response. The growth of a beef-and-wheat export economy concentrated socioeconomic power in the hands of a landed elite which believed that the political order should reflect the socioeconomic order, rather than provide some sort of counterweight to it. By taking place *prior* to the establishment of democratic institutions, these processes helped lay down the traditional rules of the political game—rules which democratic structures went on to break in 1916–30, provoking some sectors to seek salvation (and restoration) in a corporate society.

Furthermore, the high proportion of immigrants among the urban laborers made it possible for the country's leadership to meet the pre-1912 participation crisis, and establish competitive politics, without having to effectively enfranchise the working class. These economic and demographic conditions thus gave rise to a *limited* crisis in 1912; they also permitted a response which would ultimately prove to be severely limited in its flexibility and capability. Paradoxically, the same conditions which facilitated the 1912 solution also aggravated further crises after 1930.[55] Suddenly the sons of immigrants, now native Argentines and members of the working class, swelled the ranks of eligible voters—but the traditional parties except for the Socialists, offered no effective representation of their needs. Frustrated by this situation, workers understandably accepted an authoritarian solution when it came. What had facilitated the rise of Argentine democracy, *de facto* exclusion of the working class, also helped bring about its downfall. In the long run, Argentina's pattern of socioeconomic development may have been more conducive to authoritarian, corporatist, and even Fascist politics than to a lasting democracy.

NOTES

1. These assumptions have been so prevalent, especially in the literature of the 1960s, as to defy citation. For some recent alternative views, see Phillipe C. Schmitter, "Paths to Political Development in Latin America," in *Changing Latin America: New Interpretations of Its Politics and Society,* ed. Douglas A. Chalmers, *Proceedings of the Academy of Political Science* 30, no. 4 (August 1972): 83–105; and Guillermo A. O'Donnell, *Modernization and Bureaucratic-Authoritarianism: Studies in South American Politics* (Berkeley: Institute of International Studies, University of California, 1973) esp. chaps. 1 and 2.

2. The definition is taken from Juan J. Linz, "An Authoritarian Regime: Spain," most easily consulted in *Mass Politics: Studies in Political Sociology,* ed. Erik Allardt and Stein Rokkan (New York: The Free Press, 1970), pp. 254–55. Robert A. Dahl also writes of Argentina in this period as a "polyarchy" or *relatively* democratized regime. See his *Polyarchy: Participation and Opposition* (New Haven: Yale University Press, 1972), esp. pp. 132–40.

3. For an excellent analysis of this electoral reform, see Darío Cantón, "Universal Suffrage as an Agent of Mobilization" (paper delivered at the Sixth World Congress of Sociology, Evian, France, 4–11 September 1966). Voter turnout figures appear on pp. 13 and 16.

4. I shall use the terms *coup* and *revolution* interchangeably in this paper, since the 1930 movement meets my definition of a revolution: an illegal seizure of political power through the use or threat of violence by groups seeking to make structural changes in the distribution of political, social, or economic power.

5. See the controversial chapter by Seymour M. Lipset on "Economic Development and Democracy" in his *Political Man: The Social Bases of Politics* (Garden City, N.Y.: Doubleday, 1963), pp. 27–63.

6. Estimates of GNP per capita are in United Nations, Economic Commission for Latin America, *El desarrollo económico de la Argentina,* mimeographed (Santiago de Chile, 1958) E/CN. 12/429. Add. 4, p. 4; the conversion to dollars is based on data in Carlos Díaz Alejandro, *Essays on the Economic History of the Argentine Republic* (New Haven: Yale University Press, 1970), p. 485.

7. See the tables in my article on "Social Mobilization, Political Participation, and the Rise of Juan Perón," *Political Science Quarterly* 84, no. 1 (March 1969): 33, and the data in Gino Germani, *Estructura social de la Argentina: Análisis estadístico* (Buenos Aires: Raigal, 1955), pp. 198 and 220–22.

8. Dahl, *Polyarchy,* Chap. 1.

9. For expressions of this widespread view, see Arthur P. Whitaker, *Argentina* (Englewood Cliffs, N.J.: Prentice-Hall, 1964), pp. 81–82; and Darío Cantón, José L. Moreno, and Alberto Ciria, *Argentina: La democracia constitucional y su crisis* (Buenos Aires: Paidós, 1972), pp. 121–23. The most recent (and sophisticated) version of this argument appears in David Rock, *Politics in Argentina, 1890–1930: The Rise and Fall of Radicalism* (Cambridge: Cambridge University Press, 1975), pp. 252–64. Rock clearly demonstrates that there were economic pressures on the government in 1930, but his assertion that they comprised "the great factor" behind the coup is unconvincing for at least two reasons: first, he does not pay sufficient attention to the *timing* of events (specifically regarding the emergence of pro-coup sentiment, which antedated most of the economic problems); second, as he himself acknowledges (p. 262 n.), he does not analyze the coup from the viewpoint of the elite groups that perpetrated and supported it.

10. Peter H. Smith, *Politics and Beef in Argentina: Patterns of Conflict and Change* (New York: Columbia University Press, 1969), pp. 48–49, 137.

11. Carl Solberg, "Rural Unrest and Agrarian Policy in Argentina, 1916–1930," *Journal of Inter-American Studies and World Affairs* 13, no. 1 (January 1971): 18–52.

12. Ricardo M. Ortiz, "El aspecto económico-social de la crisis de 1930," *Revista de historia* 3 (1958): 63–64.

13. For data on strikes, strikers, and real wages, see Peter H. Smith, *Argentina and the Failure of Democracy: Conflict among Political Elites, 1904–1955* (Madison: University of Wisconsin Press, 1974), pp. 16, 101.

14. Cantón et al., *Argentina*, p. 122; and Rock, *Politics*, pp. 252–64. Rock emphasizes the way that budgetary limitations restricted the growth of the bureaucracy and, consequently, the distribution of patronage; the point is well taken, but in my view, he carries it much too far.

15. See José María Sarobe, *Memorias de la revolución del 6 de septiembre de 1930* (Buenos Aires: Gure, 1957); José Félix Uriburu, *La palabra del General Uriburu*, 2d ed. (Buenos Aires: Roldán, 1933); and statements by various participants in the *Revista de historia* 3 (1958): 95–138.

16. Dahl, *Polyarchy*, pp. 134–35.

17. Leonard Binder et al., *Crises and Sequences in Political Development* (Princeton, N.J.: Princeton University Press, 1971).

18. An aristocracy is here defined as a group of people who hold predominant shares of both economic and social power, who recognize a common bond with other members of the group, and who regulate admission to the group. Whether or not to pursue political power is a matter of choice. For further discussion see Smith, *Argentina*, Appendix A.

19. See his comment in Ministerio del Interior, *Las fuerzas armadas restituyen el imperio de la soberanía popular* (Buenos Aires: Ministerio del Interior, 1946), vol. 1, p. 9; and the discussion in Darío Cantón, *Elecciones y partidos políticos en la Argentina. Historia, interpretación y balance: 1910–1966* (Buenos Aires: Siglo XXI, 1973), chap. 4.

20. Smith, *Argentina*, pp. 11–12.

21. Documentation for this sort of statement is virtually impossible, since people rarely announce their adherence to "codes" which (in many instances) might not have been consciously perceived. In this case I am imputing attitudes from contemporary behavior and from indirect statements made during and *after* the fact (some of which are quoted).

22. This is a little different from Dahl's version of the credo, which is: "I believe in elections as long as I can be sure that my opponents will not win" (*Polyarchy*, p. 140). The fact is that Conservatives *did* accept Radical triumphs in 1916, 1922, and 1928; it was only when these rules were broken that the opposition's victory became intolerable.

23. For narrative background on the Radicals, see Gabriel del Mazo, *El radicalismo: Ensayo sobre su historia y doctrina*, 3 vols. (Buenos Aires: Gure, 1957); Manuel Gálvez, *Vida de Hipólito Yrigoyen: El hombre del misterio*, 5th ed. (Buenos Aires: Tor, 1959); and Félix Luna, *Yrigoyen* (Buenos Aires: Raigal, 1964). On the social background of early Radical leaders, see Ezequiel Gallo y Silvia Sigal, "La formación de los partidos políticos contemporáneos: La U.C.R., 1890–1916," in *Argentina, sociedad de masas*, ed. Torcuato S. di Tella, Gino Germani, and Jorge Graciarena (Buenos Aires: Editorial Universitaria de Buenos Aires, 1965), pp. 124–76; Smith, *Argentina*, chap. 2, esp. table 2-2; and Rock, *Politics*, esp. chap. 3.

24. See the debates in Ministerio del Interior, *Las fuerzas armadas,* vol. 1, pp. 36–303; one specific reference to "coalition government" is on p. 74.
25. Cantón, "Universal Suffrage," esp. pp. 16–22.
26. Darío Cantón, *Materiales para el estudio de la sociología política en la Argentina,* 2 vols. (Buenos Aires: Instituto Torcuato di Tella, 1968); Smith, *Argentina,* p. 10.
27. Smith, *Argentina,* pp. 18–19. For an impressionistic statement about the vigor of the Argentine Congress in 1916–22, see Matías G. Sánchez Sorondo's comment in the *Revista de historia* 3 (1958): 103.
28. Because of its construction I would construe an index of .50 as being very high. The computational procedures were as follows: for each legislative session, I first factor-analyzed all contested roll-call votes, with each deputy obtaining an individual score on each factor; second, I found the maximum proportion of variance in factor scores explained by the optimal dichotomous party grouping; third, I computed the mean proportion of variance explained (R^2), weighted by the statistical importance of the factors. For an extended discussion of this methodology, see Smith, *Argentina,* Appendix B.
29. Here the operational distinction between Personalists and Antipersonalists is based on the roll-call vote for president of the Chamber of Deputies; see Cámara de Diputados, *Diario de Sesiones, 1924* 1 (12 June): 430; a different procedure appears in Smith, *Argentina,* pp. 77–78, with "aristocrats" defined in Appendix A.
30. Mariano Bosch, *Historia del Partido Radical: La U.C.R., 1891–1930* (Buenos Aires: by the author, 1931), p. 214.
31. Rosendo A. Gómez, "Intervention in Argentina, 1860–1930," *Inter-American Economic Affairs* 1, no. 3 (December 1947): 55–73. Interventions were permitted by Article 5 of the constitution, which stated: "The federal government shall have the right to intervene in the territory of the provinces in order to guarantee the republican form of government or to repel foreign invasions; and when requested by the constituted authorities, to maintain them in power, or to reestablish them if they shall have been deposed by sedition or by invasion from another province."
32. Cámara de Diputados, *Diario de Sesiones, 1932* 7 (1 December): 142.
33. Smith, *Politics and Beef*; Solberg, "Rural Unrest." In the prevailing atmosphere of mutual distrust, however, Conservatives may well have feared that Yrigoyenist policies would become detrimental to them in the future—especially in the event of serious economic crisis.
34. Cantón makes this point in *Elecciones,* principally on pp. 149–52. I construe this argument as tentative, however, since Cantón uses rank-order correlation coefficients to measure relationships between conceptually imprecise variables *on the provincial level* (with fifteen observations or less).
35. In a telling expression of Conservative disenchantment with democratic procedure, Joaquín Costa declared—even while accepting his party's nomination to the Chamber of Deputies—that the secret ballot was like "a subterranean mechanism which belongs... to sanitation works—it is a water-tight master pipe which carries impassible currents of all parties mixed with the debris of the social organism, among which gloriously stand out the human refuse, the most apt for fertilization of the soil" (*La Nación,* 31 March 1928; quoted in Cantón, "Universal Suffrage," p. 26).
36. Important studies of Argentine military history can be found in Marvin Goldwert, "The Rise of Modern Militarism in Argentina," *Hispanic American Historical Review* 48, no. 2 (May 1968): 184–205; Robert A. Potash, *The Army and Politics in Argentina, 1928–1945* (Stanford, Ca.: Stanford University Press, 1969); Darío Cantón, *La política de los militares argentinos, 1900–1971* (Buenos Aires: Siglo XXI, 1971); and Marvin Goldwert, *Democracy, Militarism, and Nationalism in Argentina, 1930–1966: An Interpretation* (Austin: University of Texas Press, 1972).
37. Potash, *Army,* p. 20; José Luis de Imaz, *Los que mandan* (Buenos Aires: Eudeba, 1964), pp. 56–57.
38. Peter G. Snow, *Political Forces in Argentina* (Boston: Allyn and Bacon, 1971), p. 53; Potash, *Army,* pp. 8, 34, 99; and George I. Blanksten, *Perón's Argentina* (Chicago: University of Chicago Press, 1953), p. 311.
39. In particular see Goldwert, "Rise of Modern Militarism."
40. Evidence for this interpretation is indirect and circumstantial since (to the best of my

knowledge) Justo and his colleagues issued no clear public statement of political purpose; the best available account is in Sarobe, *Memorias*.

41. Sarobe, *Memorias*, pp. 19–38, 44–50, 56–78; Uriburu, *La palabra del General Uriburu*, esp. pp. 22–23, 95–100, 167–68.

42. For descriptions of these events, see J. Beresford Crawkes, *533 días de historia argentina: 6 de septiembre de 1930—20 de febrero de 1932* (Buenos Aires: Mercatali, 1932); Sarobe, *Memorias;* and Potash, *Army*, pp. 39–54.

43. Sarobe, *Memorias*, pp. 271–72. Rock quotes only the clauses relating to economic difficulties, thus removing them from their broader political context (*Politics*, p. 262). In support of his argument he also cites the statement by Enrique Martínez, Yrigoyen's vice-president, to the effect that "The economic crisis was the great factor that made the revolution possible . . . " (p. 262 n.). But this declaration must be interpreted with great caution, not to say skepticism, since it would be natural for prominent Radicals to insist that the coup was due to uncontrollable external forces rather than a failure of the party or the system that they led. And I myself would agree that the economic crisis made the revolution possible; what I would deny, and what Rock concludes, is that the crisis was the primary and determining cause of the coup.

44. Sarobe, *Memorias*, facsimile reproduction between pp. 144–45.

45. Ibid., pp. 273–74.

46. See del Mazo, *Radicalismo*, vol. 2, pp. 149–50.

47. Unfortunately we know very little about the social composition of the crowds which hailed the coup.

48. Potash, *Army*, pp. 42–43.

49. I would not call the electoral interlude of 1958–66 democratic because the Peronists were not allowed to run their own candidates—except in 1962, when the armed forces annulled the results and seized power.

50. See the figures in Cantón, *Elecciones*, pp. 267–69. I have counted votes for local pro–status quo parties as part of the "Conservative" total; otherwise the decline in party strength would appear to be even more drastic.

51. A preliminary analysis of this phenomenon appears in Oscar Cornblit, "El fracaso del Conservadorismo en la política argentina," Trabajo Interno no. 14 of the Centro de Investigaciones Sociales, Instituto Torcuato di Tella, 1973.

52. Actually, Dellepiane did not suggest a coalition cabinet; he merely warned Yrigoyen to replace apparently disloyal aides.

53. It is not at all clear that Yrigoyen was in fact senile: see Rock, *Politics*, pp. 260–61.

54. As Yrigoyen said near the end of his first presidential term: "I did not expect to end up here. I expected to remain in the agreeable role of an opponent [*el papel simpático de opositor*] . . ." (Luna, *Yrigoyen*, p. 182).

55. For discussion of post-1930 crises see Smith, *Argentina*, chap. 6.

2.

Conversations among Gentlemen: Oligarchical Democracy in Colombia

Alexander W. Wilde*

The truth is that the Conservatives have officially terminated the negotiations [for peace], in spite of our having made known, through several very respectable channels, our desire to continue them. That is the absolute truth, and if I do not give you publicly more facts and evidence to corroborate it, it is because I want to be true to the confidentiality that it was appropriate to maintain in a conversation among gentlemen. Carlos Lleras Restrepo, October 1949.

In the 1940s, when the world still seemed divided into democracies and dictatorships, Colombia loomed larger to those studying politics than it does now. It had a two-party system, regular elections, and a record of democratic reforms in the depression of the thirties. Diplomats and political scientists called Bogotá the "Athens of the Americas." They considered Colombia an outpost of Western political culture in a region that in general seemed politically pathological.[1] Hence, the shock was great when that democracy came to an end in November 1949, to be followed by a quasi-corporatist dictatorship (Laureano Gómez, 1950–53) and a Peronist-style military regime (Gustavo Rojas Pinilla, 1953–57). And there was horror and disbelief as what had seemed one of the most democratic of nations fell, over the course of a decade, into the greatest political violence in the hemisphere since the Mexican Revolution.

The basic questions about these events are as alive today as they were then,

*The research on which this chapter is based was completed in March 1974 and made possible in part by a grant from the Ibero-American Program, University of Wisconsin–Madison. A book-length version of this chapter, with fuller documentation, will be published as *Conversaciones de caballeros* (Bogotá: Universidad de los Andes, 1978). The author is grateful for critical comments on earlier drafts from the editors and from Charles W. Anderson, R. Booth Fowler, Richard Weinert, James Scott, Leon Epstein, Thomas Bossert, R. Van Whiting, and especially from Francisco Leal.

because they involve problems not only of politics but of political analysis. What is "democracy" in the first place? How is democracy created and sustained? What are its requisites—what social and economic conditions, what political structures, bargains, and leadership? How does democracy break down? What is the role of socioeconomic change? What is the impact of more "political" factors—of the perceptions and choices of politicians, of the character of institutions they operate, of the specific rules of their own democratic game? What kinds of changes would permit a democracy that has broken down to be reestablished? And what, finally, might the study of such a case contribute to our broader understanding of the nature of democracy?

Democracy in Colombia

There are various traditions in democratic theory. One conceives of "democracy" as a kind of civilization, which allows the development of rational, autonomous, and fulfilled individuals. A narrower approach, in part in reaction to the first, defines democracy primarily as a kind of political system—a method for regulating conflict and power.[2] The problem with the former as a standard is that all polities that have existed inevitably fall short. The latter allows us to make a relatively clear distinction between historical cases, with some falling above the threshold of democracy and others below, rather than merely at varying distances from an ideal. Although it can be debated that the latter approach neglects an element that is quintessentially "democratic," it does at least make possible the comparative analysis of historical "democracies."

"Democracy" can be defined in more restricted, procedural terms as those rules that allow (though they do not necessarily bring about) genuine competition for authoritative political roles. No effective political office should be excluded from such competition, nor should opposition be suppressed by force.[3] More specifically, such rules would include freedom of speech, press, and assembly, and the provision of regular institutional mechanisms for obtaining consent and permitting change of political personnel (normally, elections).

Colombia shared with the rest of Latin America the usual supposed impediments to democracy: a high rate of illiteracy, widespread poverty, a powerful Catholic church, a dominant landowning class, poor national integration, and a nineteenth-century heritage of political violence second to none. Despite the lack of the appropriate "requisites,"[4] however, she managed to achieve, between 1910 and 1949, a political system of notable stability, openness, and competitiveness.[5]

Elections were held regularly throughout the period at national, departmental, and municipal levels. The opposition party twice won presidential elections, in 1930 and 1946, and twice took office. Until the breakdown process of 1948–49, all significant political actors regarded elections as the legitimate source of authority. Colombia was one of only two countries in all Latin America (the other was Uruguay) not to suffer a single successful military coup throughout this period. All elections were direct, except senatorial elections (which were made so in 1945); the president appointed departmental governors, who in turn appointed municipal mayors. Literacy restricted the franchise for national elections until 1936. Even so, perhaps half the adult males participated in national elections as early as 1922, and this proportion had risen sharply to nearly three-quarters by the 1940s.[6]

Colombia can be conceived as having evolved from the competitive oligarchy it was in 1910 to the more inclusive "oligarchical democracy" it had become by the 1940s. Figure 1 depicts this evolution in terms of Dahl's schematic classification of political systems.

Even for such a simple, dichotomous characterization, however, considerable qualifications must be entered. Concerning contestation, even a cursory survey of presidential elections during the period shows four—1914, 1926, 1934, and 1938—in which there was only one serious candidate because the opposition refused to run. There are, in addition, two other elections—1918 and 1942—that were competitive only because the governing party nominated two candidates. Indeed, during the period only three presidential elections were fought between nominees of the two parties—1922, 1930, and 1946. These variations in contestation produced parallel variations in electoral participation. The episodic character of participation means that the "inclusive-

Figure 1.   The Evolution of Democracy in Colombia, 1910–49

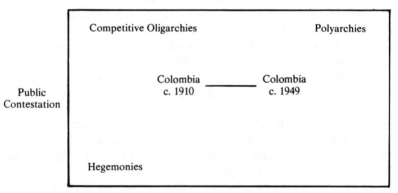

Inclusiveness (Participation)

SOURCE: Adapted from Robert Dahl, *Polyarchy* (New Haven: Yale University Press, 1971), figure 1.2, p. 7.

Figure 2.   Competition and Participation in Presidential Elections, 1910–49

Turnout
(in thousands)

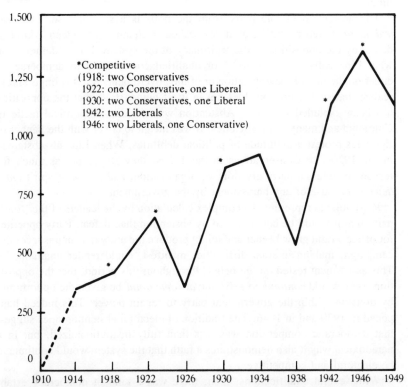

```
*Competitive
(1918: two Conservatives
 1922: one Conservative, one Liberal
 1930: two Conservatives, one Liberal
 1942: two Liberals
 1946: two Liberals, one Conservative)
```

SOURCES: DANE (Departamento Administrativo Nacional de Estadística), *Colombia política: Estadísticas 1935–1970* (Bogotá: DANE, 1972), table 8.1.1, for data from 1936–49; data from earlier elections are from Jesús María Henao and Gerardo Arrubla, *Historia de Colombia*, 8th ed. (Bogotá: Librería Voluntad, 1967), pp. 838–98 *passim* (from figures gathered from the *Archivo del congreso, Diario oficial*, etc.).

ness'' of the system cannot be inferred directly from the formal franchise or electoral laws.

Fraud was always present, as was periodic coercion against the opposition.[7] On balance, however, neither should be taken as reason to deny Colombia its place among historical ''democracies.'' Fraud was, at least, more than a matter of spurious electoral accounting. Peasants were actually mobilized to vote in substantial numbers, and traditional kinds of influence decreased in importance as the society became more urban in the 1930s and 1940s. There were elements in both parties that aspired to permanent hegemony, but the competition of elites over electoral capabilities prevented it. Fraud and coercion never destroyed the institutional framework that permitted two alternations of the parties in power and the significant expansion of participation over time.

The abstention of one party from the polls is a special case. Such *retraimiento* ("retirement"), as it was called in Spain, was indeed a kind of denial by the opposition of the legitimacy of the system. It may demonstrate what Linz calls "semiloyalty," or qualified commitment to democracy—either on the part of the opposition or of the government. But it is important to realize that such a boycott does not in itself demonstrate that the opposition has been excluded by force. Abstention was a recurrent political tactic in Colombia and many Latin societies. It was meant to cover with the banner of righteous protest a multitude of political debilities. When Liberals abstained in the 1920s, or Conservatives in the 1930s, they stayed out as much for reasons of internal party division, disorganization, and a lack of spirit (*mística*) as because of any harassment by the government.

Retraimiento represented a complex calculation by the leaders of the "out" party that it would be better served by abstention than defeat. Party appetites for office would grow keener and might produce the unity that an unsuccessful campaign, making internal difficulties manifest, could render unattainable. This assessment rested on the belief, throughout this period, that the opposition party would *continue to exist* and *at some point* be given the opportunity by division within the government party to regain power. This indeed happened in 1930 and in 1946. The tradition of electoral abstention does suggest that democratic competition was less than fully institutionalized, but in a paradoxical way it also demonstrates a faith that the system would continue to be electoral and competitive.

With several qualifications, then, there was a kind of democracy established and operating in Colombia before November 1949. The foundations constructed in those years proved more durable than most would have believed possible through the breakdown, widespread violence, one-party dictatorship, and military rule that prevailed from 1949 to 1958. In the generation since 1958, the two traditional parties have returned and continued to dominate a political system that has been, despite some restrictions on competition, relatively open and democratic.[8] This regime (the "National Front") has had many shortcomings and failures, but these mean less that it has been undemocratic than that procedural democracy is no panacea.

Colombian Politics and "Infra-Democracy"

When democracy was lost in 1949, much of Colombian politics did not change. The system remained oligarchical, the economy capitalist, the institutions republican, the military civilianist. Above all, party politicians (albeit of only one party) continued to reign. Similarly, the democracy that emerged in the decades after 1910 was not a tabula rasa, but incorporated many elements of previous politics. The convulsive traumas of European democracies, which succeeded or gave way to quite different kinds of regimes, did not suggest such continuities. Analysis of them tended conceptually to equate "democracy" with the "political system" of the given case. In more developmental perspective, for a country without such sharp regime shifts, one should distinguish between the two. The democratic era in Colombia can be seen as a phase of a larger, continuing political system.[9]

When democracy breaks down anywhere, it is because certain rules concerning competition and consent, which we regard as inherent in the general definition of the concept, no longer hold. When democracy breaks down in any particular instance, it is because the specific rules for *that* democracy no longer obtain and have, as a consequence, removed the foundation for the more universal rules. These more specific rules are a product of the historical conditions and agreements that surrounded the creation of democracy in that country, and also of those that existed during subsequent crises when democracy was tested and sustained. To understand the breakdown of democracy in any particular case, we should focus our analysis first on the level of these more specific rules.

Democracy, within the overall development of a political system, is supported by a special configuration of that system—an "infra-democracy"—which makes it possible. Infra-democracy is specific to a particular system; there are many different infra-democracies underlying the different systems we would call "democratic." Part of an infra-democracy is structural. It might associate democracy with a particular kind of economy, a certain distribution of power within society, a particular set of political institutions, a specific kind of social structure. A democracy founded with a two-party system might be threatened by its transformation into a three-party system, or it might survive such change. If politics has any autonomy at all as a social activity, it must be possible for the initial assumptions of a system to be modified, and for the "rules" of the infra-democracy to be amended.

The other part of infra-democracy is experiential. A democracy is created and maintained by people who, for a variety of reasons, are committed to its rules of competition and consent. In a given case that commitment is to a series of historical, often quite specific, memories, understandings, symbols, and experiences.[10] They represent modifications or qualifications to the more general rules of democracy that permit *that* democracy to operate. Whether a democracy breaks down or survives in crisis depends not only on structural considerations but also on the experiential rules of infra-democracy—the expectations and perceptions that political actors have of one another.[11]

For Colombia the most important of the experiential rules was that democracy must be, in Lijphart's useful term, "consociational" between the two traditional parties.[12] Though some fraud and coercion would be accepted from the party in government, it was not expected to rule as a party government, but rather to share power with the elites of the other party. Majoritarianism was qualified. Neither party expected to be a permanent minority without at least some participation in government. In moments of crisis, this tacit norm would often be voiced explicitly, particularly by the opposition. Then it could lead to the strongest sort of consociational mechanism, a bipartisan coalition government. Partisan symbols would be muted, and moderate elites of both parties, emphasizing their common stakes in democracy, would swing party troops behind the fusion ticket.

Oligarchical democracy had its origins in such a coalition, the "Republican Union" of 1909.[13] Both parties had been brought into government by Rafael Reyes in 1904, following the last of the great party civil wars (1899–1903; 100,000 dead) and the loss of the Panamá state. When Reyes ruled as a dictator, civilian politicians composed their ideological differences and forced him out.[14] Although the coalition did not endure, Liberals continued to receive a share of the portfolios in succeeding Conservative governments.[15] The benefits of the interparty peace were abundant. Coffee receipts and foreign investment fueled a surge of rapid economic growth; Colombian exports increased in value more than ten-fold between 1905 and 1928.[16] Elites had strong economic incentives to prevent the renewal of fratricidal warfare.

In 1922 the Conservatives employed all the resources of government to maintain their hegemony, but by 1930 they had split, and a Liberal came to power. In the political and economic crisis of that year, party elites found a new basis for *convivencia* in the National Concentration coalition of Enrique Olaya Herrera, who had been part of the earlier Republican Union of 1910–14. In 1946, a similar division in the ruling Liberals allowed Conservative Mariano Ospina Pérez to become president at the head of the National Union coalition. None of these arrangements was really intended to become a new party; they were, rather, attempts to give a share of power to those committed to the system.

The consociational character of Colombian democracy was clearly oligarchical. It assumed the continuing control of mass mobilization by traditional party elites. Convivencia was primarily a matter of agreement between national factional leaders and depended to a great degree on personal relationships among them. They had to recognize when intra-elite conflict had gone too far and to forge a new consensus when it did. Making that operative, in turn, depended on their ability to retain control of the party machinery and, more generally, of party followers. There were characteristic tensions here: the pull on one side toward compromise with the extremes within one's own party, toward the solidarity that was the basis of political success in normal times; and the pull on the other side toward the more moderate elements of the other party, toward the consensus that made preservation of the system possible in a crisis. They were tensions that could be exacerbated by changes in the other parameters of the infra-democracy.

The most important structural element of the infra-democracy was the party system. The two historical parties, the Liberals and the Conservatives, were the central, inescapable basis of political life for over a century. They defined and shaped nearly all conflict. They were, in some sense, the most fundamental national institutions in society. They were more significant structurally, culturally, and behaviorally than other social groupings (such as regions, classes, and strata) and other national institutions (such as the army, the church, or even the state itself). They possessed, in Anderson's terms, the greatest range of "power capabilities," including symbols, violence, electoral mobilization, and economic resources (patronage).[17]

The dominance of the two parties antedated oligarchical democracy. In contrast to virtually all other Latin American countries (except for Chile), elections were from the very beginnings of the republic significant for transferring political leadership. By the 1850s parties had developed amazing capabilities for electoral mobilization.[18] A parallel capacity, one used as often in these times, was the ability to mobilize considerable violence. Most of the many civil wars of the nineteenth century consisted of conventional battles fought between irregular civilian party armies—a violent extension of electoral conflict.[19]

Thus, when party politicians created a democratic system after 1910, they were accustomed to standing at the center of politics to an unusual degree.[20] They commanded a traditional, largely rural, society. Bogotá in 1912 had a population of 121,000; Medellín, the next largest city, 71,000.[21] Modernization and economic change had barely begun to make society more differentiated, to throw up new forces, new elites, and new organizations to challenge them.

The traditional institutional rivals to parties in more praetorian politics had been thoroughly subordinated. Even in the civil conflicts of the nineteenth century, which frequently had religious aspects, the Catholic church demonstrated little independence or monolithic strength. It was deeply divided over party politics until 1886, when a new constitution gave it a series of public guarantees. Its institutional interests thus protected, the church then confined its political activities largely within the Conservative party until the 1940s.[22]

In contrast to the role of its counterparts in Brazil or Venezuela, the army was ineffectual militarily and marginal politically.[23] It had been reduced by the Liberals to a force of some five hundred men around 1850 (just at the time the parties were formed). As late as 1899 it was disgraced by Liberal party irregulars (led by trained Liberal officers) in the War of 1,000 Days.[24] It gradually became professionalized in the twentieth century; it was 1943 before the first graduate of the *Escuela Militar* reached top rank. The army fought and won an international war with Peru in 1933 and was proud that it was not used for internal police functions. A support for elected government, it arrogated no autonomous "moderating power" to itself. Party politicians for their part almost never knocked at the barracks door.[25] The solution in a crisis was not to provoke a military coup but to find a new consociational convivencia.

The potential for severe party conflict remained, in part because the stakes were high. As in much of nineteenth-century Latin America, the Colombian economy only slowly created new career possibilities for the upwardly mobile. In this context, government offered an unparalleled source of advancement.[26] In Eduardo Santa's memorable phrase, "the budget is the only industry in a country without industries."[27] The Colombian state, in the tradition of the Spanish empire, had an extensive administrative apparatus. It dispensed salaries, licenses, exemptions, profits, privileges, contracts— opportunities, in short, available nowhere else.

Control of this bounty turned on the capture of the national presidency.[28] The president appointed governors, who in turn appointed mayors, and each of these controlled the police at his respective level. Almost every administrative position at all levels of government was filled through patronage, down to the humblest municipal employees.[29] The state was the prize of the parties; it was important for what the parties could obtain from it. In itself it was little institutionalized; it lacked, in Huntington's term, "autonomy."[30] Like Neustadt's weak American president, it was an indispensable clerk.[31] Its own structures and institutions, its own potential public values, were subordinated to the collected particularistic goals of the clientelistic party. One of the assumptions of infra-democracy was that the state had limited capacities, but what resources it did possess were the rightful property of the party of government.

Parties, not government, formed the most significant links between the top and bottom of society.[32] They did so in spite of a lack of strong formal organization. National party bureaucracies began to appear only at the very end of the nineteenth century and remained nascent throughout the period of oligarchical democracy. The parties consisted of various national factions, each of which was a kind of diffuse, vertical hierarchy of various brokers forming a pyramid from local gamonales to regional bosses to national elites. Lower-level brokers furnished bodies for battles, both electoral and martial, and their superiors, when in power, responded with jobs and favors from the government. The quest for these stakes tied together the most diverse groups and strata of the society within both of the parties. They could not readily be distinguished from one another on the basis of their social followings; both were "poly-class."

The stakes of the party battle were apparent not only to elites but also to the masses who composed their shock troops. Party mobilization for elections, and particularly for the many internal wars of the nineteenth century, had produced a deep party identification at the grass roots. Although it would be excessive to call the resultant groupings "subcultures," partisan identification was a primary element of social cleavage.[33] Children were socialized into the antagonism of the preceding generations, and recurring armed conflicts reinforced these "hereditary hatreds."[34] By the end of the nineteenth century geography had come to reflect these political and social cleavages: the countryside was increasingly divided between communities that were nearly uniformly Liberal or Conservative. Neighboring villages, often socioeconomically indistinguishable, were often bitterly hostile to one another because of different party loyalties.[35]

It is a mistake to read too much specific content into party identities, especially at the mass level. Among elites something akin to "ideologies" did affect nineteenth-century conflict—particularly over the whole Spanish colonial heritage—but such differences had played themselves out by 1910.[36] The consociational bases of the oligarchical democracy were founded on the muting of such ideology. The identification of the elites with the parties, and their capacity to activate their followers, were based instead on a kind of mística—a "party spirit" that might invoke certain symbols that were part of the history of a band. This identity was of a traditional sort not closely related to existing social or economic distinctions.

Events and Indicators of the Breakdown

The period of political decay for oligarchical democracy began with the second presidency of Alfonso López Pumarejo (1942-45).[37] A triumphant Liberal reformist in the 1930s, López received the presidential sash in 1942 only after a bitter split in his own party of government. It was wartime, and social reform came to an end, replaced by wild speculation and the making of private fortunes.[38] Laureano Gómez, the leader of the opposition Conservatives, talked openly of the need for revolution and justified such acts as the bombing of the Palace of Justice. At one point Gómez was jailed for slandering the interior minister; the judge who sentenced him was nearly assassinated by a seminarian.[39] In 1944 the president was seized and held by an army garrison, in the first attempted military coup in generations, and this was followed by an attempted general strike.[40] The instability of cabinets rose sharply (and would increase further in the subsequent period).

In an atmosphere of intrigue and plotting, of rumor and scandal surrounding his whole government (and including even his family), López resigned from office in 1945. A makeshift government was put together under Liberal Alberto Lleras Camargo to fill the remainder of his term. Lleras took several Conservatives into his cabinet, the bipartisan gesture usual in such a crisis.

Figure 3.   Cabinet Changes, 1930–70

Resignation
Crises

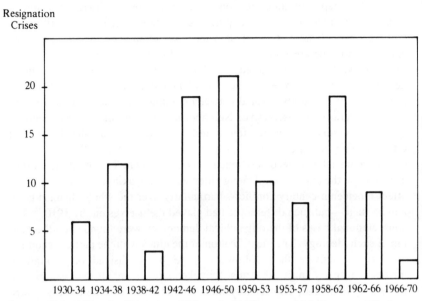

1930-34 1934-38 1938-42 1942-46 1946-50 1950-53 1953-57 1958-62 1962-66 1966-70

SOURCE: Richard Hartwig, University of Wisconsin–Madison, unpublished paper, 1972, from data collected by the Departamento de Ciencias Políticas, Universidad de los Andes, Bogotá.

NOTE: The simultaneous resignation of several ministers is designated a "resignation crisis." Serious crises, in which five or more ministers resign, are weighted by a factor of three; less serious crises, involving three or four resignations, by a factor of two.

Almost immediately his government faced the most serious strikes in the nation's history, tying up its transportation system and its oil supplies. He survived and held the 1946 elections as scheduled.

The 1946 presidential campaign marked a milestone in the development of democracy. It witnessed the brilliant rise of the populist demagogue, Jorge Eliécer Gaitán, who ceaselessly attacked the corruption and bankruptcy of the whole oligarchical system. Running as a dissident Liberal, Gaitán finished third but became presumptive leader of his party soon after the elections. His candidacy split the majority Liberal vote and gave victory to the Conservative, Mariano Ospina Pérez, who formed a coalition National Union government. There were massive strikes before the end of his first year. The army had to be called in to deal with a riot in Bogotá in October 1946 and another in Cali in November. In the countryside violence broke out in many different regions as Conservatives gradually assumed control of the administrative apparatus.[41]

Gaitán walked an uneasy line between cooperation and opposition. Several times he forced the resignations of Liberal ministers who had participated, as individuals, in the National Union. A general strike was called by the Liberal

Colombian Workers' Federation (CTC) in May 1947, and Gaitán equivocated before finally disassociating his party from it. The urban police seemed unable (or unwilling) to deal with riots in the cities, just as their rural counterparts (with the opposite affiliation) were unable to deal with the growing violence in the countryside. The Liberals blamed the government for repressing dissent; the Conservatives blamed the Liberals for supporting subversion. The Liberal majority in Congress tried to wrest control of the National Police from the executive, and the interior minister replied that the government would defend itself with "blood and fire" if necessary.[42] In January 1948 the Liberals presented the government with a long petition of grievances, listing dozens of incidents of violence against their fellow party members, and in March they left the government.

The crisis of oligarchical democracy began when Gaitán was assassinated, by a lone gunman, in April 1948.[43] His death set off the riot called the *bogotazo*, which destroyed most of the center of the capital and left perhaps thousands dead. Violence spread to other cities, and a general strike was called. The country appeared to be on the edge of collapse. The army, at the urging of Gómez, suggested a military government. Instead, Ospina declared a state of siege and brought the Liberals back into coalition. As the process that had become known as *la Violencia* continued to mount in the countryside, Congress spent its energies for the rest of the year on a complete reform of the electoral system, changing the dates for the next election and ordering a complete new registration of voters.

Despite the efforts of the coalition government, violence was rapidly becoming an "unsolvable problem" for the system.[44] The final phase of the process of breakdown began when the Liberals left the National Union for the last time in May 1949. In June the Liberals won another congressional majority, in the largest voter turnout in Colombian history. From this base they launched a systematic attack on the powers of the president, including reorganization of the police, congressional approval of cabinet ministers, and election of governors and mayors. Most significantly, they introduced yet another electoral reform, which advanced the presidential election to November 1949. The legislature and the executive were locked in constitutional crisis.

All institutional norms were lost in the face of escalating violence and party polarization. Insults, epithets, and threats filled the halls of Congress. Gómez called it the "center of subversion" in the country and demanded that Ospina close it. Deputies came to debates drunk and armed. In September 1949 the Liberal deputy Gustavo Jiménez was killed in a gun battle on the chamber floor in which more than one hundred shots were fired. Four former Liberal presidents attended his funeral; Gómez seated the deputy who had killed the Liberal on his right at a gala dinner. The "neutral powers" in government (in Linz's term)—the Supreme Court, the Council of State, the national Electoral

Registrar—were all politicized along straight party lines. The desperate, behind-the-scenes negotiations between the parties to save the system had failed by October, and the Liberals announced they were boycotting the elections. On 9 November Ospina, in the face of a pending congressional motion for his impeachment, declared a state of siege, closed Congress and the provincial assemblies, and suspended civil liberties. These decrees were essentially just formal confirmation that the system had already broken down.[45]

Backdrop to Breakdown: Structural Change

Beneath these events lay a changing structure of infra-democracy. The presuppositions of the game were shifting. Democracy had begun and had long operated in a traditional, rural economy. Now urbanization had altered the relations between elites and masses. Economic development was creating new sources of power in society. Traditional politics had been limited in its complexity and scope, but now modernization was making possible much greater participation and a much more extensive state. Both resources and demands increased. The pace of change quickened greatly. The place of politics, and of political elites, in national life, became something different. The breakdown of oligarchical democracy occurred, in the last analysis, because political elites decided it would not work. But that decision, that perception, that event, was significantly shaped by change in the whole structure of the situation. Ultimately, it was politicians who acted, but many of the parameters of that choice had been set for them.

Much of existing social science literature about breakdown—theories of revolution, for example—tends to see social and economic factors as the "underlying" causes, as somehow more "fundamental" than politics, which is perceived as reactive and dependent.[46] Other theory in recent years (such as Linz's) has insisted that political factors—institutional quality, leadership, ideology, coalitional skills—are variable quite independently of socioeconomic factors.[47] In reality the two are often difficult to separate.

Naturally, socioeconomic change imposes certain "loads" on a political system, but these loads interact with the political system—they do not simply flow into it. They are defined and redefined over time by this interaction. The Colombian case is one in which political factors clearly made an important and independent contribution to breakdown.

That vast societal process, modernization, came later to Colombia than to much of Latin America. It began in the 1920s, with the first large foreign investments made in Colombia.[48] The economy grew very rapidly.[49] Extensive public investments began to create the communications and infrastructure for a truly national society.[50] A process of urbanization began, which, with some fluctuations, was sustained at a high level through the subsequent decades. Between 1918 and 1953, the urban population grew at an annual rate of 4.2 percent (the rural rate was 1.2 percent), while the urban proportion of the total population rose from 21 to 43 percent.[51] However, Colombia never received the massive influx of European immigrants whose presence had so changed countries like Argentina and Brazil.

These processes, slowed by the depression, accelerated again in the 1940s. Transportation indices of railroads and particularly of airlines, considered indicators of national integration, increased spectacularly during the decade.[52] The gross product generated in the transport sector went from an annual average of 166 million pesos in 1939–45 to 394 million pesos in 1946–53.[53] Economic growth was held back by the war but spurted ahead immediately afterward. The GNP rose 2.2 percent annually between 1939 and 1944, and 6.2 percent annually between 1945 and 1949.[54] The economy was increasingly oriented toward the external market, with exports (led by coffee) nearly doubling from 592 million pesos in 1939–44 to 1,000 million in 1945–53 (in 1950 pesos).[55]

Other kinds of modernization were greatly quickened by la Violencia, the initial origins of which were primarily political. The percentage of the labor force engaged in agriculture, which had declined from 70 percent to 62 percent between 1925 and 1945, dropped more sharply as peasants fled the land, and had reached 55.5 percent by 1951.[56] Between 1945 and 1953 the urban population grew at a rate of 5.2 percent annually, while the rural population grew at 0.4 percent.[57] Bogotá was a city of 650,000 in 1951; Medellín had a population of 360,000. Employment in the secondary sector of the economy increased from 15.2 percent in 1945 to 18.8 percent in 1951.[58] Labor union membership grew rapidly, from 42,678 in 1935 to 94,190 in 1941 to 165,595 in 1947.[59]

The large-scale strikes, the urban riots, and the rural violence of the late 1940s seem to reflect these underlying processes. They represent, in their inchoate way, greater "demands" on the political system. But the political system was also changing. Political change accompanied social and economic change—as a response to it, as a cause of it, and in interaction with it. Late in the process of disintegration, in the periods of "crisis" and "breakdown," some of the changes in the structure of politics were activated and others became more acute. To get at this we need a dynamic analysis of process, of sequence, of dialectics. But the structural changes in the rules, which underlay the whole process, must first be understood.

These changes involved the beginnings of a modern state and the rise of populist politics. The former greatly affected the stakes of politics; the latter, the character of participation. Both altered the scope and style of the political game, shifted the cleavages on which conflict was fought, and challenged the adequacy of traditional mechanisms.

After Conservative governments of the 1920s had laid the foundations, the Liberal administration of Alfonso López Pumarejo (1934–38) began in earnest the construction of the modern state.[60] This meant, above all, the extension of central political authority. The state assumed new functions; it began to regulate the organization of labor, agrarian property relations, and the electoral franchise. It strengthened its controls over commerce and banking, and in the world crisis of the 1930s it asserted its primacy in the direction of the economy. To administer these new functions it created new structures—public agencies and semipublic institutes. And to finance this structural expansion, it laid a solid fiscal groundwork of new direct taxation.

The result, by the time of the crisis in the 1940s, was a state far more extensive than that which had existed during much of the period of oligarchical democracy. On one hand, government had more resources than ever before to meet growing demands. National revenues nearly quadrupled between 1941 and 1949, doubling between 1945 and 1949. Particularly impressive were the gains in revenues obtained through direct taxation, which by 1949 nearly equaled the level of all revenues in 1945 (see table 1). There was no fiscal crisis of the state in the background to breakdown.

On the other hand, however, the differentiation of the state undercut the influence of the parties. They still stood at center stage, but now the apron was filling up with new characters. Bureaucratic agencies, interest groups, and *gremios* were organized, which both expressed and satisfied demands that had been channeled through the parties in simpler times. Even nominally "private" bodies (such as the National Federation of Coffee Growers) characteristically possessed a corporatist kind of relationship to government, with a guaranteed direct representation, support, and often authority.[61] Although it was probably not until the 1960s that they came to constitute what amounted to a parallel government for social and economic affairs, the "decentralized institutes" of many stripes had a significant impact on total public policy much earlier.[62] They insulated many of the new economic functions of government from the party struggle. This may well have removed a major incentive for nongovernmental elites to try to save democracy in the 1940s.[63]

The rise of populist politics was a more direct and obvious challenge to the parties.[64] Unprecedented numbers were drawn into the political system. Voter turnout reached 60 percent of adult males in the presidential election of 1946 and 73 percent in the congressional elections of 1949 (see table 2).[65]

This increase was by no means restricted to urban areas. The rural violence represented, in its own way, another manifestation of the explosion of participation—and an inescapable part of the backdrop to breakdown.

In one sense the traditional parties responded to this opportunity with great success; they recruited the new participants to their old labels.[66] But the sheer size of the increase threatened their oligarchical presuppositions, and changed the character of participation. What the parties were able to establish with the

Table 1. Government Revenues through Direct Taxation, Selected Years, 1935–49 (in millions of Colombian pesos)

	1	2	3	4	5	6	7
Year	All Revenues, Public Sector	All Revenues, National Government	Direct Taxes, National Government	Indirect Taxes, National Government	All Revenues, Public Sector (1950 pesos)	Direct Taxes, Public Sector (1950 pesos)	Indirect Taxes, Public Sector (1950 pesos)
1935	118.7	61.8	5.3 (9%)	41.8	292.7	23.5	269.3
1936	135.8	73.1	14.0 (19%)	45.7	329.6	54.2	275.4
1940	156.8	82.2	25.0 (31%)	45.7	333.1	81.0	252.0
1945	309.2	165.1	67.1 (34%)	75.9	376.1	126.8	249.3
1946	381.3	227.5	87.6 (32%)	93.9	428.5	151.5	277.0
1947	520.0	305.5	130.1 (34%)	123.6	499.9	193.5	306.3
1948	584.6	335.2	155.7 (39%)	126.7	498.8	204.0	294.6
1949	670.0	379.0	187.6 (46%)	133.2	543.6	227.1	316.5

SOURCE: CEPAL (Comisión Económica para América Latina), *El desarrollo económico de Colombia: Anexo estadístico*. From the ''Análisis y proyecciones del desarrollo económico,'' reprinted by the Colombian Departamento Administrativo Nacional de Estadística (Bogotá: DANE, n.d.), tables 46, 47, 50.

NOTE: All amounts given in current pesos except where noted. ''Public Sector'' revenues include taxes and other revenues at all levels of government. Columns 3 and 4 do not add up to 2 because national revenues include more than taxes. Adjusted revenues—columns 5, 6, and 7—downplay the effects of direct taxation because they include departmental and municipal government, where direct taxation was almost nonexistent. Figures adjusted for inflation were not available for the national government alone.

Table 2. Electoral Participation in the 1940s

Years	Type of Election[a]	Adult Males	Total Votes	Electoral Participation[b]	Registered Voters	Electoral Participation[c]
1935	C	1,834,314	430,728	23.5	1,288,441	33.4
1937	C	1,906,551	550,726	28.9	1,692,004	32.5
1938	P	1,943,729	513,520	26.4	1,700,171	30.2
1939	C	1,981,632	919,568	46.4	—	—
1941	C	2,059,381	885,525	43.0	—	—
1942	P	2,099,227	1,147,806	54.7	2,056,366	55.8
1943	C	2,141,017	882,647	41.2	—	—
1945	C	2,225,570	875,856	39.4	2,279,510	38.4
1946	P	2,260,304	1,366,272	60.2	2,450,596	55.7
1947	C	2,313,038	1,472,689	63.7	2,613,586	56.3
1949	C	2,403,421	1,751,804	72.9	2,773,804	63.1
1949	P	2,403,421	1,140,646	47.4	2,856,339	39.9
1951	C	2,497,905	934,580	37.4	—	—
1953	C	2,632,792	1,028,323	39.0	—	—

SOURCE: DANE (Departamento Administrativo Nacional de Estadística), *Colombia política: Estadísticas 1935–1970* (Bogotá: DANE, 1972), table 8.1.1.

[a]C = congressional, P = presidential.
[b]Votes as percentage of adult males.
[c]Votes as percentage of registered voters.

new participants, urban and rural, were linkages of label, sentiment, and symbol. What they found much more difficult to extend were mechanisms of control. Colombia stood, in some sense, between oligarchical democracy and a more modern, participatory democracy. Its society was still relatively undifferentiated and lacking in intermediate structures. Its participation was more "activated," in the short run, by the political crisis, than "mobilized," for sustained involvement, by social change long underway.[67] Political organization was still primitive. The populist style of politics was indeed new, but the old continued to coexist alongside it.

The rise of trade unions illustrates the extent to which populism challenged oligarchical democracy, and the extent to which it was resisted. The CTC national labor federation, founded in 1936, was involved in party politics from the beginning. Initially, it was clearly a new "power capability" of the Liberals, and to some extent it remained so. The ambiguity of its relationship with the party, however, had emerged by 1945. With Law 6 of that year, the caretaker coalition of Alberto Lleras Camargo consolidated labor gains and prohibited formation of any competing federation. But later that year the same government dealt a crippling blow to the CTC as a national organization when it used the army to break a strike called by the Magdalena River workers.[68]

This was a sign from the "oligarchical" leaders of the Liberal party (above all, López) that they recognized the potential dangers of this new organization. They said to the Conservatives, in effect, that they remained fundamentally committed to the old game. There were others in the party who wanted to use the unions, and all the new participants in the political process, to rewrite the rules in the Liberals' favor. They encouraged the direct action tactics of the CTC as a way of putting continuing pressure on party leadership. The "oligarchical" line prevailed, however, particularly after the death of Gaitán in 1948. The party directorate did not support union desires at several key points—as in the general strike calls of 1947 and 1948 (after the bogotazo, when Echandía led the party back into coalition with the Conservatives).

Nevertheless, the unions did contribute to the breakdown of oligarchical democracy. They did not do this by transforming the nature of politics, as they might have done. They did not decisively shift the cleavages of the system nor become the new base of the Liberal party, for their organization was too weak. They were torn apart in struggles between Liberal and Communist leadership, and they never in this period organized more than a minuscule proportion (perhaps three percent) of the labor force.[69]

Their presence, however, was constantly unsettling. The CTC could compromise the Liberals, they could force the party leadership to choose to support or repudiate them, and could strain party commitment to oligarchical convivencia in a situation of obviously changed conditions. Conservatives distrusted Liberal leaders who professed loyalty to the system on one hand and seemed to take advantage of threats to it on the other. However credible they found the Liberal retreat from the unions after 1945, Conservatives could still doubt the extent to which their oligarchical counterparts actually controlled their movement, particularly in the deteriorating situation of 1948–49.[70]

The rise of populism also meant the reintroduction of ideology, in a broad sense, into politics. After the self-proclaimed "Revolution on the March" of Alfonso López in 1934–38, slogans of class, revolution, and socialism came easily to the lips of Liberal politicians. Conservatives opposed this with increasingly reactionary appeals for the defense of a traditional, orderly, Catholic Colombia. Symbols that had historically separated the two parties (such as the church) were recalled in a new setting of world ideological polarization. As in the Spain of the 1930s (a parallel consciously invoked in Colombia), political conflict could be presented as Armageddon.

Ideology exacerbated weaknesses already present in oligarchical democracy. The system was predicated on the assumption that one party would not become a permanently excluded minority. Liberal governments in the 1930s seemed to challenge that assumption. In the face of Conservative abstention after five years of participation in the executive, López welcomed the "Liberal Republic" as a "convenient, new, obligatory fact."[71] He extended suffrage and completely reformed the system of electoral registration. This made rural fraud more difficult and greatly expanded the urban vote. As Conservatives saw it, the Liberal motive was a highly partisan—one preventing the "true Conservative majority" of the country from being heard. Worse yet, inexorable demographic change supported Liberal designs. As Colombia became more urban, the Liberals' historical strength in the cities would assure their continuing dominance.[72]

Ideology was a fillip on top of this cup. The mainstay of consociational sharing was faith between the elites of the two parties. That faith was subject to very tangible tensions due to the changing structure of the situation: fears of exclusion, temptations to hegemony. An increasingly ideological style put a further burden on these personal relationships. It strengthened the mística of the party, and by strengthening party solidarity, it weakened identification with the larger system.

It is typical, finally, of populist politics that the parties did not significantly modernize as organizations. They remained vertical collections of factions, coordinated at the national level, and dependent on consensus between elites there. They possessed no more ability to discipline rebels at any level in the party than they ever had.

The changed conditions of the 1930s and 1940s—the rapid growth of participation, the rise of new political entrepreneurs within the old parties, and eventually the Violencia—exposed the vulnerability of the traditional structures.

The *Bogotazo* and the Crisis

The assassination of the populist Liberal leader Gaitán on 9 April 1948, was a watershed for oligarchical democracy. The bogotazo which followed the act was the greatest urban riot in the history of the Western hemisphere, a revolution that died in the agonies of birth. After it, Colombian politics would never look the same. To Laureano Gómez it was the end of politics and the beginning of civil war;[73] he called for a military junta and fled the country. To Mariano Ospina Pérez and to the Liberal leaders, it was more ambiguous. On the one hand both could see it as an attack on the president's authority (either justified, for the Liberals, or illegitimate, for Ospina). On the other hand they perceived it as a threat to the system in which they both had a stake. For the great "semiloyal" social institutions—the church and the military—the bogotazo accelerated a dynamic that thrust them deeper into politics.

Politics since the victory of Ospina in 1946 had been dominated by the question of coalition. Violence had begun between Liberals and Conservatives in the countryside, as it had in the past, over administrative spoils. The bipartisan National Union faced a dilemma on an almost daily basis in trying to control it, as the reports of massacres and atrocities reached the capital: were the police the instrument of governmental authority (i.e., "neutral") or of partisan advantage (i.e., Conservative)? This tension was heightened by the Liberal control of Congress, which they retained in the 1947 elections.[74]

There were elements in both parties who wanted an end to Liberal participation in the Ospina government. For the *laureanista* Conservatives, Liberal participation made reconquest of the administration painfully slow[75] and prevented the elimination of the corrupt basis of Liberal electoral success—some 1,800,000 false registrations, they alleged.[76] For the *gaitanista* Liberals, participation meant collaboration in their party's own demolition, as they saw the government gradually destroying the bases for political competition. The antiparticipation line had won out by March 1948, and the Liberals left the first National Union.[77]

Less than a month later, the bogotazo made politicians realize that the system itself was at stake. The Violencia had seemed earlier a traditional, rural sort of partisan conflict; now it threatened to turn into something much more dangerous and immediate. Gaitán's death had removed the figure most menacing to the Conservatives (and to oligarchical Liberals). He was replaced as Liberal leader by Darío Echandía, a man of reserved charm, much less abrasive than Gaitán.[78] Against the desires of the CTC labor federation, Echandía led his party into the second National Union coalition the day after Gaitán's assassination. He received the key post of minister of the interior (*Gobierno*) in the Ospina government, with authority over the country's internal order. Liberals were named to other cabinet posts and various governorships. At lower levels in the administration a pattern of *cruce* ("crossover") was to be instituted. Ministers, governors, and mayors were to name secretaries of the opposite party—a way of giving both parties stakes in the system, with checks on each other.

The elements of both parties that composed the second National Union perceived consociational guarantees as the central problem of politics. The government spent most of its energies during 1948 on one key to that problem, electoral reform.[79] In 1947 the Liberal congressional majority had not supported Gaitán, who wanted electoral reform;[80] they felt confident of their dominance of the old system. By 1948 they were willing to give up the local electoral juries, most of which they controlled, in favor of municipal registrars, whose posts would be split between the two parties and rotated.[81] They agreed to a new registration of voters, with a new, impartial, national registrar. There was to be a National Electoral Court, composed of prestigious and moderate members of both parties, and congressional and municipal elections were to be postponed from March to June of 1949. Soon after the reform finally passed Congress, in December 1948, Ospina lifted the state of siege.

The second National Union came to an end a few months later, however, in May 1949, and the electoral engineering did not save democratic competition. One reason it failed was another reform that the government did *not* make, that of the police. There was no central control over the six different kinds of police forces that existed in the late 1940s.[82] By 1947 the Liberals had tried, unsuccessfully, to remove the control of governors and majors over their own police forces, which Liberals believed were used against them. The bogotazo in 1948, during which many of the police had joined the mobs, made clear that the traditional police system, based on partisanship and patronage, could threaten Conservatives as well.

No nonpartisan reorganization of the police resulted, however, despite a foreign technical mission sent to assist in the effort. Instead, the police were simply gradually purged of Liberals by the executive. A parallel kind of winnowing occurred within the Conservative party, as the more collaborationist, moderate officeholders were forced out in favor of more sectarian types.[83] Violence in the countryside escalated. Armed Liberal bands confronted Conservative *pájaros* and *chulavitas,* the departmental guards that the Liberals called the "political police."[84] Much of this violence from both sides must have been condoned and even actively supported by party elites.[85]

The factional character of the parties undermined the second National Union and subsequent attempts at convivencia. On the Liberal side the leadership situation was confused and competitive; no single figure could dominate the national party as a whole. Much of the weakness and vacillation of the Liberals during 1948 and 1949 can be traced to this. Echandía assumed leadership of the party-in-government but never established his hold over the party machinery throughout the country—the brokers and bosses, clienteles and *militantes.*[86] In government he faced great pressure from Liberals in the provinces, who felt themselves victims of governmental violence, either to protect them or to get out. He was never able to protect them, though he was interior minister, because he could not control the Conservative governors and mayors nominally under his authority. The Liberals eventually left the coalition in May 1949, over no great event but simply over the continued failure of the executive to institute the agreed-upon consociational cruce in several localities. With congressional elections approaching in June 1949, there was probably no other way the leadership could have held troops in line at the grass roots, where the party battle was most devastating.[87]

On the Conservative side, Mariano Ospina commanded the party-in-government as chief executive. He represented the party's "moderate" elements, those with some commitment to the system. He stood, in some sense, for the class interests of the oligarchy—as did the Liberals López and Santos, by this time—against the *país político,* those who could only understand the deepening conflict as a clash of party interests. Contrary to later Liberal allegations, his presidency is replete with evidence of a sincere desire for party cooperation.[88] If he could not make provincial officials responsive to Echandía, it was probably largely because he himself lacked authority over them; they were primarily loyal to Laureano Gómez.

Gómez dominated the Conservative party machinery from 1939 on. Despite his periodic absences from the country, he remained the *jefe único,* hero of the militants and friend of the uncounted *gamonales* who were the backbone of the party's electoral strength. He could not himself run for president in 1946, for fear of uniting the Liberals, but Ospina never threatened his hold over the party, even though he commanded all the political resources of the executive. The Conservatives were in opposition, in fact or in spirit, until the breakdown, and Gómez was the ideal opposition politician. As much as Ospina may have asked his officials to maintain institutional authority, Gómez was always able to appeal to their deeper loyalty to their party.

The bogotazo thrust the church back into politics more deeply than it had been since the civil wars of the nineteenth century. The archbishop's palace, the Nunciatura, the old *colegio* of LaSalle, and the Pontifical Bolivarian University of Medellín were all burned by the mob. In the continuing violence in the countryside priests were murdered and sanctuaries sacked. The church felt itself caught in a civil war waged by a people it was accustomed to considering, in its complacent triumphalism, *"culto y cristiano."*

In its reactions, the church was divided within itself. A significant part, the most visible, reverted, as in past crises, to alliance with the Conservative party. The violence was not for them so much a threat to be overcome as an opportunity to conquer; death to terror and to enemies of the church. At the grass roots there were *párrocos* who mobilized their flocks against Liberals, who called for holy war, who swore "safe-conduct" passes for certified Conservatives in zones of violence.[89] They found considerable support among their bishops, led by Miguel Ángel Builes of Santa Rosa de Osos. Builes, in his Lenten message of 1949, called the Liberal party "communist . . . the enemy of Christ and his Church." No Colombian, he said, could at the same time be a Catholic and a Liberal. He was joined by many of his fellow bishops in forbidding Catholics to vote for Liberal candidates in the 1949 congressional elections.[90]

The archbishop, Ismael Perdomo, led the forces that opposed this polarization. He encouraged the clergy who attempted to mediate between the warring parties and to minister to the sick and needy. He forbade priests to issue safe-conducts or even to mention party in sermons or sacraments.[91] "The immense majority of Conservatives and Liberals," he wrote in his April 1949 pastoral, ". . . defends the same creed, is educated under identical moral norms, and feels equal veneration for the spiritual jurisdiction of the Catholic religion."[92] With a principal episcopal ally, the bishop of Manizales, Luis Concha Córdoba (significantly, later to become Archbishop of Bogotá under the National Front), Perdomo had good political, as well as religious, reasons for his stand. In 1949 he already understood the threat the Violencia posed to the institutional church. He perceived that it could be torn apart if convivencia between the parties—guarantor of the whole public order with which the church identified—were not preserved.

Although Perdomo moved the Episcopal Conference gradually to his view, the church, on balance, probably made some contribution to breakdown.[93]

The Collective Pastoral of 3 October 1949 and the archbishop's final plea for peace on 23 October had no visible effect on the course of events.[94] That triumphalist part of the church represented by Builes, on the other hand, fed the Violencia. They reactivated the traditional cleavages separating the parties, which undoubtedly exacerbated local conflict. It is important to note, however, that this invocation of the old místicas does not seem significantly to have affected elite relationships at the political center during the breakdown. The church was not the controverted symbol between them it had been in the past century. Indeed, the Liberals made clear both in the nomination of Echandía and in private negotiations in October 1949 that they accepted the public role of the church as one of the common principles shared by the parties.[95]

For the army, the bogotazo gave added impetus to a politicization that had begun earlier. The military as an institution was created during the long Conservative hegemony (1886–1930). In the 1930s and 1940s, Liberal governments had tried in various ways to neutralize its Conservative sentiment by creating the new National Police, by favoring Liberals in promotions, and above all by emphasizing its nonpartisan professionalism. López praised the army for remaining loyal during the attempted coup of 1944 and stressed that the large number of (Conservative) officers retired were being punished strictly as individuals (despite the fact that many so treated were in no way linked to the conspiracy).[96]

The army faced strong Conservative pressures intended to reinforce its long-standing partisan feeling. Conservative politicians were implicated in the Pasto coup of 1944 and the earlier conspiracy of 1936.[97] After the bogotazo, during Ospina's presidency, known Liberals were purged from the officer corps. Party polarization and the mounting violence, to which the police had contributed, pushed the army further into politics. By 1946 military men had been appointed to nearly one-quarter of the mayoralties in the country.[98] In 1948 one general was made minister of war, another was appointed head of the National Police, and several were made governors of departments.[99] In May of the following year three military men were included in the cabinet following resignation of all the Liberals (after requesting military replacements for various Conservative provincial officials).

Despite some professionalist resentment at this politicization, and despite rapid growth in the size of the institution,[100] the army played no autonomous role in the breakdown of 1949. Indeed, military loyalty to the regime had allowed Conservatives to persecute Liberals as harshly as they did without feeling the need to maintain consensus with other moderate civilians they might have felt if the army had been institutionally more self-confident. In the years after 1949 Gómez systematically tried to ensure that recruitment of officers and men was wholly Conservative (at the same time that junior officers were cooperating with Liberal guerrillas).[101] It was not until 1953 that military resistance to being used in partisan fashion finally pushed the army past the limits of its traditional deference to civilian control.[102]

Breakdown

The backdrop to the drama played out from May to November 1949 was in some ways unexpected. Traditional rural society was disintegrating, the political arrangements of generations were collapsing, and yet much in Colombian life went on as before. Government revenues were rising in a prosperous economy (see table 1). Per capita income was increasing at an unprecedented rate.[103] Exports were little affected through the end of 1949, either in the quantities that could be exported through the ports or in the receipts for the goods. Total kilo weight for exports was considerably higher in 1949 than ever before in Colombian history, and their value was more than twice that of 1945. Vital coffee exports, which composed between 70 and 80 percent of export earnings, were slightly lower in weight in 1949 than in some previous years, but receipts were the greatest ever, the result of a high market price (see table 3). If there had been a crisis in 1948, by 1949 the economy was bullish.[104] The collapse of 1949 was not economic but political.

The overriding concern in the process that took place between May and November was control of the national executive—retention for the Conservatives, recapture for the Liberals. Lacking the presidency, the Liberals used Congress as a power base. After leaving the coalition government in May, they were able to retain their congressional majority in the June elections.[105] From there they launched, in July, a series of "heroic projects" intended to

Table 3. Export Capacity and Earnings: Selected Years, 1940–49

Year	Value[a]	Index for (1) (1930 = 100)	Weight (millions of tons)	Index (1930 = 100)	Coffee, Value[a]	Coffee, Quantity (thousands of bags)
1940	126.0	121	3.57	115	—	—
1942	170.9	164	1.36	44	144.9	4,310
1944	227.1	218	2.99	97	164.7	4,924
1945	246.2	236	3.13	101	183.2	4,924
1946	351.8	338	2.92	94	274.4	5,149
1947	446.3	428	3.17	102	344.8	5,339
1948	504.9	484	3.10	100	412.1	5,588
1949	625.9	601	3.89	125	473.3	5,410

SOURCES: All information except for the last two columns is from *Anuario general de estadística, 1949* (Bogotá: DANE, 1949), table 129; data on coffee were calculated from idem, 1945, table 187, and idem, 1949, table 179.

[a] In millions of Colombian pesos.

enable them to win the next presidential election. To do this they had to circumvent a Conservative president and the system that gave him such great power. They introduced bills calling for nationalization of the police under congressional aegis, the elections of governors and mayors, the institution of a parliamentary style of cabinet, and above all, yet another electoral reform. This "counterreform" (as the Conservatives called it) in effect negated the hard-won accord of the previous year. It moved up the presidential election to November 1949 (instead of June 1950), a time when Congress was still in session and could, presumably, offer some protection against possible abuses. Moving up the date would, however, make it impossible to complete reform of the electoral register, which had been the major Conservative goal in the previous reform.

This offensive was intended by the Liberal leadership as an answer to the charges of "ingenuousness" that had been leveled at them by more partisan *copartidarios* during the second National Union.[106] It was accompanied by a new posture of truculent opposition—ranging from calculated slights of protocol when the president opened Congress in July to expressions of solidarity with the "political prisoners" jailed during the riots of the bogotazo.[107] While all of this was more a matter of style than of substance, it had very real consequences.

For Ospina and the Conservatives, what the Liberals played was a "two-faced game" (*un juego doble*).[108] On one hand they pretended to support democratic institutions, while on the other they fomented rebellion against legitimate authority for their own partisan purposes.[109] They were, at best, "semiloyal." But the Conservatives played a double game as well.[110] The government wanted to wear the cloak of constitutional authority while it allowed its provincial officials and police to try to perpetuate Conservative power by force. Gómez, who had returned to the country from Spain in June, denied that Congress had any legitimacy whatsoever and demanded that the president close it.[111] His son distributed whistles to drown out Liberal speakers in debates. Both sides were guilty of trading on the authority of their institutional bases, thereby undermining whatever autonomy those structures possessed. They were less and less institutions with values of their own, arenas where the parties could resolve differences, and more and more instruments subordinated to "higher" (i.e., partisan) ends.[112]

The eminently political issue of the electoral "counterreform" was debated in constitutional terms (thereby reserving the ultimate decision to the Supreme Court, one of Linz's "neutral powers"). The Conservatives contended that the law it affected, the electoral law of 1948, was a code and required a two-thirds congressional majority for amendment. The Liberals, with less than such a majority, held that the previous reform was an ordinary law and its amendment required only a simple majority plus one. The law was passed by Congress at the end of August with a simple majority and vetoed by Ospina a few days later.

While conflict occurred in the legislature and between Congress and the president, the process Linz calls "the reduction of the arena" had already begun. Moderates interested in achieving convivencia between the parties had begun to realize that the formal, public sites were inadequate. A bipartisan "Pro-Peace Committee," with strong representation from business and financial elites (and the blessing of the archbishop of Bogotá), took the first step in mid-August.[113] On 23 August Ospina responded to them by sending out a general statement of principles, presumably a basis for discussion. He asked that, while conversations were being held, Liberals hold up electoral reform, then being debated. The Liberals saw no definite guarantees to them in the president's message and believed the reform would strengthen their bargaining position. They put it through, and it was vetoed.

On 6 September Ospina told the National Conservative Directorate that he would accept the Liberal electoral reform if it were held to be constitutional by the Supreme Court. His stand was rejected by the *laureanista* directorate, which attacked, both in Congress and in public posters, all other Conservatives who declared themselves in favor of an acuerdo.[114] Ospina went further on 12 September and offered the Liberals a bipartisan Commission of Guarantees charged with examining the state of the country, particularly the activities of "lower authorities" of the government. But the shooting of the Liberal deputy, Gustavo Jiménez, on 8 September, had embittered party relations. Senate Liberals rejected the president's offer and repassed the electoral reform on 13 September. But informal conversations continued.

On 23 September, in what was openly a straight party vote, the Supreme Court accepted the constitutionality of the new Liberal electoral reform. Gómez's *El Siglo* called the court "a contemptible political committee,"[115] but the presidential election was fixed for 27 November. The dialectic of events public and private then developed very rapidly, the two spheres spilling over into one another. The pressures eventually proved too great for the crisis mechanisms of oligarchical democracy, but the defenders of the system made one last attempt to save it.

On 7 October Ospina proposed a sweeping constitutional reform, rather like the one on which the subsequent National Front (1958–74) would be based. Presidential elections would be postponed for four years, with the country ruled in the interim by a bipartisan four-man government council. The Supreme Court, Council of State, and the Electoral Court would be shared equally between the parties, and a two-thirds majority would be required to pass legislation. The reform was discussed privately between four party leaders: Gómez and Urdaneta Arbeláez for the Conservatives, López and Echandía for the Liberals.[116] The first stage of these conversations (another of Linz's "small c's") failed.

The proposal must have been difficult for the Liberal leaders to take entirely seriously. It did not come from Ospina directly but was relayed through Gómez, who later clearly indicated his disagreement with it. Though an apparent concession from the government, it was contradicted by other evidence at about the same time of hardening partisanship, as Gómez exerted his influence more and more directly. At the end of September the key Interior Ministry was given to a hard-line laureanista (a former editor of Gómez's *El Siglo*). On 2 October the governors of six departments were replaced with (in the words of a Conservative commentator) "the most radical personages that could be found in the Conservative party."[117] On 7 October, the same day Ospina's proposal was made, the new Interior Minister on his own initiative retired one Liberal general from the general staff, sent another to Europe, and promoted the notorious anti-Liberal, Gustavo Rojas Pinilla.[118]

The Liberals were confused about the best course. On one hand the "heroic projects," which were still in the legislature, suggested that the party saw defeat as almost inevitable. They implied that only extraordinary steps, which broke with the institutions of oligarchical democracy, could preserve a Liberal victory.[119] But in a contradictory way the Liberals also seemed overly confident. They had, after all, left the government before the congressional elections in June and had won them anyway; surely things could get no worse. "There is no reason to doubt victory," Carlos Lleras Restrepo told a party meeting.[120] The later official party report passes very quickly over this first stage of discussions, in early October, noting simply that "no resolution was reached" and that López called the presidential arrangement "dictatorship by covenant."[121] It may well have been the Liberals who torpedoed agreement at this point, because they thought they could win or because any partisan course—fighting the election or even "retiring"—would at least unite the deeply divided party, while another coalition with the Conservatives threatened to tear it apart from within. They seemed caught between two opposed postures in a crisis in which the rules were rapidly changing.

The situation became increasingly clear after the nomination of Gómez as the Conservative standard-bearer on 12 October. The Liberals finally realized that their only hope, short of revolution, lay in some kind of accord; the Conservatives did not want one. The conversations were renewed, now enlarged to include four more leaders (Lleras Restrepo among them). The Conservatives stalled, making and breaking several appointments. Finally the Liberals decided to make the whole matter public. On radio on 21 October Echandía presented a "peace formula" which closely corresponded to Ospina's earlier proposal. The Pro-Peace Committee, accepting the formula as a solid base for progress, asked the president to mediate a truce between the parties.

This Ospina attempted to do, naming on 24 October a bipartisan committee of senators who were also members of their respective party directorates to study the Echandía plan and to report to him in two days. But on 22 October the police had made an unprovoked attack on the Liberal headquarters in the city of Cali, killing twenty-four and wounding sixty.[122] On 23 October the national electoral registrar, a distinguished moderate Liberal, protested to the government that local violence made his task impossible and that the upcoming election would be a "bloody farce."[123] On 24 October the Council of State (another "neutral power") was consulted by the government about declaring a state of siege. It replied in the negative, in a party vote, blaming much of the violence on the government's own officials.[124] On 26 October the Liberal members of the bipartisan committee on Ospina's proposal suggested an agreement including not only constitutional mechanics but also broad principles shared by the two parties (e.g., the special place of the Catholic church in Colombian society). The Conservatives did not sign, finally arguing that the decision rested not with them but with Laureano Gómez.[125]

There were other eleventh-hour attempts to reach some accord (including a personal call by López on Gómez at his home), but the die was cast. On 28 October Lleras Restrepo announced on the floor of the Senate that the Liberals were withdrawing from all the bipartisan electoral machinery, from the national to the local level, and breaking off all relationships, even personal ones, with all Conservatives:

No relation will we have from now on with the members of the Conservative party; while they do not offer us a different Republic, guarantees that put an end to this infamy, the relations between Liberals and Conservatives, already broken in the public sphere, must be so also in the private sphere as well.[126]

On 29 October and again more emphatically on 2 November Gómez publicly rejected any possibility of an accord.[127]

Facing the impending state of siege, the Liberals were desperate. They came to the decision, formalized in their statement of 7 November, to abstain entirely from the election. They explicitly denied any legitimacy to the government that came to power in them:

Colombian Liberalism will never recognize as legitimate, in any form, the result . . . and declares that the electoral farce that they intend to carry out on the 27th of November will never give anyone the right to exercise power with valid title nor to be obeyed nor respected by a free people.[128]

There were dark threats about a battle just beginning and fights to the death.[129] The Liberals laid their case before the United Nations in New York, and in the Colombian Congress they prepared to impeach the president. Ospina's reaction on 9 November—the declaration of state of siege, the closing of Congress and the provincial legislatures, the banning of public meetings, and the censorship of press and radio—formally established that the oligarchical democracy was at an end.

Need this have happened? What, in the last analysis, caused the conversations between the parties to fail? Are there any conditions under which they might have produced an accord? And when no agreement could be reached, did the Liberals have no choice but to abstain? Could they have gone to the polls? These are questions for which there are no definitive answers, but in historical retrospect, some plausible guesses can be made.

The only way that informal negotiations might have worked would have been if moderates, committed to the defense of the system, had been able to control both parties. The informal, factional structure of the parties—accompanied by the depth of party identification—made this very difficult. Factionalism within the parties—rather than the existence of multiple separate parties—blurred distinctions between who was and was not loyal to the system. Factions did not put forth competing programs, did not represent recognizable social groupings. Claiming only to act in the "true interests" of the larger party, "disloyal" extremists always knew they had a great resource in the traditional partisan loyalties of the masses. The organizational weaknesses of the parties—particularly under conditions of the Violence—allowed such forces considerable security from any real discipline.[130]

On the Conservative side all these forces were concentrated in Gómez, who worked long and assidously to put himself into the presidency. He was the unquestioned leader of the party machinery. His weak support for the institutions of democracy had long been evident, not only in his flamboyant encomiums to the Spanish *Falange* but in his deeds. It was Gómez who was ready to give up democracy during the bogotazo in 1948 in favor of a military junta and who left the country immediately when Ospina resolutely remained in office.[131]

It was Gómez who sabotaged all efforts by Ospina to achieve convivencia with the Liberals.[132] It was Gómez's *El Siglo* that editorialized, on the eve of the elections, "We have not destroyed the myth of Liberal majorities in order to halt in a whirlpool of words. . . . We look not for peace but for victory."[133] It was Gómez who stood behind the Conservative National Directorate in October 1949 and proclaimed, six weeks before the election: "let the nation be saved, though democracy be lost in the saving"[134] Democracy was probably not a great historical evil for Gómez, as more ideologically inclined commentators sometimes argue. He once said of himself: "I don't know how to do anything but foul things up" (a somewhat euphemistic rendering of *poner pereques*).[135] Democracy, in 1949, was simply in his way.

There is still the question, however, of why he got his way. Ospina gave many signs throughout his presidency of wanting to preserve intact the system he had inherited. In addition, he had good reason to fear and dislike Gómez, who had deserted him in April 1948, in his moment of greatest need. But when the sticking point was reached, in September and October 1949, Ospina capitulated. His radical initiative of 7 October might have found a much more positive response from the Liberals if he had not preceded it by naming hard-line laureanistas to the Interior Ministry and six governorships. If he had been able, at that point, to name military officers to those positions—as he had done in his cabinet before the June congressional elections—the Liberals would have been much more persuaded of his neutrality. By taking away with one hand what he had given with the other, Ospina undercut those within the Liberal party who wanted somehow to save the system.

Assuming that he did share that desire, why could Ospina not handle Gómez? Why, with all the resources of the presidency at his disposal, was he unable to control the Conservative party? Aside from personal factors, the answer is in part that he could *not* command all the resources of the presidency. Liberal control of Congress and many of the provincial and local assemblies would not allow him to be as partisan as he might otherwise have wished. He chose a strategy of conciliation and coalition. What this meant in very concrete terms was that Liberals demanded and received much of the patronage available at all levels. Ospina could not deliver the administrative spoils that parties were accustomed to receiving upon conquest of the executive. He faced continuous pressure from within his own ranks. He was undermined as party leader by his position as coalition president.[136]

He was also undercut by the Liberals. Their implicit denial of his authority as a "minority president" did nothing to facilitate his potential for arbitration between the parties. More directly, their whole strategy of the electoral counterreform played into the hands of the most sectarian elements in the Conservative party. It moved up the date of the election and prevented a thorough, neutral renovation of registration. It said to the Conservatives, in effect, that the game would be played under the rules the Liberals had written over four successive governments, which included a generous cushion of fictitious registrations.[137] Ospina, who ultimately accepted the Liberal counterreform, was unable to protect his party through the laws. If they wanted to win the presidential election, the Conservatives had strong incentives to use more direct methods to eliminate what they regarded as a "phantom majority."

For the Liberal leadership, the "heroic projects" offensive represented an attempt to build the most militant strategy possible within the limits of the constitution. Still directed essentially toward winning power through the election, it was intended to answer those within the party who urged armed insurrection. But the leadership could maintain neither control of the party nor confidence in the president. It could not bring itself to condemn manifestations of Liberal disloyalty (in Linz's sense), but neither could it stand by, ultimately, as its fellow party members were persecuted by the police and army.[138] At the end of October 1949, as the last interparty negotiations collapsed, as reports of preelectoral violence reached the capital, party loyalty prevailed:

How are we going to accept being called tomorrow to erect national *convivencia* upon this bloody base? No! There will not be *convivencia* this way; because the dead upon which one tried to build it would rise to cry out to the Liberal leaders, "Don't be cowards! Don't be so accommodating! We perished for the ideas that you defended;

we fell in the battle to which you invited us. Over our dead bodies and the grief of our memory one cannot make a pact with the supreme author of the deed. . . .'' Our fellow party members who are falling under the hail of bullets and daggers are not victims of isolated individuals but victims of a party and of a system.[139]

It was not sheer humanitarianism, of course, that made the Liberal leaders decide to abstain, but realistic political calculation. With no representation in the electoral machinery, they were defenseless at the polls. If the Conservatives were to eliminate their majority by brute force, better not to lend the undertaking the legitimacy of their participation. Despite their frequently radical, sectarian rhetoric, the Liberal leaders put little that was concrete behind it.[140] Thus, when agreement could not be reached with the Conservatives, revolution was really no alternative to abstention.

Democracy broke down in Colombia in 1949 because the mechanisms upon which it rested were too informal, personalistic, and narrowly based. When governmental institutions offered no solution in a crisis, leaders from the two parties had to find some new basis for ad hoc consensus. This was a typically oligarchical mechanism, created in simpler times in a much less mobilized society. During the National Union period, "conversations among gentlemen" produced pacts between the parties in August 1947, April 1948, and April 1949.[141] None of them had any lasting effect, and the last efforts, which took place between August and October of 1949, did not even result in documentary agreement. The weight of saving the whole system rested on a few men, with uncertain control over their own subordinates and fellow elites,[142] in conditions of considerable general violence.[143] When the Liberals broke off personal relations with Conservatives at the end of October—even before the declaration of abstention and the state of siege—the last fragile support for oligarchical democracy was removed.

Reestablishing Democracy

Following the loss of democracy in November 1949, Colombian politics went through three phases before the National Front was installed in August 1958. The first consisted of the remainder of Ospina Pérez's term and the presidency of Laureano Gómez, from 1950 to 1953. It was a period of increasing violence and deepening dictatorship. It was ended by a widely welcomed military coup, led by Gustavo Rojas Pinilla. In this second phase, from 1953 to 1957, Rojas gradually alienated virtually all those who had exercised power in the previous regime and failed to establish an alternative base for his own authority. After lengthy negotiations, leaders of the political parties assumed the leadership of the opposition to Rojas and ousted him in May 1957.

In the third and final phase, presided over by a military junta from May 1957 to August 1958, the parties reestablished their former primacy in politics. A national plebiscite in December 1957 overwhelmingly endorsed the consociational National Front, which shared all legislative and administrative posts equally between the parties while alternating the presidency. Despite an abortive military coup in May 1958, a refurbished version of oligarchical democracy was successfully reinstalled by the presidency of Alberto Lleras Camargo (1958–62). Whatever its manifold faults and weaknesses, it endured, throughout its constitutional term of sixteen years, until 1974.

What explains this remarkable reincarnation? In the years from 1950 to 1958 both Gómez and Rojas—supported by significant elements within the church, the military, and the Conservative party—attempted to create new corporatist alternatives to oligarchical democracy. There were others who believed the Violencia could be made the catalyst for social revolution. They all failed. What enabled the politicians of the two parties to reconstruct the old game, very much on their own terms? And what brought them together in a common effort after the bitter divisions that led to breakdown?

The central social phenomenon of the period was the Violence. Although even today its historiography remains confusing and incomplete, the ways in which the Violence was understood and the way it affected contemporary events are fairly clear.[144] The dialectic of Liberal support for the guerrilla rebels and Conservative government repression had produced a situation, by the early 1950s, that had escaped from the hands of the political parties. Violence spread and intensified. Despite official optimism, government efforts to control it were of no avail. It increasingly took on the character of an incipient social revolution, a danger against which Alfonso López began to warn in 1952.[145] Rojas Pinilla offered amnesty to those who would lay down their arms, and for some time in 1953 and early 1954 hostilities lessened.

There was a sharp economic downturn in mid-1954, as world coffee prices plummeted, and the Violence flared up again. Pressures for a return to normalcy and to the previous regime began to appear among economic elites, who previously had had little incentive for opposition to either the Gómez or Rojas governments. Although the rural guerrillas never achieved a self-sustained revolutionary insurrection or even a unified command, they were a continuing source of disorder and insecurity in society. The army alone could not eliminate them. In the face of this failure, the arbitrary actions of the Rojas government in the cities—against the parties, newspapers, unions, students, and church—became progressively less tolerable. The return to oligarchical democracy was in part the result of the failure of other kinds of government to solve the fundamental social problem of the era.

There was also a decisive shift within the central social institutions that had previously been, in Linz's term, only "semiloyal." The church had nursed a long hostility to the Liberal party. It was, at best, divided and wavering in its support of democracy. But in the 1950s, the church tried to maintain some autonomy from both Gómez and Rojas, despite the fact that both courted it assiduously. With its traditional *Realpolitik,* the church accepted the Rojas government after the coup of 1953, and in Gómez's choleric reaction from exile in Spain, it may have recognized more clearly than ever before the dangers of close identification with any partisan force.[146]

The church began to become a more coherent, national organization in the course of the 1950s. The Jesuits pushed forward initiatives in several new fields of social action, notably the UTC labor federation. The National Bishops' Conference self-consciously examined contemporary events and their implications for the church's whole mission. The continuing Violence destroyed its triumphalist pride in a people *culto y cristiano* and threatened its institutional existence with the specter of revolution. It became specifically alienated from Rojas, who had fired on student demonstrators from the Jesuit Javeriana University, challenged the UTC with his own labor federation, and tear-gassed a packed Mass on Palm Sunday. The church was squarely behind his overthrow in May 1957. More fundamentally, it gave full support to the National Front, which, besides enshrining the church as the "religion of the nation," also guaranteed future Liberal governments. With an institutional coherence absent heretofore, it gave a significant endorsement to oligarchical democracy.[147]

The military had traditionally put a low value on its own status and competence vis-à-vis civilian politicians.[148] Professionalization had complemented this attitude by explicitly defining institutional functions within a limited sphere. Populist politics and the spread of the Violencia had challenged that valuation. As politics became more partisan, the army became more politicized; as politics became more violent, the army became more important. Its institutional professionalism threatened by Gómez's overt partisanship, the army under Rojas felt called upon to deliver the nation from the tragedy of its party hatreds.

That it was not able to do, in part because it was badly led. Rojas began by making the army the primary guarantor of order. He incorporated the police into its structure—neutralizing a key instrument of the old partisanship—and used the army initially as a broker between existing political forces. But he failed when he tried more actively to realign the bases of the polity. His quasi-Peronist "Third Force," characterized by a mixture of populism and corporatism, frightened almost all those who had benefited from oligarchical democracy without ever gaining the organizational strength to resist them. At the same time Rojas's personalist stance, with its cronyism and corruption, threatened the institutional unity of the armed services.[149] As civilian opposition grew and the Violencia continued, the officer corps came to believe that Rojas himself was a major cause of disorder. The junta that removed him in 1957 saw itself as a surgeon and then as a caretaker: order was primarily a political problem and the military would need party politicians to solve it.[150] In return, officers received assurances that any failings or excesses committed by the army in the past would be considered Rojas's personal responsibility, not that of the military institution.[151] The army and the National Front needed each other.

The National Front was the product of negotiations between the two historical parties beginning in 1956. To get to that point, politicians on both sides had to learn to recognize, between 1950 and 1956, their common stake in oligarchical democracy. In the early years Ospina and Gómez rebuffed the attempts of the Liberals to begin a return to democracy by reconvening Congress. By 1952, when police stood by while urban mobs burned down the offices of the Liberal daily *El Tiempo* and the homes of López and Lleras Restrepo, it had become clear that there would be no easy restoration. At the same time Gómez moved seriously toward installing a new corporatist order in his National Constituent Assembly (ANAC). This would have been a break not simply with liberal institutions but, perhaps most importantly, with the historical presumption of oligarchical politics against *continuismo*. Gómez's corporatist constitution was perceived as a thinly disguised means of keeping himself in power. It created opposition not only among the demoralized Liberals but—more dangerously—within his own party of government, above all from Ospina Pérez. Anti-laureanista Conservatives were a key support for the coup of 1953.[152]

Rojas frightened oligarchical politicians with his Peronist gestures and his attempts to bypass the parties altogether and forge a new kind of mechanism linking "the people" directly with the armed forces. But it was probably his determination to remain in office, his continuismo, that contributed the critical mass to the coalition that ousted him. Construction was begun by Alberto Lleras Camargo, the old López protégé, and Laureano Gómez.[153] Lleras used his prestige as a figure above the divisive intraparty battles of the 1940s to assume the leadership of the Liberals in 1956. His predominance was made easier by changes in the party in the intervening years: the old gaitanistas had scattered; the labor movement had been split and debilitated; and, with the changes in the Violencia, paramilitary forces were no longer key cadres to return the party to power. On the other side Gómez, surprisingly, was the obvious counterpart. Any movement to restore oligarchical democracy would have to begin with a common party opposition to Rojas. But in 1956 the *ospinista* Conservatives worked with and supported the Rojas government. Gómez, who still commanded great reserves of sentiment within his party, remained in exile in Spain.

From the Pact of Benidorm, which Lleras Camargo and Gómez signed in Spain in July 1956, to the so-called Civic Front statement of March 1957, to the Pact of Sitges of July 1957, there was a consistent development of the understandings that resurrected oligarchical democracy.[154] They represented lessons learned throughout the whole process of breakdown, both before and after November 1949. Their central theme was consociational guarantees. The principal cause of the sad plight of the nation, of the violence and dictatorship, was seen to have been each party's fear of exclusion and repression by the other.

Their understandings were reflected in the plebiscite of December 1957, overwhelmingly approved by the electorate,[155] which became part of the restored 1886 constitution. The parties were incorporated into the constitution itself, recognized as fundamental elements of the polity. A whole series of mechanisms implemented parity between the parties as a check on partisanship. Both parties were to receive half the membership of all legislative bodies, whatever their vote in a given district or election. A special majority of two-thirds was required for ordinary legislation. In addition, parity was to be maintained in the cabinet, the Council of State, the Supreme Court, governorships and mayoralties, and the whole administrative and bureaucratic apparatus of the executive.[156] These mutual checks within institutions were supplemented by those between them, notably in the effort to strengthen congressional (vs. presidential) controls over the executive (a lesson learned from the Liberal experience of the 1940s as well as from opposition to Rojas).

The National Front gave institutional substance to what, in the previous infra-democracy, had depended upon personal relationships. It represented a solution to one critical problem of the old oligarchical democracy, that of guaranteeing that neither party would be excluded from the stakes available in the state. What was most remarkable was that it represented little more than that. It was essentially an institutionalized elaboration of the old system, despite all the changes that had taken place in the society and the economy. The structural changes had unsettled politics and contributed to breakdown, but they never found the leadership or the organization to force a fundamental transformation. Those who aspired to channel the new currents in society fell before the combined forces of the oligarchical parties.

The Pact of Sitges had called the National Front *"convivencia* for a generation,'' an ''ordered and respectable democracy for those to come.'' It did solve the most basic problem of the nation, political order; the Violence gradually came to an end. But it was a conservative victory. Minority guarantees were more important than majority rule. The majority Liberals coopted their Conservative opposition, in a sense, but at the potential cost of casting the system in concrete.[157] It remains for future historians to decide whether this form of ''democratic convalescence'' made possible—or actually prevented—a fuller democracy, with a broader distribution of the power and wealth of society.[158]

Conclusion: Alternative Perspectives on Breakdown

Oligarchical democracy broke down because traditional party solidarity was strengthened at the expense of identification with the system—but without a concomitant increase in party organization and discipline. It did not break down, despite the claims of most existing commentaries, primarily because of the malevolent intentions of one party or the other.[159] Nor did it collapse, with some inevitable determinism, simply because social and economic change were so massive.[160] Rather, breakdown was a complex process of interaction between the structures of society and politics that reduced the options of the political elite and undermined the mechanisms of consensus between them. It was shaped most fundamentally by the character of the instruments operated by political elites—above all, the parties—and the experiential rules of the game within which they tried to make them work.

This analysis owes much to Juan Linz's general theoretical framework. It encountered many correspondences to the sequence of events he suggests precede a breakdown. More broadly, it found in his emphasis on the *politics* of breakdown—the explicitly political institutions and arenas, the political actors and their perceptions—the most persuasive explanation for why breakdown occurred in Colombia.[161] Thus this case study lends plausibility to Linz's scheme both by being consistent with it and by finding it demonstrably more useful than various alternative approaches to why breakdown occurred. Several of those rejected alternatives should be considered briefly here.

One perspective increasingly in use in studying Latin American politics is class analysis. A class-oriented interpretation might see breakdown as the result of pressures on the system from below, from masses mobilized by the modernization of the 1930s and 1940s whose needs (or "demands") were not met within the oligarchical democracy. The political expression of these pressures would be populism, and its instrument, Gaitán. The defeat of his social and economic reforms in 1947 and his assassination in 1948, in such a view, unleashed the tremendous popular frustration that became the Violencia. In confronting this popular rebellion, the ruling class was divided between strategies of cooptation and of repression. The breakdown, class analysts would argue, was the result of the failure of the ruling class to unite to protect their common interest.[162]

Such an interpretation would be most plausible if oligarchical democracy had collapsed in 1948, following the bogotazo, and not 1949. Significant inflation accompanied the gains in real wages in 1946 and 1947. When inflation accelerated in 1948, as real wages fell, there were very sharp increases in the cost of living in March 1948 in the major cities (see table 4).[163] The urban rioting that broke out all over the republic following Gaitán's death unquestionably expressed genuine popular suffering and anger against the system. It was the high point of populism, if populism is understood as a class phenomenon.[164] From that point on it declined rapidly as a significant force in politics. The gaitanista movement had been largely personalist, but now the *persona* was removed. Perhaps it was also undercut by the improving economy in 1949, when the material conditions of the masses were getting better (see table 4). The demands pressed from below on Liberal leaders in the second

Table 4. Cost of Living and Real Wages, 1940–50

Year	1 Cost of Living Index, Working Class Bogotá (1937 = 100)	2 Medellín	3 Real Wage Index, Working Class Manufacturing	4 Manufacturing	5 Industrial/Service	6 Real Salary Index, Nat'l Govt. Employees (1961 = 100)
1940	—	—	102	102	—	77
1941	113	99	101	100	—	80
1942	123	106	101	101	—	100
1943	142	124	107	108	—	86
1944	171	139	106	107	—	n.a.
1945	191	162	108	110	—	n.a.
1946	208	187	112	115	107	n.a.
1947	246	218	118	120	110	93
1948	287	262	109	112	107	89
1949	306	278	116	120	124	104
1950	—	—	114	119	142	98

SOURCES: Data for columns 1 and 2 from *Anuario general de estadística, 1945* (Bogotá: DANE, 1945), table 187; idem, 1949, tables 180 and 185. Data for columns 3, 4, and 6 from Albert Berry and Miguel Urrutia. "Salarios reales en la industria manufacturera y en el sector gobierno, 1915–1963," in *Compendio de estadísticas históricas de Colombia*, ed. Miguel Urrutia and Mario Arrubla (Bogotá: Dirección de Divulgación Cultural, Universidad Nacional de Colombia, 1970), tables 13 and 15. Data for column 5 from Economic Commission for Latin America (ECLA), *The Economic Development of Colombia*, vol. 3 of *Analyses and Projections of Economic Development* (Geneva: United Nations, 1957), table 75.

NOTE: Except where noted, 1938 = 100. Column 4 index includes various government-guaranteed fringe benefits (*prestaciones sociales*) not taken into account in column 3. Columns 3 and 4 apply to manufacturing workers in the departments of Cundinamarca, Boyacá, Norte de Santander, and Santander. The majority of the sample was probably drawn from Bogotá (Cundinamarca).

National Union coalition (April 1948–May 1949) were political in nature, not social. They concerned above all the need for protection from partisan government persecution (hence, the call for electoral and police reform). The Violence could never have taken on the scope it did if there had not been significant earlier social change, but in 1948 and 1949 it was still an escalation of the traditional party struggle more than any new kind of class warfare.

Events from 1950 to 1958 confirm the weakness of class as an explanation for breakdown. The Violence never became a social revolution. It consisted essentially of groups of peasants killing one another. The antigovernment guerrillas were never brought together under a unified command; the Liberal rebels resisted incorporation with Communist bands and retained the "false consciousness" of their historical partisan identification. Class unquestionably became more prominent in the Violencia of the 1950s, but the phenomenon as a whole remained ambiguous and contradictory. The localization of violence in the prosperous coffee regions and the seizures of land by peasant bands suggest one thing; the absence of violence from regions which lacked historical grass-roots party competition (as on the Caribbean coast) and the use of peasants by one landlord to seize the lands of another suggest something quite different.[165] In general these years demonstrate that, whatever its very real sufferings, *el pueblo* never became a self-conscious class. In December 1957 it voted overwhelmingly to return to oligarchical democracy.

Another perspective on the Colombian breakdown would have given greater prominence to the role of ideology. According to such an approach, the fundamental source of the breakdown would be seen as the redefinition of partisan cleavage in the 1930s and 1940s in socioeconomic terms, away from the old issues which had been largely depoliticized. A simple version of this approach—based on many of the parties' explicit statements about each other—might see the two collectivities as representing diametrically opposing views about society, with breakdown simply the showdown between them. It would take the rhetoric of politicians as a serious indication of what each of the parties wanted and intended to bring about, given the opportunity. More concretely, it would assume that what was at stake in the struggle between the parties in the late 1940s was the choice between (in their opponent's eyes) a godless, foreign, socialistic mobocracy and a reactionary, repressive, theocratic dictatorship. A more sophisticated version of this interpretation might argue that, in the course of the political crisis, it was the most ideological elements *within* each of the parties that came to the fore, moving each party toward an increasingly ideological self-definition. In either case, polarization and breakdown would be seen as the result of the ideological stakes each party had in the political game.

Political "ideology" implies a fairly coherent body of ideas about the social purposes of politics; it implies, furthermore, that those ideas significantly shape behavior and, more particularly, policy. If any force in Colombian politics should be understood in those terms, it is Laureano Gómez. His whole career as the leader of the Conservative party was shot through with visions of impending apocalypse.[166] No other politician—not even Gaitán—so consistently invoked ultimate ends and Manichean symbolism in his public discourse. His political life was a series of great moral crusades: against Yankee imperialism, against atheistic communism (Liberalism), against majoritarian democracy.

Yet, when he became president in 1950, he did not behave in a particularly ideological way. He did not embark immediately on the construction of a corporate, nondemocratic state. He did not even bother to apologize for his very successful campaign to attract American investment. He did favor a triumphalist Catholic church and persecution of Protestants; he did repress Liberals; he did rule as a dictator. But there was very little in his presidency to suggest a coherent plan or program. Most of what he did can be understood best as opportunism—he did what it took to put him in office and keep him there. What Gómez sought, ultimately, was not power for its social uses, but simply power for its own sake.[167]

Ideology played only a peripheral role in Colombian politics in the 1940s in general. Colombian politics had the appearance of "modern" politics elsewhere—contemporary Europe for example—with parties, organized interests, slogans of class. But the reality was more akin to politics in Renaissance Italy or classical Rome.[168] The operative groupings were more diffuse, the dominant motivations more particularistic, the characteristic style more private and traditional. The elites who excoriated each other so ferociously in public maintained personal relations in private—their *conversaciones de caballeros*—up until the breakdown itself. This atmosphere was encouraged by the lack of a social basis for true class or ideological politics. Like its nineteenth-century liberalism, Colombia's ideology did not grow organically out of indigenous conflict, but was imported from a different environment.[169]

The party factions sometimes clothed themselves in the rhetoric of ideology (for example, the "Left Command" of the 1949 Liberals), but for the most part they were known by personalist designations ("gaitanistas," "lopistas," "santistas," "laureanistas," etc.) after their leaders. Such groupings might well have represented different social interests in some general way, but it would be an overstatement to characterize their differences as ideological. They were not given to manifestoes or programs (in contrast, for example, to Chilean parties in the early 1970s). They did, however, have clear differences over tactical and strategic considerations and, above all, over who would enjoy the fruits of office.

Emotionally charged symbols and perhaps different mentalities did contribute to breakdown by reinforcing the mística of each of the parties. But it was ultimately identification with the band per se, devoid of any real ideological content, that mattered. This more traditional sort of identification lay behind the dialectic of the Violencia. The initial battles of 1946, which occurred at the lowest level of the system, principally involved the humble stakes of municipal patronage. Within little more than a year, violence had begotten more violence, in a kind of "defensive feud."[170] In a pattern of attack and revenge, of kill or be killed, the basis of solidarity (and safety) became partisan identification. It is romantic projection, unsupported by the known facts, to claim that the masses, who provided cannon fodder for the conflict, viewed it as a "holy war." It was not the revolutionary ideas of Liberal peasants that threatened Conservative peasants; it was their guns and machetes.[171]

Ultimately the best argument for emphasizing that political institutions and rules (rather than class or ideology) explain the breakdown of 1949 is the way democracy was reestablished in 1958. There were important changes, certainly, during the hiatus. The trauma of the Violençe made the value of order, for its own sake, apparent to virtually the whole society. It is significant, however, that the National Front represented (1) solutions that had been perceived (though not implemented) in 1949; (2) almost exclusively political guarantees, with no notable social character; and (3) an enduring settlement engineered by party politicians—in fact, even the same generation—intimately involved in the breakdown. This does not mean, necessarily, that there would never have been a breakdown if the Ospina plan of October 1949 had been accepted; it could have failed at some later point, just as the second National Union coalition had earlier. But the political content of the National Front, and the way the system was established by party politicians in 1957 and 1958, do suggest quite clearly that it was *political* factors (and political failures) that were central to the breakdown in 1948 and 1949.

Conclusion: Democracy and the Colombian Breakdown

Democracy in Colombia died as it had lived, oligarchical, and so it rose again. Founded in a society that comparative aggregate analysis would argue was unpropitious for its survival, it nevertheless worked for a considerable period of time. It broke down when it could not make the transition from its informal, diffuse, particularistic mechanisms to ones that were broader and more institutionalized. It was undone by the way modernization reactivated old problems on a scale unanticipated by the traditional rules. Colombia thus stands as an important case among a small number of democracies in societies with little modern differentiation—the oligarchical democracies.

Crisis in the system had to be handled oligarchically, by ad hoc agreement among party leaders. Elites committed to the system did exist in the 1940s and they understood very well the specific mechanisms that could have regulated their conflict.[172] Their failure tells us something about the limits of such political engineering. It can be vitiated if there are other leaders who lack such commitment to the system present, particularly if they are not clearly identifiable as "disloyal" and are able to use the same partisan identifications as the "loyal" leaders. More generally, political engineering encounters difficulty if there is competition and conflict among the top leaders within each of the negotiating collectivities.

To the degree that such competition exists, elites may not be able to control nonelites, neither masses nor middle-level brokers; but such control must exist before convivencia can be realized among leaders. Colombian democratic politicians, particularly the Liberals, showed many signs of insecurity in their party leadership. The problem was not simply, as Linz sometimes seems to imply, that "moderates" were lacking in courage or resolve. It was rather that, given the depth of partisan identifications, any conciliatory gesture could be the occasion of a deep split in the party or a repudiation of the leadership. On the other hand, the temptation to achieve party goals by domination rather than cooperation was high. Becoming the hegemonic "majority" was easy to envision when the only significant political cleavage simply divided the polity in two.[173] Trying to stay at the head of their own troops, anxious party leaders (especially the Liberals) may well have transferred the hostilities they felt toward internal challengers to a more acceptable target, the other party.[174]

Over the course of the oligarchical democracy, leaders had controlled followers essentially through a clientelistic system of concrete rewards. They had also been able to count on the traditional deference and apoliticism of much of the population.[175] Some of the new structures of incipient modernization—such as the trade unions—challenged these mechanisms. The Violencia destroyed traditional social controls. But none of the changes in the structure of politics was enough, ultimately, to effect a transition to a new level of organization. When oligarchical party elites reasserted their predominance over the new social forces by forming the National Front, they did so without any significant mass organization.[176] That oligarchical democracy survived is a tribute not only to the skill of these leaders but at least as much testimony to the weakness of the challenge they faced—the lack of explicit and organized alternatives to their system.[177] How much longer the system can continue on such foundations is an open question.

Another open question is the value of "democracy" for such a country as Colombia. There is a strong presumption among students of democracy that a democratic political system is fundamental to the realization of other social values, such as freedom, justice, and equality.[178] Clearly, democracy has not brought such blessings to Colombia in any great measure. It has not notably helped the country to identify and deal with its most important problems.[179] It has served to maintain stability in a social structure that the Catholic church, among others, has come to believe is highly exploitative and unjust.[180] In the breakdown of 1949 it was not clear even to elites, to say nothing of the masses, that a consociational democracy was preferable to various authoritarian possibilities of the Right or Left.

By 1957 it had become so. In the Hobbesian war of the Violencia, the value of order for its own sake became apparent. The National Front did bring about basic social peace, in a society that had long demonstrated an extraordinary capacity for unrevolutionary self-destruction. It did so with a political system of relatively low repressiveness. Latin America and the world have surely experienced many far worse regimes in the past twenty years. The oligarchical democracy is, at least, an open political system; it retains some capacity for change that has been lost in most of the rest of the continent. Whether Colombia can tolerate meaningful change will surely be tested in the near future. The results will be another piece of evidence as to whether "democracy" is a historically specific stage of Western political development or a more permanent, universal form of polity to which peoples will always aspire.

NOTES

1. John Gunther described Colombia in 1941 as "one of the most democratic and progressive nations in the Americas" (*Inside Latin America* [New York: Harper and Row, 1941], p. 161). Cf. the survey of "expert" opinion done by Russell H. Fitzgibbon, "Measurement of Latin American Political Phenomena: A Statistical Experiment," *American Political Science Review* 45 (1951): 517–23, which concluded that Colombia was the fourth most democratic country in the region in 1945.

2. The classic example of a more restricted, procedural definition is Joseph Schumpeter, *Capitalism, Socialism, and Democracy,* 2d ed. rev. (London: George Allen and Unwin, 1947), pt. 4. Recent works that stress the importance of participation for individual and social development are Peter Bachrach, *The Theory of Democratic Elitism* (Boston: Little, Brown, 1967), and Carole Pateman, *Participation and Democratic Theory* (Cambridge: Cambridge University Press, 1970).

3. Marxists have long argued that the conditions that can prevent free competition go much beyond overt force. Historically they pointed to the undemocratic nature of the control of information, an argument updated in sophisticated form by Herbert Marcuse, as in, e.g., (with Robert Paul Wolff and Barrington Moore, Jr.) *A Critique of Pure Tolerance* (Boston: Beacon Press, 1965).

4. The landmark article on the "requisites" of democracy (usually misread as the "prerequisites" for its creation) is Seymour Martin Lipset, "Some Social Requisites of Democracy: Economic Development and Political Legitimacy," rptd. in *Empirical Democratic Theory*, ed. Charles F. Cnudde and Deane E. Neubauer (Chicago: Markham Publishing, 1969), a very useful collection of the evidence on this and related questions.

5. Although voting for the presidency was made direct in 1910, the first election affected was that of 1914.

6. Colombian women first voted in 1957.

7. Before the late 1940s, the election campaign that involved the greatest violence against the opposition was that of the Conservative government of 1922. The Liberals produced a whole book of incidents, entitled *Los partidos en Colombia* (Bogotá: Editorial "Águila Negra," 1922).

8. The requirement that candidates adopt the label of one of the two traditional parties was an insignificant limitation in practice. The lack of party discipline made it possible for anyone

who wished to run to appropriate a Conservative or Liberal label. National Front governments defended themselves by force from revolutionary opponents, such as guerrillas. They did harass critics like Camilo Torres and may have deprived Rojas Pinilla of the presidency in 1970 by fraud. (The final margin was small and the trend of early returns reversed itself in middle-of-the-night counting—a scenario rather like that of Illinois in the U.S. election of 1960.) On the whole these governments permitted a comparatively wide range of civil liberties, though they became observably more arbitrary and repressive after 1970.

9. Such an analysis comes easily to those who study Latin America and are forced to reconcile the "instability" of its politics at one level with its many examples of continuity at another. The most influential description of the "Latin American political system" that exists beyond shifting appearances was Charles W. Anderson, *Politics and Economic Change in Latin America* (Englewood Cliffs, N.J.: Van Nostrand, 1967) chap. 4.

10. Dankwart Rustow emphasizes these specific historical circumstances in "Transitions to Democracy," *Comparative Politics* 2, no. 3 (April 1970): 337–63. A more general, comparative treatment of the creation of democracies is the sensitive and insightful study by Eric A. Nordlinger, *Conflict Regulation in Divided Societies,* Occasional Papers in International Affairs, no. 29 (Cambridge, Mass., Harvard University, January 1972).

11. The "rules of the game" as used here are imputed partly on the basis of expressed sentiments and partly on regularities in behavior. Such an analytical characterization attempts to go beyond the conscious norms of contemporary actors to include latent assumptions that later became manifest. It is not intended to describe an elite "political culture" (in the sense of general background dispositions) so much as an operative code growing out of the way political actors have perceived past problems and attempted to solve them. Cf. Daniel H. Levine, *Conflict and Political Change in Venezuela* (Princeton, N.J.: Princeton University Press, 1973) esp. pp. 231–54; and Philippe Schmitter, "O Sistema," in *Interest Conflict and Political Change in Brazil* (Stanford, Ca.: Stanford University Press, 1971), pp. 376–86.

12. Cf. Arend Lijphart, "Consociational Democracy," *World Politics* 21, no. 2 (January 1969): 207–25.

13. There were similar coalitions in the nineteenth century, of which the most important was the so-called National Party of Rafael Núñez in the 1880s. It brought together moderate elements of both parties around a new Conservative consensus, which was subsequently reflected in the 1886 constitution.

14. In 1909 an agreement was signed by key leaders of both parties that established a common set of principles on formerly divisive issues (e.g., the place of the church in national life). See Francisco de Paula Pérez, *Derecho constitucional colombiano,* 5th ed. (Bogotá: Librería Voluntad, 1967), pp. 230–31.

15. See Jesús María Henao and Gerardo Arrubla, *Historia de Colombia,* 8th ed. (Bogotá: Librería Voluntad, 1967), pp. 818–61 passim.

16. Jorge E. Rodríguez R. and William P. McGreevey, "Colombia: Comercio exterior, 1835–1962," in *Compendio de estadísticas históricas de Colombia* ed. Miguel Urrutia M. and Mario Arrubla (Bogotá: Universidad Nacional de Colombia, 1970), table 9, following p. 208. Coffee rose from 39 percent of export earnings in 1905 to 75–80 percent in 1924–26, after which oil also became a significant exchange earner.

17. Anderson, *Politics and Economic Change.*

18. Some 210,000 votes were cast in the 1856 presidential election, in which universal male suffrage prevailed. This figure represented perhaps 40 percent of the adult male population, certainly very high by world standards of the day. See David Bushnell, "Elecciones presidenciales colombianas 1825–1856," in Urrutia and Arrubla, *Compendio,* p. 310. On the origins of the parties and on electoral organization in this period, see Eduardo Santa, *Sociología política de Colombia* (Bogotá: Ediciones Tercer Mundo, 1964), pp. 39–70; Orlando Fals Borda, *Subversion and Social Change in Colombia,* trans. J. Skiles (New York: Columbia University Press, 1969), pp. 67–92; and Germán Colmenares, *Partidos políticos y clases sociales* (Bogotá: Ediciones Universidad de los Andes, 1968). Although corruption and fraud were commonplace, local electoral organization had continuing significance. See the good description by Helen Delpar in "The Liberal Party of Colombia, 1863–1903" (Ph.D. diss., Columbia University, 1967).

19. The 1876-77 conflict, for example, may have involved as many as 62,000 men, and the 1885 rebellion more than 50,000. See Luis Eduardo Nieto Arteta, *Economía y cultura en la historia de Colombia,* 2d ed. (Bogotá: Tercer Mundo, 1962), p. 383. Julio Holguín Arboleda, *21 años de vida colombiana* (Bogotá: Ediciones Tercer Mundo, 1967), p. 248, and William P. McGreevey, *An Economic History of Colombia, 1845-1930* (Cambridge: Cambridge University Press, 1971), p. 88, give lower estimates. A traditional *copla* from the nineteenth century runs: "In Colombia, that is the land/ of singular things,/ soldiers bring peace/ and civilians war". Quoted by Víctor M. Salazar, *Memorias de la guerra (1899-1902)* (Bogotá: Editorial ABC, 1943), p. 361.

20. Latin American parties in general have had a peripheral role in politics compared, say, to their European counterparts. See Robert Scott, "Parties and Policy-Making in Latin America," in *Political Parties and Political Development* ed. Joseph LaPalombara and Myron Weiner (Princeton, N.J.: Princeton University Press, 1966), pp. 331-67.

21. Edward Friedel and Michael F. Jiménez, "Colombia," in *The Urban Development of Latin America, 1750-1920* ed. Richard M. Morse (Stanford, Ca.: Stanford University Center for Latin American Studies, 1971), p. 62.

22. Alexander W. Wilde, "A Traditional Church and Politics: Colombia" (Ph.D. diss. Columbia University, 1972), chaps. 4 and 5. *Politics and the Church in Colombia* (Durham, N.C.: Duke University Press, 1979), is an expanded and revised version.

23. In Brazil or Venezuela, the military antedated political parties both as institution and as central political actor. See Ronald Schneider, *The Political System of Brazil* (New York: Columbia University Press, 1971), esp. chap. 2; Alfred Stepan, *The Military in Politics: Changing Patterns in Brazil* (Princeton, N.J.: Princeton University Press, 1971); Robert Gilmore, *Caudillismo and Militarism in Venezuela* (Athens: Ohio University Press, 1964); and Winfield Burggraaff, *The Venezuelan Armed Forces in Politics, 1935-1959* (Columbia: Missouri University Press, 1972).

24. See James L. Payne, *Patterns of Conflict in Colombia* (New Haven: Yale University Press, 1968), pp. 111-33, for an insightful analysis of the relation between the parties and the military, with a good short bibliography. See also Anthony Maingot, "Colombia: Civil-Military Relations in a Political Culture of Conflict" (Ph.D. diss., University of Florida, Gainesville, 1967); Richard Maullin, *Soldiers, Guerrillas, and Politics in Colombia* (Lexington, Mass.: Lexington Books, Heath, 1973); Francisco Leal Buitrago, "Política e intervención militar en Colombia," *Revista Mexicana de Sociología* 32, no. 3 (May-June 1970): 491-538.

25. There were reportedly attempts to have Conservative president Miguel Abadía Méndez call in the army in 1929 to prevent a Liberal government from coming to power in 1930. Abadía Méndez refused. See J. A. Osorio Lizarazo, *Gaitán: Vida, muerta, y permanente presencia,* 2d ed. (Buenos Aires: Ediciones Negri, 1952), p. 133. Of the various plots against Liberal governments between 1930 and 1946, the abortive Pasto coup of 10 July 1944 went furthest. President Alfonso López was held prisoner for several days, until it became clear that the army as a whole remained loyal. After this, however, the military was in some sense discredited and was doubly anxious to avoid intervention, despite Liberal overtures from 1949 on.

26. Cf. Merle Kling, "Toward a Theory of Power and Political Instability in Latin America," *Western Political Quarterly* 9, no. 7 (March 1956): 21-35.

27. Cited from Santa's *Sociología política de Colombia* (1955 edition), p. 73, by Germán Guzmán, *La violencia en Colombia: Parte descriptiva* (Cali: Ediciones Progreso, 1968), p. 358.

28. Malcolm Deas sees an important shift in this game with the great increase in central governmental resources that occurred beginning in the 1920s. See his rich, sensitive article on the structure and stakes of parties until the 1930s, "Algunas notas sobre la historia del caciquismo en Colombia," *Revista de Occidente* [Madrid] no. 127 (October 1973), pp. 118-40.

29. See Payne, *Patterns of Conflict,* pp. 51-73 and 185-237, for a provocative (though sometimes perverse) treatment of stakes and factions in Colombia. Payne estimated that posts based on merit comprised less than 4 percent of the total bureaucracy in the 1960s (p. 64).

30. Samuel P. Huntington, *Political Order in Changing Societies* (New Haven, Conn: Yale University Press, 1968), pp. 20-22.

31. Richard Neustadt, *Presidential Power* (New York: Wiley, 1960), Chap. 1.
32. See Fernando Guillén Martínez, *Raíz y futuro de la revolución* (Bogotá: Tercer Mundo, 1963), especially pt. 2, "Los modos de preferir."
33. The followings of the Conservative and Liberal parties were not fully comparable to, say, the Austrian *Lager* or the Weimar *Weltanschauungs gesinnungsgemeinschaften* because partisan identification did not reinforce a whole range of other social, economic, and status distinctions. Nevertheless, the strength of party identification down through society did make these followings the functional equivalent of Lijphart's "subcultures"—the vertical social groupings that had to be manipulated by elites to make consociational agreements work. See Lijphart, "Consociational Democracy."
34. The phrase is that of the nineteenth-century Conservative intellectual and president, Miguel Antonio Caro, himself often blamed for causing the 1895 civil war by his sectarian exclusion of Liberals from his administration. Certainly the most vivid and perhaps the most percipient description of Colombia's traditional political violence is in Gabriel García Márquez's magnificent novel, *One Hundred Years of Solitude,* trans. Gregory Rabassa (New York: Harper and Row, 1970).
35. See Orlando Fals Borda, *Campesinos de los Andes* (Bogotá: Facultad de Sociología, Universidad Nacional; Editorial Iqueima, 1961), pp. 260, 297–302. He writes of the village of Saucío, "open warfare caused each locality [within the area] to strengthen its internal political bonds as a way to survive in social conflicts. In this way, politics became for the *saucita* as important as life itself, since it was identified with his struggle for existence" (p. 299). See also Robert H. Dix, *Colombia: The Political Dimensions of Change* (New Haven: Yale University Press, 1967), pp. 213–14, where several other village-level studies on this point are cited. The feud, in the absence of any significant governmental penetration to most of the countryside, seems the most persuasive explanation of Colombia's singular pattern of vertical cleavage at the village level. Comparably intense party identification in other Latin American countries seems almost always to have had a regional basis—e.g., the Colorados and Blancos in Uruguay, the Apristas in Peru.
36. Even among the causes of the nineteenth-century civil wars, ideology was frequently less important than material stakes. See, e.g., Guillén Martínez, *Raíz,* p. 134. For a more general discussion of the nature of nineteenth-century political conflict, see Wilde, "A Traditional Church," pp. 132–41.
37. On "political decay" see Huntington, *Political Order,* chaps. 1, 4.
38. See Antonio García, *Gaitán y el problema de la revolución colombiana* (Bogotá: M.S.C., 1955), pp. 286–91, for a vivid description, and also *Los elegidos* (Bogotá: Tercer Mundo, 1967), a novel by Alfonso López Michelsen, son of the wartime president and himself president from 1974 to 1978.
39. Abelardo Patiño B., "The Political Ideas of the Liberal and Conservative Parties in Colombia during the 1946–53 Crisis" (Ph.D. diss., American University, 1954), p. 66: Gilberto Zapata Isaza, *¿Patricios o asesinos?* (Medellín? Editorial Ital Torino, 1969), pp. 119–20.
40. Maullin asserts, on the basis of an unpublished manuscript, that the coup attempt was jointly plotted by officers and Conservative politicians (*Soldiers in Colombia,* p. 58). Leal Buitrago, however, argues on the basis of his own interviews that the officers involved acted on their own initiative, reacting against what they regarded as López's politicization of the army. The president had some months earlier—amid constant rumors of coups—broken with civilianist tradition and appointed a trusted officer as his minister of war, ("Política e intervención," pp. 505, 533, n. 58).
41. This violence mirrored that which occurred in 1930–32, when Liberals replaced Conservatives in public administration. The major difference between it and that of the later period is that in the 1930s violence remained localized in only three departments and exhausted itself within a few years. Conservatives later claimed that it was the basis of their policy of abstention, but tactical considerations, primarily the need to allow Laureano Gómez to assert sole control over his badly divided party, were probably more important. On the party violence, see the good summary in Guzmán, *Violencia,* pp. 15–39, and Laureano Gómez's *Comentarios a un régimen,* 2d ed. (Bogotá: Editorial Centro, 1935). On the state of the Conservative party during this period, see Augusto Ramírez Moreno, *La crisis del partido conservador* (Bogotá: Tip. Granada, 1937) and the extremely valuable biography

of the Antioqueño Conservative politician, Fernando Martínez Gómez, *Don Fernando* (Medellín: Editorial Granamérica, 1963), by Pedronel Giraldo Londoño.

42. The interior minister's statement, interpreted as justification for repression, became a powerful cry of Liberals against any cooperation with Conservatives. The logic of the minister's full argument—as distinct from its political context—seems admirable enough on the face of it. See Rafael Azula Barrera, *De la revolución al órden nuevo* (Bogotá: Editorial Kelly, 1956), p. 292.

43. "Crisis" is used here in the sense employed by Douglas Chalmers in "Crisis and Change in Latin America," *Journal of International Affairs* 23, no. 1 [1969]: 78, i.e., to denote a period of emergency of which political actors are contemporaneously aware. This is in contrast to the usage of the influential Committee on Comparative Politics of the Social Science Research Council, which employs the term as equivalent to "structural problem." See, e.g., Leonard Binder et al., *Crises and Sequences in Political Development* (Princeton, N.J.: Princeton University Press, 1971).

44. Linz appears to define the "unsolvable problem" more narrowly, as one dealing with substantive policy and usually "created" in some sense by politicians. In Colombia the "unsolvable problem" was the problem of guarantees of the opposition and authority for the government—the problem of order itself.

45. "The die was already cast": "La suerte estaba ya echada. . ." (Carlos Lleras Restrepo, *De la república a la dictadura* [Bogotá: Editorial Argra, 1955] p. 306). The identical phrase is used to characterize this point at the beginning of November in two additional first-person accounts, that of the prominent laureanista Conservative, Joaquín Estrada Monsalve, *Así fué la revolución,* 2d ed. (Bogotá: Editorial Iqueima, 1950), p. 113; and that of the moderate Liberal congressman, Guillermo Fonnegra Sierra, *El parlamento colombiano* (Bogota: Gráficas "Centauro," 1952 [1953]), p. 250. These three accounts, with Azula Barrera, *De la revolución,* are all valuable for their insights into events and perceptions among the elite. So, too, is the political biography by Giraldo Londoño, *Don Fernando.* The most useful secondary accounts in English are John Martz, *Colombia: A Contemporary Political Survey* (Chapel Hill, N.C.: University of North Carolina Press, 1962), which draws heavily on contemporary journalistic sources; Vernon Fluharty, *Dance of the Millions* (Pittsburgh, Pa.: Pittsburgh University Press, 1957) by an author who was in Colombia for some of the events; Patiño, "Political Ideas," which also uses primary sources extensively; and Dix, *Colombia: Political Dimensions.*

46. Many authors could be cited, but Chalmers Johnson, *Revolutionary Change* (Boston: Little, Brown, 1966) is a convenient example. See, e.g., pp. 64–70, 106.

47. In addition to Linz one might list Huntington, *Political Order;* Nordlinger, *Conflict Regulation;* Rustow, "Transitions to Democracy"; Gabriel Almond, Scott C. Flanagan, and Robert J. Mundt, eds., *Crisis, Choice, and Change* (Boston: Little, Brown, 1973); John R. Gillis, "Political Decay and the European Revolutions, 1789–1848," *World Politics* 22, no. 3 (April 1970): 344–70; and Mark Kesselman, "Over-institutionalization and Political Constraints: The Case of France," *Comparative Politics,* 3, no. 1 (October 1970): 21–44.

48. Miguel Urrutia, a Colombian economist, argues that in 1913 there was probably less American capital in Colombia than in any other Latin American country. See *The Development of the Colombian Labor Movement* (New Haven: Yale University Press, 1969), p. 85. Between 1923 and 1929 U.S. investments increased from $4 million to $280 million; see J. Fred Rippy, *The Capitalists and Colombia* (New York: Vanguard Press, 1931), p. 152.

49. Colombia's per capita exports more than doubled in the 1920s, from 52.7 million pesos in 1922 to 132.5 million in 1928; see Urrutia, *Colombian Labor,* p. 84. The national budget increased from 43.5 million pesos to 107.5 million between 1923 and 1928, as the GNP grew at an annual rate of 7.3 percent between 1925 and 1929; see García, *Gaitán,* p. 241; and Dix, *Colombia: Political Dimensions,* p. 32, citing a Colombian economic plan.

50. The length of railroad track increased from 1,511 km. in 1921 to 3,122 in 1931 (still only a small fraction of the track at that time in Brazil, Argentina, or Mexico). Telephone line mileage increased from 5,095 in 1913 to 34,680 in 1927, while the number of phones went from 11,860 to 20,066; Fluharty, *Dance,* p. 32.

51. ECLA figures, cited by Juan Luis DeLannoy and Gustavo Pérez, *Estructuras demográficas y sociales de Colombia* (Bogotá: CIS, 1961), p. 72.
52. The number of airline passengers increased from 6,685 in 1933 to 103,136 in 1944 to 775,812 in 1949. Air freight grew from 0.7 million kg. in 1933 to 12.6 in 1944 to 139.4 in 1949. See DANE (Departamento Administrativo Nacional de Estadística), *Anuario general de estadística* (Bogotá: DANE, 1949) The airplane also made the Bogotá dailies a national press for the first time.
53. ECLA (Economic Commission for Latin America), *Analyses and Projections of Economic Development; 3, The Economic Development of Colombia* (Geneva: United Nations, 1957), p. 369.
54. Cited in Dix, *Colombia: Political Dimensions,* p. 32.
55. ECLA, *Economic Development of Colombia,* pp. 11, 32, 33.
56. DeLannoy and Pérez, *Estructuras,* p. 93. Figures are actually for employment in the primary sector, but mining can for all practical purposes be ignored here.
57. DeLannoy and Pérez, *Estructuras,* p. 70. Camilo Torres pointed out that peasants sought the cities in these times for the same reason that they had in the Middle Ages: security. See "Social Change and Rural Violence in Colombia," *Studies in Comparative International Development* 4, no. 12 (1968-69).
58. DeLannoy and Pérez, *Estructuras,* p. 93.
59. Cited in Urrutia, *Colombian Labor,* p. 183, from a government labor census.
60. The best analysis is found in Francisco Leal Buitrago, *Análisis histórico del desarrollo político nacional, 1930-1970,* vol. 1 of "Estudio del comportamiento legislativo en Colombia" (Bogotá: Tercer Mundo, 1973). See also Dix, *Colombia: Political Dimensions,* and Fluharty, *Dance.*
61. Leal provides a brief but provocative description of what he calls the "oligarchical corporativist system" in *Desarrollo político,* pp. 48-52. A convenient survey of the most relevant structures created by the Liberals is given by Carlos Lleras Restrepo, "La obra económica y fiscal del liberalismo," in *El liberalismo en el gobierno,* vol. 2, *Sus realizaciones, 1930-1946,* ed. Plinio Mendoza Neira and Alberto Camacho Angarita (Bogotá: Editorial Minerva, 1946), pp. 9-80. On the coffee growers' federation, see Christopher Abel, "Conservative Politics in Twentieth-Century Antioquia (1910-1953)," (Latin American Centre, St. Antony's College, Occasional Paper 3 (Oxford, 1973), pp. 15-16.
62. See Lynton K. Caldwell, "Technical Assistance and Administrative Reform in Colombia," *American Political Science Review* 47, no. 2 (June 1953): 503-5. The best study of this development is a private document not for citation.
63. It may be significant that the National Federation of Coffee Growers, the most powerful economic interest group in the country, did not take part in the initiative by economic elites in August-October 1949, represented by the "Pro-Peace Committee." Mariano Ospina Pérez, who had been the president of the federation for four years, said in 1946, "The coffee industry is neither Liberal nor Conservative. . . . Party politics have never penetrated into the Federation of Coffee Growers" (cited by Hugo Velasco A., *Mariano Ospina Pérez* [Bogotá: Editorial Cosmos, 1953], pp. 81-82).
64. It should be pointed out explicitly that the concept "populism" is used differently in Latin America than elsewhere, particularly in that it refers to *urban* mass-based movements. See Torquato di Tella, "Populism and Reform in Latin America," in *Obstacles to Change in Latin America,* ed. Claudio Véliz (London: Oxford University Press, 1965); and Alistair Hennessey, "Latin America," in *Populism,* ed. Ghita Ionescu and Ernest Gellner (London: Weidenfeld and Nicolson, 1969). There has been much popular and polemical literature on "populism" in Colombia in recent years.
65. The first "Electoral Participation" column in table 2 is more meaningful than the second because of corruption. By the late 1940s registration substantially exceeded eligible population.
66. The greatest challenge by new parties to Liberal and Conservative electoral dominance was registered in the 1945 congressional election, when the Communists and all other parties together received 3.5 percent of the vote. See *Colombia política: Estadísticas 1935-1970* (Bogotá: DANE, 1972) p. 154.

To found a new party was seen in time as essentially a device to enhance one's power within one of the traditional parties. Compare, e.g., Liberal Jorge Eliécer Gaitán's UNIR (Unión Nacionalista Izquierdista Revolucionaria), 1932–35, and Conservative Gilberto Alzate Avendaño and Silvio Villegas' reactionary ANP (Acción Nacionalista Popular), 1936–39. A more recent example is that of the MRL (Movimiento Revolucionario Liberal) of Liberal Alfonso López Michelsen in the 1960s. Both Gaitán and López Michelsen were eventually Liberal presidential nominees (López becoming president in 1974). Alzate would have had a strong bid to a Conservative candidacy in the 1950s if Gómez had not been overthrown.

67. The distinction is made by Chalmers in "Crises and Change," p. 78.

68. See Urrutia, *Colombian Labor,* and the Communist account of Edgar Caicedo, *Historia de las luchas sindicales en Colombia* (Bogotá: Ediciones CEIS, 1971), chap. 3.

69. Calculated from Urrutia, *Colombian Labor*, p. 183.

70. The creation of the Jesuit-sponsored UTC labor federation in 1946, to parallel the Liberal-Communist CTC, seems to have had little immediate effect on Conservative perceptions or strategies. There was still much opposition within the party in the 1940s to any kind of labor organizing. Although Ospina's government tolerated the UTC, illegal under Law 6 of 1945, it did not extend legal recognition until late 1949. With its tactics of economic unionism, the UTC never became a political arm of the Conservative party in the way the CTC was to the Liberal party in the 1930s. See Urrutia, *Colombian Labor;* Abel, "Conservative Politics"; and James Backer, "La historia de las influencias de la Iglesia sobre el sindicalismo colombiano," *Razón y fábula* [Bogotá], no. 22 (November-December 1970), pp. 6–27.

71. Cited in García, *Gaitán,* p. 272. A table listing the proportion of ministries and governorships for each party and for the military, by year, from 1930 to 1958, is given in Leal, *Desarrollo político,* Appendix.

72. The Liberal dominance of the cities was augmented only slightly between 1933 and 1949, although it may have accelerated between 1946 and 1949. See Richard S. Weinert, "Violence in Pre-Modern Societies: Rural Colombia," *American Political Science Review* 60, no. 2 (June 1966): 341, table 1. The proportion of the population residing in the departmental capitals had grown from 31 percent in 1933 to 39 percent in 1951. (See DANE, *XIII Censo nacional de población [Julio 15 de 1964]; Resumen General* [Bogotá: Imprenta Nacional, 1967], p. 31.) But one should not exaggerate the demographic side of the "permanent minority" danger for the Conservatives. Registration continued much lower in the cities than the countryside. Urban registration constituted less than 19 percent of the total at the end of 1947. See DANE, *Anuario general de estadística, 1947* (Bogotá: Imprenta Nacional, 1948), pp. 732–33. Despite the visibility of the new urban populism, the game was still won or lost in the *campo*.

73. "I compare this moment in Colombia with that of Spain during the revolution of '34. I think that, as [it was] here, civil war is inevitable. May God grant that we win" (Laureano Gómez, in Spain, August 1948, cited in Lleras Restrepo, *De la república,* p. 509).

74. As Conservative Roberto Urdaneta Arbeláez (later to become acting president under Gómez) remarked of the event, "Liberalism believe[d] that it ha[d] lost nothing, and Conservatism that it ha[d] gained everything" (Azula Barrera, *De la revolución,* p. 177). Azula's own analysis at this point, from a Conservative perspective, is cogent.

75. See Conservative complaints in, e.g., Velasco, *Ospina,* pp. 105, 118, 145.

76. The figure of 1,800,000 false Liberal registrations was frequently repeated by Laureano Gómez (see, e.g., Velasco, *Ospina,* pp. 176–77). For the most colorful description of electoral corruption, the plume must go to Conservative Gilberto Alzate Avendaño: "in Colombia, due to the voting of the absent and the dead, elections look more like a gathering in the Valley of Jehoshaphat!" (Estrada Monsalve, *Así fué,* p. 88).

77. Gaitán submitted a lengthy "Memoria de Agravios," documenting incidents of violence against Liberals, to the Ospina government in January 1948 and held a gigantic silent rally of protest in February. The text of his address on the latter occasion is reprinted in *Gaitán: Antología de su pensamiento económico y social* (Bogotá: Ediciones Suramérica, 1968), pp. 411–15, and an earlier "Memorial de Agravios," from April 1947, at pp. 399–410.

78. Echandía had been Santos's representative in negotiating a new Concordat with the Vatican

between 1938 and 1942. Even in Rome the Liberal impressed the Curia with his daily attendance at Mass and his knowledge of the Latin classics (see Giraldo Londoño, *Don Fernando,* pp. 136–37). The initial expectations of the Conservatives, and their later disillusion, is reported in Estrada Monsalve, *Así fué,* pp. 9–10.

79. The only other significant legislation of 1948 granted emergency economic powers to the president.

80. Azula Barrera, *De la revolución,* p. 279.

81. Part of the Liberals' willingness to consider reform may have been based on their losses to the Conservatives in municipal elections. Conservative municipal councils rose from 194 to about 350 after the 1947 elections, while the Liberals dropped from 607 to some 450. See Azula Barrera, *De la revolución,* p. 283.

82. Guzmán, *Violencia,* p. 366. On the organization of the police, see also Special Operations Research Office, *U.S. Army Handbook for Colombia,* 2d ed. (Washington, D.C.: Government Printing Office, 1964), pp. 396–97. The police were not fully nationalized until 1953, when Rojas Pinilla, in one of his first acts in office, removed them from the Interior Ministry and put them under the Armed Forces Ministry.

83. See Abel, ''Conservative Politics,'' pp. 34 ff.

84. Army officers keenly felt a difference between their professionalism and the partisan character of the police. See the review by Col. Alvaro Valencia Tovar of the first edition of Guzmán, *Violencia,* ''Informe sobre el libro, 'La Violencia en Colombia,' '' *Revista la nueva prensa,* nos. 85–86, (January-February 1963). It is interesting to note the confirmation of this view from within the police. See the judgment of a police captain quoted in Guzmán, *Violencia,* pp. 367–68.

85. Alberto Lleras Camargo, later president under the National Front (1958–62), spoke of the Violencia as ''unleashed, ordered, stimulated, without any risk, by remote control,'' consuming the countryside with the ''flames of madness,'' fed by fuel ''dispatched from urban offices'' (Azula Barrera, *De la revolución,* p. 231). There were many allegations of urban direction and supply of the guerrillas (see, e.g., Guzmán, *Violencia,* passim) but available evidence seems to indicate that this became significant only after the Liberals dropped out of the 1949 election.

86. After the 1946 election, Gabriel Turbay, the other Liberal in the race against Gaitán and Ospina, left the country and soon died in exile. Older oligarchical leaders, such as López, had undercut their position within the Liberal party by supporting Ospina against the Liberal candidates. Although Gaitán had control of the party machinery by 1947, he never commanded the party-in-government. In any case, he was removed from the scene in 1948. The lack of Liberal unity, even under very threatening conditions, was demonstrated in the 1949 congressional elections. The Liberals ran an average of 2.2 competing lists per department, the Conservatives only 1.1. See Payne, *Patterns of Conflict,,* p. 202.

87. See Lleras Restrepo, *De la república,* pp. 154–55.

88. Ospina opened Congress in July 1948, against the explicit demands of the Conservative party convention of that year, and in 1949 he resisted his party's repeated calls to close Congress from July on. On the first, see Martz, *Colombia,* p. 71.

89. See Martz, *Colombia,* p. 92. Most of the priests in novels about the Violencia are of this partisan type. See Gerardo Suárez Rondón, *La novela sobre la Violencia* (Bogotá: Ed. Luis F. Serrano A., 1966) pp. 61–80, for a discussion of various perspectives.

90. Cited in James E. Goff, *The Persecution of Protestant Christians in Colombia, 1948–1958* (Cuernavaca, Mexico: CIDOC, Sondeos No. 23, 1968), chap. 2, p. 47. Martz, *Colombia,* p. 84, lists at least five other bishops besides Builes who took this action.

91. Germán Arciniegas, *The State of Latin America* (New York: Knopf, 1952), p. 167. Examples of good and nonpartisan priests are found in Guzmán, *Violencia,* pp. 65–66, and Zapata Isaza, *¿Patricios?* p. 278.

92. *El Catolicismo,* 30 April 1949, cited in Martz, *Colombia,* pp. 83–84.

93. The first response of the Episcopal Conference to the bogotazo was narrow and institutional—a protest against such attacks on its buildings and personnel. Its later collective pastoral of 1948 had long refutations of ''Doctrinaire Liberalism'' and of communism, and an implicit warning against the Colombian Liberal party. See *Conferencias episcopales,* vol. 1 (1908–1953) (Bogotá: Editorial El Catolicismo, 1956), pp. 464–67, 469–

87. See also the Jesuit view, in an article published soon after the bogotazo, Francisco José González, S. J., "Persecución religiosa en Colombia en el golpe terrorista de Abril 9, 1948," *Revista Javeriana* 29, no. 145, (June 1948). Red-baiting articles in this publication are conveniently indexed in this issue, pp. 268–72.

94. The bishops expressed the hope that 1950 would bring peace to their land, torn apart "by passion and hatreds which are not only anti-Christian but antihuman, drenched with the blood of fratricidal battles . . ." (*Conferencias episcopales*, vol. 1, p. 492).

95. Lleras Restrepo, *De la república*, pp. 190–91, 295.

96. See Leal Buitrago, "Política e intervención," esp. pp. 502–3, and Gonzalo Canal Ramírez, *Del 13 de Junio al 10 de Mayo en las fuerzas armadas* (Bogotá: Editorial Antares, 1955), p. 18.

97. Maullin, *Soldiers in Colombia*, p. 58, and General Amadeo Rodríguez, *Caminos de guerra y conspiración* (Barcelona: Gráficas Claret, 1955), bk. 2.

98. Cited in Maullin, *Soldiers in Colombia*, p. 58.

99. The alternative of a military junta after the bogotazo was rejected by both Ospina and the Liberal leaders as contrary to Colombia's civilianist traditions. See Azula Barrera, *De la revolución*, pp. 386, 400–404; and Leal Buitrago, "Política e intervención," p. 507 and n. 68.

100. Leal Buitrago claims it had reached 20,000 men by 1949 ("Política e intervención," p. 508), while Maullin puts the figure at 15,000 (*Soldiers in Colombia*, p. 82), up from some 10,000 in 1944.

101. Guzmán, *Violencia*, pp. 372–73; Maullin, *Soldiers in Colombia*, p. 59; and Eduardo Franco Isaza, *Las guerrillas del llano* (Bogotá: Librería Mundial, [1959]), pp. 94, 145–46, and passim.

102. See Canal Ramírez, *Las fuerzas armadas*, pp. 22–25. Martz argues that even in 1953 intervention hinged on personal factors and was not inevitable (*Colombia*, pp. 167–69). This view is supported, from a perspective favorable to Gómez, in Camilo Vázquez Cobo Carrizosa, *El frente nacional: Su origen y desarrollo* (Cali: Carvajal, n.d.), pp. 83–124 passim.

103. The average increase was 5.8 percent annually between 1945 and 1954. See ECLA, *Economic Development of Colombia*, p. 12.

104. See, for example, the "Comentarios económicos" of Humberto Mesa González in the section on "The Month" in the *Revista Javeriana* 32, no. 159 (October 1949): (173–86), and idem, vol. 33, no. 161 (January 1950): 44–49, in which he concluded that, despite the political and social upheaval, the economy was in good shape and getting better.

105. A Liberal perspective in the final break with the National Union government is found in Fonnegra Sierra, *El parlamento*, pp. 213–16. The Conservative view is given in Estrada Monsalve, *Así fué*, pp. 47–57. Ospina, who had often resisted pressures from his own party, blamed the Liberal ministers and parliamentarians for giving in to those from their own.

106. Fonnegra Sierra, *El parlamento*, p. 218.

107. A Liberal congressman had suggested in 1947 that Ospina deserved the same fate as Bolivian president Villarroel, who had been hanged on a lamppost by a mob in 1946. Ospina later wrote that the Liberal salutation to the bogotazo prisoners, the "*nueveabrileños,*" finally convinced him of their disloyalty to democratic norms. See República de Colombia, *La oposición y el gobierno* (Bogotá: Imprenta Nacional, 1950), pp. 36–37.

108. "With one hand, [Liberalism] was throwing rocks, while with the other waving the white flag of peace." Of the 1947 general strike: "In spite of collaborating with the government, the Liberal party supported and was pleased by preparations for the strike" (Velasco, *Ospina Pérez*, pp. 196, 125). The phrase "*juego doble*" was often invoked by Conservatives.

109. Liberal leaders frequently condemned the Violencia. See, e.g., Lleras Restrepo, *De la república*, pp. 115–22.

110. "In many places the agents of authority have believed that in order to achieve institutional stability they should put force at the electoral service of the party of government" (Council of State, October 1949, cited in Fonnegra Sierra, *El parlamento*, p. 264).

111. Lleras Restrepo, *De la república*, p. 275; Fonnegra Sierra, *El parlamento*, 230–32.

112. There is a clear sense of this in the account of Fonnegra Sierra, *El parlamento*, pp. 231, 238. Whether either of the parties might have been justified in doing so is a question that this analysis does not try to answer. Nor does it attempt definitively to apportion historical blame or responsibility between the two sides.

113. The names of the most prominent of the committee's members are given by Ospina in his letter to them, reproduced in Mariano Ospina Pérez, *Historia de un proceso político*, vol. 6 of "El gobierno de Unión Nacional" (Bogotá: Imprenta Nacional, 1950), p. 236. This volume and Lleras Restrepo, *De la república*, offer the most useful documentation of the offers and counteroffers by the two sides during the "reduction of the arena."

114. Lleras Restrepo, *De la república*, p. 278.

115. Cited in "Vida Nacional," *Revista Javeriana* 32 (July-November 1949): (212).

116. Ospina Pérez, *Historia*, pp. 241–43; Lleras Restrepo, *De la república*, pp. 292–93; Giraldo Londoño, *Don Fernando*, pp. 301–3. Martz is incorrect in stating that the proposal came only after Echandía's withdrawal (*Colombia*, p. 93).

117. "The [Conservative] color blue became black in the persons of these individuals" (Giraldo Londoño, *Don Fernando*, p. 299). Bogotá's Liberal *El Tiempo* (4 October 1949) called the designation of the new governors "the most evil-tempered and unlimited demonstration of sectarianism that a government has ever dared in the Republic of Colombia" (cited in "Vida Nacional," *Revista Javeriana* 32 (July-November 1949): (208).

118. Lleras Restrepo, *De la república*, p. 279.

119. Cf. the editorial of *El Tiempo* of 25 September 1949, cited in "Vida Nacional," *Revista Javeriana*, 32 (July-November 1949); (214).

120. *De la república*, p. 182. Cf. p. 189, and the judgments of Giraldo Londoño (*Don Fernando*, p. 303) and Fonnegra Sierra (*El parlamento*, p. 217).

121. "Dictadura pactada": Lleras Restrepo, *De la república*, p. 292.

122. Daniel Caicedo's novel, *Viento seco* (Bogotá: Cooperativa Nacional de Artes Gráficas, 1954), which describes the agonies of the Liberal party in the Valle del Cauca during this period, devotes a large section to the massacre at the Casa Liberal. See also Zapata Isaza, *¿Patricios?* pp. 280-83.

123. Lleras Restrepo, *De la república*, pp. 280—81. Ospina replied, with some justification, that the registrar had made no protest when the Liberal electoral "counterreform" had greatly shortened the time available for reregistration. See "Vida Nacional," *Revista Javeriana* 33, no. 161 (February 1950): (18).

124. Fonnegra Sierra, *El parlamento*, p. 264. Cf. Lleras Restrepo's description of the government's characteristic "technique of the Violence," using thugs to intimidate Liberals after first replacing local military troops with sectarian police; *De la república*, p. 207.

125. Fonnegra Sierra, *El parlamento*, p. 248; Lleras Restrepo, *De la república*, p. 298.

126. Lleras Restrepo, *De la república*, p. 212.

127. Ibid., pp. 292-303; Giraldo Londoño, *Don Fernando*, 306-7.

128. Lleras Restrepo, *De la república*, p. 304.

129. Cf. ibid., p. 305, and editorials from *El Tiempo* cited in Fonnegra Sierra, *El parlamento*, pp. 256-57.

130. It is important to note that "disloyal opposition" to democracy may be present *within* the government (and in the party organization of an executive) as much as outside it. Linz seems to concentrate principally on the latter, drawing mainly from the European experience.

131. See Azula Barrera, *De la revolución*, pp. 384-86, and Giraldo Londoño, *Don Fernando*, pp. 276-77.

132. Cf. Guzmán, *Violencia*, p. 73, citing a Conservative source. It was very much the *exaltado* sentiment of Lucio Pabón Núñez: "Conservatism is ready to fight with force and to die as Christians and sons of Bolívar. . . . our motto is to triumph with the Government [of Ospina Pérez] or in spite of the Government" (cited in Patiño, "Political Ideas," p. 144).

133. Cited in Patiño, "Political Ideas," p. 150.

134. Ibid., pp. 200-201.

135. Ramírez Moreno, *La crisis*, p. 25.

136. Actually, Ospina was probably able to provide a very large number of Conservatives with government jobs without displacing many Liberals, due to the great expansion of revenues

that occurred in these years. This should have contributed to the possibilities of convivencia between the parties, and probably did. It may not have been enough in the end because both parties continued to *think* in terms of a zero-sum—rather than an expanding-sum—game.

137. The official figures of DANE, the national office of statistics, show that registrations exceeded the number of eligible voters (males over twenty-one) by nearly 20 percent by 1949. See table 2, above.

138. For examples of Liberal extremism, see Guzmán, *Violencia,* pp. 352–53, and the discussion on pp. 358–59 of the fanatical pamphlets (of perhaps dubious authenticity). Note the tacit admission by Lleras Restrepo concerning the congressional elites: "*in general* the *authorized* leaders of the party in the chambers did not propose nor accept but very moderate formulas..." (*De la república,* p. 267, emphasis added).

139. Lleras Restrepo, *De la república,* pp. 211, 212.

140. Consider the brilliant excoriation by Juan Lozano y Lozano of the "eminent public men of Liberalism... until yesterday so valiant, demanding, and dissatisfied," who failed to support the resistance of country people to "official violence" and instead "either hid themselves in their houses and private occupations or chose circumspection, moderation, good manners, cool heads, friendly approaches and respectful petitions" ("Prólogo" in Franco Isaza, *Las guerrillas del llano,* p. iv).

141. The phrase is from Lleras Restrepo, reporting on negotiations with the Conservatives, (*De la república,* p. 188). It was also used by *El Tiempo* concerning the Gómez-Gaitán agreement of 1947 ("Vida Nacional," *Revista Javeriana* 29, no. 141 [February 1948]: (10)). A notable feature of this early pact was a provision for a bipartisan tribunal of guarantees. The text of this accord is given in the *Revista Javeriana* 28, no. 139 (Octubre 1947): (146–52). That of the later two pacts is in Lleras Restrepo, *De la república,* pp. 91–93, 115–22.

142. See Lleras Restrepo, *De la república,* pp. 283–84, 300, for documents that reflect the existence of such problems in the Liberal party.

143. It was the *relationship* between the Violencia and the political parties—rather than the presence of massive violence *per se*—that led to breakdown. Elite consensus would have been affected very differently by equally great mobilization and conflict associated, say, with *fidelista* guerrilla revolutionaries instead of identifiably Liberal and Conservative partisans.

144. A convenient descriptive survey on the Violencia, particularly sensitive to its military aspects, is Russell W. Ramsey, "Critical Bibliography on La Violencia in Colombia," *Latin American Research Review* 8, no. 1 (Spring 1973): 3–44.

145. Cited in Leal Buitrago, *Desarrollo político,* p. 88.

146. Wilde, "A Traditional Church," pp. 246–47.

147. Ibid., pp. 251–53.

148: Maingot, "Civil-Military Relations."

149. Maullin, *Solders in Colombia,* pp. 61–64 and 139 (n. 33); and *El proceso contra Gustavo Rojas Pinilla ante el congreso de Colombia* (Bogotá: Imprenta Nacional, 1960), passim.

150. The failure of a pro-Conservative coup from within the army in May 1958, during the period of junta government, confirmed for the officer corps the dangers of rule for the military institution.

151. Dix, *Colombia: Political Dimensions,* p. 128. Cf. the "theory of *desvinculación*" in Canal Ramírez, *Fuerzas Armadas.*

152. Leal Buitrago, *Desarrollo político,* pp. 87–90.

153. The most intimate account of the negotiations between Alberto Lleras and Laureano Gómez and subsequent negotiations between the parties is Vázquez Carrizosa, *Frente nacional,* the memoirs of a Conservative politician who served as an important intermediary, particularly in the early stages.

154. The central passages of all these agreements are conveniently gathered in Jorge Cárdenas García, *El frente nacional y los partidos políticos* (Tunja: Imprenta Departamental, 1958 [1959]), pp. 93–115. Fuller versions of the pacts of Benidorm and Sitges are given in Vázquez Carrizosa, *Frente nacional,* pp. 164–65, 277–83.

155. The vote was some four million in favor, two hundred thousand against. The text of the plebiscite is given in Cárdenas García, *Frente nacional y los partidos,* pp. 117–23; Cárdenas García also provides a useful constitutional analysis, passim.

156. Articles 2 and 4 of the reform anticipate the problems that would be faced in implementing parity, given the unstable, factional character of the parties. See Cárdenas García on *"lentejismo": Frente nacional y los partidos,* pp. 70–71.

157. Cf. Levine's analysis of the reestablishment of democracy in Venezuela after 1958.

158. The phrase is from the party pact of 3 March 1957.

159. Cf. most of the Colombian commentaries; Arciniegas, *State of Latin America,* and Martz, *Colombia,* are probably the most influential accounts in English.

160. Cf. Fluharty, *Dance,* and Orlando Fals Borda, "Violence and the Break-up of Tradition in Colombia," in *Obstacles to Change in Latin America,* ed. Claudio Véliz (London: Oxford University Press, 1965).

161. Cf. Charles Tilly, "Does Modernization Breed Revolution?" *Comparative Politics* 5, no. 3 (April 1973): 425–47, esp. pp. 436–44.

162. A variant class interpretation might stress changes *within* the dominant classes, especially between commercial, agricultural, and industrial groups. See Francisco Leal Buitrago, Social Classes, International Trade, and Foreign Capital in Colombia" (Ph.D. diss., University of Wisconsin-Madison, 1974).

163. The cost of living index for the working class in Bogotá rose from 262 to 284 from January to March 1948; in Medellín it rose from 235 to 257 from January to April. The urban riots occurred in early April. See DANE, *Anuario general de estadística, 1948* (Bogotá), tables 178, 182.

164. There has been little serious social science research done on populism in Colombia, or even on the bogotazo. I could find no account of the fate of Gaitán's economic reforms in the Liberal-dominated 1947 Congress. The program is reproduced in *Gaitán,* pp. 257–328. This volume and *Los mejores discursos de Jorge Eliécer Gaitán, 1919–1938,* 2d. ed., ed. Jorge Villaveces (Bogotá: Editorial de Jorvi, 1968), are useful collections of documents.

165. Cf. Guzmán, *Violencia,* and John Pollock, "How Violence and Politics are Linked: The Political Sociology of *La Violencia* in Colombia," Livingston College, Rutgers University, 7 February 1972 (mimeographed).

166. Patiño, "Political Ideas," is replete with examples.

167. We lack a good political biography of this fascinating central figure. A psychological study that tried to link his own peculiar personality to the problems of his party and times might be quite fruitful. Among the available works are: Alfredo Cock Arango, *Las víctimas del doctor Laureano Gómez* ([Bogotá]: no publisher, 1959); Felipe Antonio Molina, *Laureano Gómez: Historia de una rebeldía* (Bogotá: Editorial Librería Voluntad, 1940); and Antonio J. Vélez M. and Domingo Jaramillo H., *El paradigma* (Medellín: Librería Nueva, n. d.).

168. Cf. Lily Ross Taylor, *Party Politics in the Age of Caesar* (Berkeley and Los Angeles: University of California Press, 1949). A focus on ideology may be deceptive in attempting to understand even those polities in which it is most apparent. See the perceptive comment by Eric Nordlinger, "Democratic Stability and Instability: The French Case," *World Politics* 23, no. 1 (October 1965): 143.

169. See Wilde, "A Traditional Church," pp. 86–88, 153–60.

170. Payne, *Patterns of Conflict,* pp. 161–77.

171. This is not to claim that changes in the countryside—e.g., in the concentration of land ownership—did not also contribute to expanding the Violencia beyond its origins in party rivalry and feuding. It is only to say that *ideological explanations* for such changes do not seem to have played a significant part in motivating the conflict. Thus, I disagree with Richard Weinert's important analysis of the Violencia, which turns on the assumption that "peasants rose to the defense of a traditional order personified by the Conservative party, against Liberal peasants whose party affiliation identified them with modernization" ("Violence in Pre-Modern Societies," p. 346). There is no evidence, however, that Conservative peasants perceived themselves as "the sector being threatened by" the modernization policies of the Liberal party—as opposed to being threatened by more traditional party hostilities.

172. Cf. Nordlinger, *Conflict Regulation,* pp. 20–41.

173. Lijphart points out that such a dual cleavage of subcultures seems inherently more unstable than a multiple one, in which the various parties were forced to bargain with each other to form majorities ("Consociational Democracy," pp. 217–18).

174. For a very provocative analysis of how the political security of leaders may affect their attitudes toward conciliation, see Nordlinger, *Conflict Regulation*, pp. 54-72.
175. See Nordlinger, *Conflict Regulation*, pp. 73-87.
176. This contrasts sharply with, say, the Austrian and Venezuelan cases, in which party elites can impose compromises upon supporting social forces and interest groups.
177. The Colombian leaders faced nothing like, for example, the strong post-Peronist trade union movement in Argentina, which made it impossible to reestablish democracy on anything resembling the old assumptions.
178. For a brief empirical exploration of the relationship, see Robert Dahl, *Polyarchy* (New Haven: Yale University Press, 1971), chap. 2.
179. For the view that National Front governments avoided all significant problems, in part because of aid from the United States, see U.S. Senate, Subcommittee on American Republics Affairs, Committee on Foreign Relations, *Colombia—A Case History of U. S. Aid*, part of *Survey of the Alliance for Progress*, 91st Cong., 1st sess. (Washington, D.C.: U. S. Government Printing Office, 1 February 1969).
180. The Colombian church has been among the most timid in Latin American in assuming a "prophetic" stance against social injustice. Nevertheless, see Conferencia Episcopal de Colombia, *La Iglesia ante el cambio*, XXV Asamblea Plenaria, (Bogotá: Secretariado Permanente del Episcopado Colombiano, 1969), esp. pp. 34-38, and idem, *La justicia en el mundo* (Bogotá: Secretariado Permanente del Episcopado Colombiano, 1972), esp. pp. 105-14.

3.
Venezuela since 1958: The Consolidation of Democratic Politics

Daniel H. Levine*

In politics as in everything else, it makes a great difference whose game we play. The rules of the game determine the requirements for success.
E. E. Schattschneider, *The Semi-Sovereign People*

In the early morning of 23 January 1958, General Marcos Pérez Jiménez fled from Venezuela. His hurried departure brought an end to ten years of military rule, permitting the reestablishment of mass democracy, a form of political life Venezuelans had only begun to know in the postwar period. The nation's single prior experience with democratic politics, from 1945 to 1948, had been brought down by the military regime now ended with Pérez Jimenez's flight.

Since throwing off dictatorship in 1958, Venezuelans have built a strong and effective democracy.[1] Their success is particularly striking given the historical record. With only three years of civilian rule in the first fifty-seven years of this century, Venezuelans have achieved one of the few stable competitive political orders in Latin America. Divided by intense conflict and widespread political violence throughout the early 1960s, they have managed four peaceful transitions of power through free elections (1958, 1963, 1968, 1973). These are the first consecutive transfers of power through popular elections in Venezuelan history. Moreover, in 1968 power passed to an opposition party, also for the first time in national history. Burdened with a long and bloody tradition of military rule, Venezuelans have nevertheless produced a complex and powerful system of mass political parties—organizations which penetrate and shape all facets of political life.

Examination of the successful transition to democracy in Venezuela, and of

*This chapter was first written in mid-1973 and substantially revised in 1974. The author is particularly indebted to Guillermo O'Donnell, Alexander Wilde, and the late Kalman H. Silvert, steadfast friend of Latin American democracy, for their careful readings, criticism, and suggestions.

its roots in history and social structure, fits nicely with comparative study of the breakdown and survival of democracies. First, the historical record is both recent and relatively clear. A notable change is apparent in the norms and methods of political leadership during the two periods of democratic rule in this century. Although substantially the same people guided organizations and dealt with problems from 1945 to 1948 as did so after 1958, the way they acted and their basic understandings of politics are dramatically different. Second, the form in which elites redefined problems and possible solutions after 1958 is strikingly similar to the experience of other nations. Although the content of conflicts is of course determined by the peculiarities of national history, the form in which they have been resolved is common to many nations. Finally, the study of Venezuelan politics lends itself to the combination of two analytical perspectives all too often kept apart: first, a focus on structural variables (social structure, mobilization patterns, organizational change) and the way in which their evolution sets up likely points of conflict; and second, a set of variables closer to the explicitly political arena, involving the norms, beliefs, and actions of leaders. The close interrelation of structural and normative elements in Venezuela is central to the evolution of the political system in its present form and to its ability to survive the sorts of crises which wrecked the initial democratic experiment of the postwar years.

Structural and normative elements come together in the study of two central and related themes: conflict and legitimacy. In the course of Venezuelan history, basic lines of conflict have undergone major shifts, whose sources must be sought in changing social and economic structures and the way in which groups emerged from them. A further question concerns the creation of institutions to deal with these conflicts. The institutionalization of conflict, providing regular and routine channels for the expression and conciliation of interests, is of course central to any society's ability to manage disputes, allowing diverse interests to coexist. It is perhaps even more important to democracies, committed by definition to the *open* expression of conflict.

Successful institutionalization depends heavily on the degree to which common political processes, criteria of power, and institutions become legitimate to key sectors of the population. An essential question facing political leaders in a new system (or in an existing system where balances and rules have undergone sudden and drastic change) then becomes how, and at what cost, are potentially disloyal oppositions neutralized, incorporated into the system, or excluded and defeated? Here, "legitimacy" means more than mere adherence to a regime or set of authorities. Conflicts over legitimacy are not only disputes over words and symbols—whole systems of action are at stake. Thus, "legitimacy" is used here in a broad sense, to refer to the evolution of shared criteria of power (e.g., money, divine sanction, force, votes, etc.), proper methods of political action, and appropriate arenas for political action and decision.[2]

The development of common norms of behavior among Venezuelan political elites is perhaps the single most important factor differentiating the abortive postwar experiment in democracy from more recent experiences. The consolidation of democracy after 1958, I would argue, is best understood not in terms of the balance among forces (whereby, for example, groups favoring democracy overwhelmed its opponents), but rather in terms of changing definitions of the proper relations among social and political forces. These changes then made possible the development of broadened support for democracy, and the isolation and defeat of opponents on the Right and the Left.

Before going into the historical roots of change in Venezuela, let me outline briefly some major characteristics of the political system established after 1958. Briefly, Venezuelan democracy is a party system. The basic tools of political action are mass parties, the crucial resources of politics are mass mobilization and votes, and power is transferred through elections in which proportional representation and closed party list voting magnify the impact of party organization.[3] Parties are the principal agents for the expression of political conflict, and most political transactions are filtered through the net of party leadership and organization.

Working within these structures, after 1958 a self-consciously prudent leadership set out to redefine the problems of politics in such a way as to make the institutionalization of conflict possible. An operational code of coexistence was developed, marking off acceptable limits and methods of conflict. In this vein, decisions were taken to reduce the level and intensity of conflict, emphasize common interests, and exclude consideration of areas of irreconcilable differences. The establishment of such common understandings made coexistence possible by making the limitation of disputes feasible. For if such agreements are not reached, conflicts easily get beyond the capacity of settlement the parties possess. Moreover, they are likely to be defined in terms which challenge the legitimacy of the system and call into question the survival of competing groups. In such circumstances, the threat of all-out conflict is visible just below the surface of every particular dispute. This is what political elites sought to avoid.

The interaction of normative and structural factors cannot be emphasized too much. Party structures in Venezuela bring people into the political arena, mobilizing large, heterogeneous groups into competing alignments. The potential created in this way can be put to many uses. In recent years, political conflict has been expressed in forms ranging from sporadic street violence and open civil war to elections, parliamentary maneuver, and interelite bargaining and negotiation. The actual form and intensity of conflict depends on the perspectives of elites. As we shall see, party leadership in Venezuela has been able to assert an independent and relatively autonomous role, making general political needs and values prevail over the more limited demands of different sectors of the party such as students, workers, peasants, or teachers. These structural factors make changes in elite norms particularly important. Through their control of organizations, elites are able to shape mass behavior, as the rank and file accept new patterns of action because of a general faith in the leadership of organizations to which they belong. Mass behavior then changes in response to new leadership perspectives. The linkage between the two is structural—the nature of party organization. But the motivating force is normative, as the transformation of elite norms triggers other, related changes.[4]

The analysis which follows is organized in terms of structural and normative changes. In structural terms, the nature of social structure prior to the emergence of mass parties will be considered, to assess the impact of social change on party formation. In other words, how did social structure shape political structures in Venezuela? In normative terms, changing definitions of problems and solutions, and the development of trust, tolerance, and mutual guarantees between competing elites will be examined in the context of specific cases and kinds of conflict.

Origins and Breakdown

From 1908 to 1935, Venezuela lived under the powerful and repressive dictatorship of Juan Vicente Gómez. Under his regime, the administrative and political unification of the country was accomplished. Reinforced by growing oil revenues, Gómez created a permanent national army and an effective state bureaucracy for the first time in Venezuelan history. With these tools in hand, his regime was able to eradicate completely the heritage of civil wars and regional and party conflict which had characterized the nineteenth century. The day of the isolated *caudillo* was ended forever, and regional uprisings passed from the scene.[5]

The dominant central state built in this way had a tremendous impact on a weakly integrated society. In political terms, the affiliations and inherited loyalties which might have carried over to help organize groups within the society were shattered. The traditional parties (Liberals and Conservatives) which had dominated politics throughout the nineteenth century simply disappeared, as their social basis in regional militarism was destroyed.[6] Indeed, it was difficult for any kind of political organization to exist under Gómez— political organization per se was suspect.[7]

Moreover, since the mid-nineteenth century, political leadership in Venezuela has rested not with a stable socioeconomic aristocracy, but rather with a succession of armed caudillos.[8] The landed aristocracy was decimated in nineteenth-century civil wars: property and position depended heavily on political power, not the reverse. The absence of a stable aristocracy was complemented by the weakness of many other institutions which often reinforce social hierarchy. Religious sanctions, for example, were negligible, as the Catholic church barely existed in most of the nation, being particularly weak in the countryside, where most Venezuelans still lived. This is not to argue, of course, that there was no social hierarchy and no inequality. Inequalities were very great, but the important point here is that bonds of loyalty and felt obligation tying upper and lower groups together were in general weak and fragile.

Important social and economic changes also began during the Gómez period. The already weak ties binding social strata together were further weakened by the impact of oil. While helping create a dominant state, oil also contributed to social change by depressing traditional agriculture and stimulating massive population movements. Until the 1920s, Venezuela was an agricultural export economy. After World War I, however, a sharp drop in production was accompanied by a decline in exports of agricultural products, both as a share of total exports and in absolute terms as well. The rapid commercialization of agriculture and the exaction of ever-increasing burdens from the peasantry further contributed to change, by stimulating migration out of the countryside and creating a pool of grievances later crystallized in a powerful peasant movement.[9]

As agricultural production and exports declined, so did rural population. As table 1 shows, the rural-urban mix of the population has been more than reversed since 1936. In addition, urban population has grown much faster than rural population. These data reflect massive internal migration which still continues to pull many Venezuelans out of their native states and regions.[10] The proportion of the work force employed in agriculture also dropped, from 71.6 percent in 1920 to 33.5 percent in 1961, while employment in industry more than doubled, and services (public and private) jumped from 7.6 percent to 24.8 percent in the same period.[11]

The weakness of traditional social ties, combined with an intensive and widespread experience of change, magnifies the impact of new organizations once the repressive lid is removed.[12] This relation, between loose traditional ties and a powerful penetration of society by new organizations, is fundamental for Venezuela. All across the social spectrum, and in all regions as well, people became available for new jobs, exposed to new experiences, and beset by new problems. But the loyalties, organizations, and identities which might have provided some continuity in a period of change were largely absent. Thus, when parties began to organize after 1936, they expanded into an organizational vacuum full of potential recruits. The broadly based nature of change made heterogeneous, multi-class parties quite effective. Moreover, political parties themselves became a central organizing principle in the society. Party affiliation links members of disparate social groups (e.g., workers, peasants, students, professionals), while at the local level, party organization serves many functions—club, social center, employment office, and political movement.[13]

Table 1. Population Distribution, 1936–71

Year	Rural	Urban
1936	71%	29%
1941	69	31
1950	52	48
1961	37	63
1971	27	73

SOURCE: Adapted from "Cuadro 7, Pobloción clasificada segun areas urbana, intermedia, y rural y aumento sobre el censo anterior, censos de 1971, 1961, 1950, 1941, y 1936," *Censo de Población y Vivienda Resúmen Nacional Características Generales,* (Caracas: Ministerio de Fomento, 1974), vol. 1, p. 53. The Venezuelan census classifies persons living in centers of over 2,500 inhabitants as "urban." "Rural" as used here combines censal definitions of "rural" (under 1,000 inhabitants) and "intermediate" (1,000 to 2,500 inhabitants).

In this way, the stage was set for a massive expansion of political organizations once the Gómez regime passed from the scene. The tremendous growth of political organization, from zero in 1935 to the present situation in which party ties penetrate and organize many spheres of life, is in good measure due to Gómez's effective destruction of old structures and ties, and his unwitting stimulation of underlying social change.

With the death of Gómez in December 1935, the political landscape began to change rapidly. While limitations of space preclude any detailed examination of the events beginning in 1936, the long-term significance of this period is clear. The years immediately following the death of Gómez saw the initial foundation of mass political organizations, the introduction of a new political resource (mass pressure), and the beginnings (under party auspices) of secondary associations of all kinds, most importantly industrial and peasant unions. Here the potential noted above begins to be realized, as organizations are created and, along party lines, begin to penetrate many areas of life. Although student leaders returning from exile played an important part in the process, the most significant political development of these years is precisely the growth of mass organizations—often directed by ex-students, but seeking power through mass organization, going far beyond the traditional bounds of student action.

Gómez was followed in office by General Eleazar López Contreras, previously minister of war. At first, López moved cautiously against the new political forces being formed. But soon new political groups had been dissolved, incipient trade unions broken up, and a major strike in the oil fields thoroughly repressed. By March 1937, most leaders of these groups were either in exile, in prison, or in hiding, preparing to begin a long struggle underground. Although the new political forces failed in their immediate goals of social and political change, they clearly found roots in society. Thus, they were able to go underground and survive, forming leadership groups, making contracts, building organizational networks, and elaborating programs for the future.

Throughout López's term in office (1936–41), there was no change in the system of power. Power continued to rest on control of the army and state machine, and politics remained closed to mass participation of any kind. López Contreras was succeeded by his minister of war, General Isias Medina Angarita. Once in power, Medina began a gradual process of political liberalization and organizational expansion, giving open expression to the sources of power nurtured underground in previous years. Seeking a base of support independent from López, and perhaps influenced by the climate of democratic struggle in World War II, he opened the doors to massive political organization. With these changes in the air, an amalgam of groups applied for legal status, and the new party was formally constituted as Acción Democrática (AD) in September 1941.

Upon formation, AD immediately began a vigorous organizational drive destined to build a comprehensive national party structure.[14] AD pioneered the development of a new kind of political party in Venezuela—a permanent organization, existing at all levels and integrating many groups into the party structure. All major parties in Venezuela have followed this basic pattern. They are vertically integrated, with organizational structures reaching from block and neighborhood to the national level; and horizontally integrated, with functional groups such as labor, students, professionals, and the like represented within the party organization. These groups, of course, are themselves divided by competing party groups.

It is important to realize that while many organizations were created after 1936, these were mainly leftist in orientation, representing new seekers after power. Traditional sectors of society did not enter the organizational race, relying instead on continued control of the army and administration to guarantee power and privilege. Economic and social elites felt effectively represented under the old system, and religious elites also failed to build mass organization, depending instead on a network of elite schools and the general sponsorship of other power groups.[15] Such groups were not oriented toward the creation of mass organizations, which indeed must have seemed superfluous in a system which rewarded regional cliques, kinship ties, and personal influence networks more than mass organization.

During the Medina period, AD created a vigorous, effective, and closely knit organization. The party began to penetrate the society on a large scale, as organizers helped to set up and mobilize industrial and peasant unions. By

1945, AD had the upper hand in these areas. But the limited and tantalizing nature of political change was profoundly frustrating to the party.

Although the potential for participation had expanded greatly, the political system remained restrictive of actual participation. Indirect elections remained the rule, female suffrage was denied, and in general mass organization yielded little in the way of effective power. In the political market then in effect, mass organization was simply not a recognized currency. Politics was structured to reward other kinds of resources, and the chances for evolutionary change seemed slim.

This context helps explain the party leadership's acceptance of an invitation to join a military conspiracy against the Medina government. They saw this as a chance to initiate rapid, far-reaching change. The coup was launched on 18 October 1945. After several days of fighting, a provisional revolutionary government was formed, with four members from AD, two military officers, and one independent civilian. The three years which followed, commonly known in Venezuela as the *trienio,* marked the introduction of a party system into Venezuela, abruptly ushering in an experiment with mass political democracy.

Politics in the trienio was characterized by a great expansion of organization set against a pattern of intense and bitter conflict. In electoral terms, all qualifications for suffrage aside from age and citizenship were eliminated. In a nation with many illiterates, this made for an instant expansion of the electorate, from 5 percent of the population before 1945 to 36 percent immediately thereafter.[16] In addition, direct election was instituted at all levels, from municipal councils and state legislatures to deputies, senators, and president. New parties were also formed, most importantly COPEI (a Christian Democratic party) and Unión Republicana Democrática (URD), a party representing the non-Communist left wing of forces that had backed Medina. In general, avenues for the expression of interests were broadened and the costs of organization cut back. The case of labor is particularly notable. Both industrial labor and peasant unions expanded greatly in terms of numbers of unions and total membership. A national Peasant Federation was organized in November 1947, forming part of the Confederation of Venezuelan Workers also organized at that time.[17]

Democracy in the trienio was flawed by the absence of a sense of trust and mutual guarantees among major social and political groups. The nature of political conflict in the period bears witness to this. Many were threatened, in material and symbolic terms, by AD and its regime. Indeed, trienio politics offers a classic example of the problems new democracies face in gaining legitimacy among established groups and institutions. I would argue that conflicts over legitimacy were inevitable in Venezuela. A revolutionary regime had taken power, committed to a radical program of union organization, control over the oil companies, agrarian reform, expanded public education, and the like. Moreover, a new set of political rules was imposed which placed a premium on mass organization. This sudden change in the "rules of the game" left previously secure groups both open to question as to their own legitimacy and ill-equipped to defend themselves, since they possessed few mass organizations.

Such an encounter of new forces with already existing groups and institutions is bound to raise basic questions concerning the form of institutions and the proper means of generating and allocating political power. Moreover, in Venezuela the same factors that gave political parties such deep popular roots also fed the fires of extreme conflict. Among new groups, organizational loyalties reinforced the commitment to struggle. The organization itself became a rallying point, a symbol of action and commitment. Meanwhile, for weakly organized traditional groups, like the church, lack of organization meant inability to control the consequences of action. Without a regular net of organization, extreme appeals may be needed to reach and activate a potential clientele not normally within the reach of organization.[18] Thus, conflicts begin at a more intense and general level, and people join them at a crisis pitch. Conflict is intensified even further, and the stakes magnified even more, by the way in which sudden change in the rules of the game cut the ground from under traditional elites. Conventional expectations of deference and understandings of effective strategies become outmoded overnight. The consequence in Venezuela was a rising sense of powerlessness and persecution, particularly among Catholic, rural, and business interests.

In this way, AD managed in three years to alienate many important power factors in Venezuela, ultimately stimulating an opposition coalition broad enough to overthrow the government of Rómulo Gallegos on 24 November 1948. A brief examination of AD's relations with several major groups will illustrate the point.

Consider the case of the church and the Catholic sector in general. Intense religious-political conflict first arose in 1946, in a dispute over educational policy. AD clashed with the Catholic church, which saw the regime's attempt to expand public education while putting tighter controls on private schools as a direct attack on the church by a Socialist, atheist political regime. For Catholic elites and their sympathizers, the legitimacy of the regime and of the political system it represented was called into question. Catholic elites asserted their right to represent the interests of the (by definition) "Catholic majority," while AD based its claim to legitimacy on the "majority of the voters." These incompatible formulae symbolize the problem of AD-Catholic relations at this time. Catholic leaders did more than attack a set of policies: they questioned the legitimacy of any political system that could produce a result which so clearly distorted the "true" interests of the Catholic majority.

In this context, negotiations, bargaining, and compromise were likely to fail, for such strategies depend on the acceptance of a common frame of reference within which groups negotiate. But the nature of this common ground was itself at issue.

AD also aroused the enmity of many former members of the Gómez, López Contreras, and Medina regimes through its unprecedented trials of former public officials for illegal enrichment while in office. The vigorous expansion of trade union organization brought opposition from economic elites, particularly in the important oil industry, where AD-led unions were very active. Meanwhile, an ambitious land reform program was begun, and the entire structure of rural power was turned around as peasant unions, backed by now-sympathetic government officials, started to push for change.

Those who stood to lose naturally moved into opposition. Opposition from such groups, threatened in positions of power and privilege, was made more effective by the alienation of competing electoral elites. Responding to its traditional critics, AD insisted that its legitimacy arose from popular elections. This overwhelming base of support was demonstrated again and again during the trienio, as a series of elections returned large AD majorities at all levels. Insisting on electoral legitimacy, how then did AD lose legitimacy in the eyes of others committed to the same principles?

In the first place, competing electoral elites despaired of ever winning power by playing according to AD's rules. The party's mass support was too great. In practice, if not in theory, the system excluded all but AD. Moreover, it is important to realize that most previously successful influence strategies (involving informal cliques, family ties, or regional sentiments) were replaced by party networks—in effect, by AD. At the local level, the close integration of party and sectors meant that in the application of programs AD used party-based, exclusive criteria. This strategy, while securing AD's own base, destroyed its legitimacy among competing electoral groups.[19]

As other electoral elites moved toward opposition, more traditional groups felt reinforced, never having accepted the legitimacy of AD in the first place. For the church, and (more gradually) the military, the criteria of power and legitimacy espoused by AD were rejected outright. The church dismissed the idea that the majority of voters could thwart the inherent interests of Catholic majorities. The military was unimpressed by AD's claim to electoral legitimacy—in their view, governments always won elections. Moreover, military leaders became increasingly concerned by reports of armed labor battalions controlled by AD.

During the trienio, AD made little attempt to soften its relations with other parties or to formulate coalitions or working agreements with them on particular issues.[20] The political actions of AD and its leadership were instead marked by the promotion of programmatic and sectoral interests over the restraint of these interests in the pursuit of more broadly based support. Few in AD spoke as did Rómulo Betancourt, at the height of the conflict with the church over education:

... the Revolutionary Government guarantees categorically that it will not go back or stop in its path of democratic achievements. At the same time, however, it invites this sector [within AD] to serene reflection, through which it may distinguish the secondary from the basic and principal. Seeking a conciliatory formula in a problem is a method which prudence and a sense of responsibility always counsel; incompatible with simple stubbornness.[21]

The overthrow of AD thus stemmed ultimately from the threat its continued rule had come to pose to a wide range of social interests. Politics in the trienio was an all-out affair. Organizations were created and new forces mobilized without the development of common rules of democratic coexistence and norms to limit conflict. In all the cases cited, more detailed analysis reveals that AD failed to establish relations of trust and to extend mutual guarantees with major groups. Not all of the blame rests with AD, but clearly the possibility of offering compromise was within its power and was not pursued. For AD, arriving on the scene in 1945 with a young, inexperienced leadership and overwhelming power, incentives to moderation, concession, and compromise were few. Backed by immense electoral majorities and secure in its alliance with the military, AD leadership on the whole saw dissent and opposition not as normal and legitimate aspects of a plural society but rather as evidence of a potential counterrevolutionary conspiracy. Secure in their majorities, AD's leaders discounted the need to compromise with intense minorities, no matter how small in size. Incentives to trust and the extension of guarantees were weak on all sides. Older elites felt threatened in their values, ways of life, and survival, while new elites saw a challenge to the revolution in any opposition. The result of this mistrust and continuous mutual provocation was that the military coup of 1948 was greeted in many sectors as a deliverance from persecution.[22]

A cursory examination of the new military regime's acts indicates that the conflicts examined above were indeed crucial to the fall of AD. Some early measures included the derogation of two major laws passed near the end of the previous regime, the Organic Law of Education and the Agrarian Reform Law. The new educational statute restored private (largely Catholic) education to its pre-1945 position. In the subsequent decade, private education grew rapidly at all levels, while official schools stagnated and their number declined. New laws on agrarian reform made expropriation and distribution of land much more difficult. In addition, previously expropriated land (along with land earmarked for distribution) was returned to private owners, while peasant families were evicted. Unions were dissolved, both in industry and in agriculture, and political party organizations, especially those of AD and the

Communist party (PCV), were suppressed. All this was backed up by a growing apparatus of terror and repression.[23]

Reestablishment and Consolidation

The dictatorship that began in 1948 had a major impact on the subsequent conduct of democratic politics. The experience of resistance to military rule gradually forced cooperation on the political parties, and many who had been bitter enemies during the trienio came to work together, both underground and in exile, against the regime. Top leadership in exile, reflecting on recent events, recognized the role intense unabated conflict had played in weakening trienio democracy. As military rule grew more harsh and personalistic, the costs of these conflicts seemed all the greater and the incentive to avoid such conflicts in the future all the more compelling.

With the overthrow of military rule, steps were taken to correct the errors of the past. The most striking feature of Venezuelan politics after 1958 is the conscious, explicit decision of political elites to reduce interparty tension and violence, accentuate common interests and procedures, and remove, insofar as possible, issues of survival and legitimacy from the political scene. This new orientation took concrete form in an agreement signed between AD, COPEI, and URD in October 1958—the Pact of Punto Fijo. As Rómulo Betancourt noted, this pact reflected a belief that extreme partisanship and intense conflict during the trienio had opened the doors to military intervention. After 1958,

Inter-party discord was kept to a minimum, and in this way leaders revealed that they had learned the harsh lesson which despotism had taught to all Venezuelans. Underground, in prison, in exile, or living a precarious liberty at home, we all understood that it was through the breach opened in the front of civility and culture that the conspiracy of November 24, 1948—unmistakably reactionary and supported by some with naive good faith—was able to pass, a conspiracy which overthrew the legitimate government of Rómulo Gallegos.[24]

The Pact of Punto Fijo contains a series of points worth examining in some detail. First, the three parties explicitly recognized the existence of various parties and of differences between them as normal and legitimate, calling for the depersonalization of political conflict and the elimination of violence. Moreover, they pledged support for a common program, emphasizing mutual interests and shelving more controversial items which might lead to renewed bitter conflict. This commitment to a common program was reinforced by agreement to participate in a coalition government after the 1958 elections, *regardless of their outcome*. In this way, all parties were committed to the defense of the system. The pact further bound the parties to defend the democratic system in case of emergency. The votes received by all three were to be considered as support for the system. In addition, the principle was established that should a party leave the coalition, it did not therefore pass automatically into all-out opposition, but rather remained tied and committed to democratic institutions.

The Pact of Punto Fijo was an attempt to begin building a set of rules of the game acceptable to major groups, committing each to the survival of all through acceptance of the same set of political processes. Thus, the issue of survival was tacitly removed from politics, at least for the signers of the pact and the forces they represented. The possible problems posed by diverse interests and intense oppositions were to be overcome through the use of coalitions, the redefinition of key substantive issues, and the reworking of procedures so as to reduce the intensity of conflict. In these measures, one begins to see a reversal of trienio patterns—now the trade-off of sectoral interests versus compromise and system stability is to be resolved in favor of the latter. During the trienio AD was seen as a threat to religious, military, business, agrarian, and competing electoral elites. After 1958, party leaders set out to bury these fears. Examination of a series of cases, parallel to those prominent in the trienio, reveals striking difference in forms of action and guiding political norms.

The church presents an interesting case. After 1958, relations of the church and the Catholic sector in general to the political system underwent fundamental change. AD mended fences, substantially increasing official subsidies to the church and sponsoring the revision of legal arrangements which had subordinated the church to the state in previous years. In the sensitive area of education, the government, while remaining committed to expansion of public education, tried to avoid raising the potentially explosive issues of organizational principles and ideological justifications for education, thus avoiding trienio-style conflicts. Emphasis was placed instead on redefining the question in technical terms.

When educational reform did arise as an issue, the way in which it was handled is revealing. A lengthy series of secret negotiations was held between the coalition parties and the church—negotiations which were intended from the beginning as a means to compromise. The talks were structured to promote compromise, by emphasizing technical issues and separating them from more intractable questions of philosophy and orientation. A potentially explosive issue was thus redefined in a manageable fashion, procedures were developed for dealing with it (the negotiations), and great efforts were made to keep the conflict in the hands of elites, out of the public eye where leaders on all sides agreed that passions could easily be inflamed, allowing the conflict to get out of hand. Privacy, centralization, and control were the watchwords.

A key factor in the reconciliation of AD and the Catholic sector was a change in the role of the Christian Democratic party, COPEI. During the trienio, COPEI was caught up in a wave of religious opposition to AD. Recently formed at the time, COPEI was not sufficiently differentiated from the rest of the Catholic sector, by virtue of being a political party with political interests and values, to serve as a mediator between Catholics and the regime. After 1948, however, many of the party's most vociferous activists abandoned COPEI, leaving party leaders feeling that they had been used by reactionary opponents of AD, people not really interested in COPEI or its program. These perspectives help explain COPEI's willingness to serve as mediator and buffer between the sectors, often restraining more militant defenders of the church with arguments as to the need for political compromise.

This mediating role was facilitated by COPEI's role in government. The party's membership in governmental coalition from 1959 to 1963 provided an implicit guarantee of survival to the Catholic sector. Moreover, under the sponsorship of COPEI, many leading Catholics participated in government. Thus, in education, labor, agriculture, and other sensitive areas, many who had been bitter enemies in the trienio began to work together on common problems.

The evolution of AD-Catholic relations is a good example of the development of a sense of trust and mutual guarantees between old enemies. As the church and Catholic leaders discovered the willingness of AD to accept initiatives of compromise and offer concrete benefits in return, they began to realize that gains could be made within the system at a cost lower than that associated with all-out conflict. As Catholic elites discovered a disposition within AD to offer and accept initiatives of compromise within a framework of felt guarantees, the old sense of exclusion and powerlessness was replaced by the hope for real possibilities within the system. Catholic elites now felt that they too could win by playing according to AD's rules. A similar feeling helped mend fences between AD and competing political groups.

After 1958, AD moved from a position of absolute electoral dominance to the status of a major party, one among several key groups in the system. As tables 2 and 3 show, in the elections held from 1958 to 1968, opposition parties gradually increased their share of the total vote in both presidential and congressional races. This greater balance is also reflected in congressional representations (see table 4). The decline in AD's vote, plus subsequent divisions of the party which cut into its congressional strength, made coalitions both feasible (as forces were more evenly distributed) and necessary to the operations of government.

Coalition strategies may be followed for several sorts of reasons. As we have seen, it may be in the interest of stability to increase the numbers of groups committed to the system and benefiting from it.[25] Coalitions are also a common response to situations of fragmentation and intense, cumulative conflict. Elite decisions to counter the effects of division often take the form of

Table 2. Percentages of the Vote in Presidential Elections, by Party (1947–73)

| | Party | | | | |
Year	AD	COPEI	URD	PCV	Other
1947	74.5	22.4	—	3.2	—
1958	49.2	15.7	30.7	3.2	—
1963	32.8	20.2	17.5	—	27.8[b]
1968	28.2	29.0	22.2[a]	—	20.3[c]
1973	48.8	36.8	3.0	—	11.4[d]

SOURCE: Data for 1947, 1958, and 1963 are drawn from Boris Bunimov-Parra, *Introducción a la sociología electoral Venezolana* (Caracas: Editorial Arte, 1968), "Cuadros Anexos." Data for 1968 are from David Myers, *Democratic Campaigning in Venezuela: Caldera's Victory* (Caracas: Editorial Natura, 1973), appendix B, table 24. Data for 1973 from *Latin America,* 21 December 1973.

[a] URD in coalition with two other parties, FND and FDP.
[b] This figure includes votes for Arturo Uslar Pietri (FND), Wolfgang Larrazábal (FDP), and several minor groups.
[c] This figure includes votes for Luis Beltrán Prieto (MEP) and several minor parties.
[d] Includes 4.2 percent for MAS, 5.1 percent for MEP, and 2.1 percent for minor parties.

Table 3. Percentages of the Vote in Congressional Elections, by Party (1958–73)

| | Party | | | | | | | | |
Year	AD	COPEI	URD	PCV	FND[a]	FDP[b]	PRIN[c]	MEP[d]	CCN[e]	Other
1958	49.5	15.2	26.8	6.2	—	—	—	—	—	2.4
1963	32.7	20.8	17.4	—	13.3	9.6	3.3	—	—	2.7
1968	25.7	24.2	9.3	2.8	2.6	5.3	2.3	13.0	11.1	—
1973	44.3	30.3	3.2	1.2	—	1.2	—	5.0	4.3	5.2

SOURCE: Data for 1958 and 1963 drawn from Boris Bunimov-Parra, *Introducción a la sociología electoral Venezolana* (Caracas: Editorial Arte, 1968), "Cuadros Anexos." Data for 1968 drawn from David Myers, *Democratic Campaigning in Venezuela: Caldera's Victory* (Caracas: Editorial Natura, 1973), appendix B, table 28. Data for 1973 are from *Latin America,* 21 December 1973.

[a] FND (Frente Nacional Democrático) is a conservative party formed around the 1963 presidential candidacy of Arturo Uslar Pietri.
[b] FDP (Fuerza Democrática Popular) is a party based on the candidacy and appeal of Wolfgang Larrazábal, head of the provisional government which followed the overthrow of Pérez Jiménez in 1958.
[c] PRIN (Partido Revolucionario de Integración Nacionalista) is a product of a division of AD in 1962.
[d] MEP (Movimiento Electoral del Pueblo) is the product of a division of AD in 1967.
[e] CCN (Cruzada Cívica Nacionalista) ran in the name of ex-president Marcos Pérez Jiménez.

Table 4. Congressional Representation, by Party (1958–73)

Party	1958 Deputies	1958 Senators	1963 Deputies	1963 Senators	1968 Deputies	1968 Senators	1973 Deputies	1973 Senators
AD	73	32	66	22	66	19	102	29
COPEI	19	6	39	8	59	16	64	14
URD	34	11	29	7	18	3	5	1
PCV	7	2	—	—	5	1	2	—
FND	—	—	22	5	4	1	—	—
FDP	—	—	16	4	10	2	—	—
MEP	—	—	—	—	24	5	8	2
CCN	—	—	—	—	21	4	7	1
Other	—	—	7	—	7	1	12	2

SOURCE: Data for 1958, 1963, and 1968 from Juan C. Rey, "El sistema de partidos Venezolano," *Politea* 1 (1972): 216, 219, 223. Data for 1973 from *Semana,* 3–9 January 1974 (Caracas).

coalitions, both limited and all-inclusive. The experience of many smaller European countries, where subcultural fragmentation has been contained through a delicate network of coalitions, speaks directly to this point.[26]

AD assumed power in 1959 in coalition with URD and COPEI. URD left the coalition in 1960, in disagreement over policy toward Cuba, while COPEI decided to pursue an independent line in the next governmental period. But despite changes in composition, the orientation to coalition on the part of AD remained firm, and a different group of partners formed the government for the 1963–68 period.

Relations with military, business, and agrarian sectors reveal a similar cautious pattern. A careful policy of compromise with the military was followed. Many real benefits were provided in training, equipment, housing, pay, and the like. Meanwhile, a purge of old-line interventionist officers was combined with a campaign of persuasion, by President Betancourt and others, to convince the military that AD was the only solution. A right-wing military coup, it was argued, would only lead to a general antimilitary coalition, producing a Cuban-style revolution and the liquidation of the traditional military, as in Cuba.[27]

To conciliate business elites, strikes were restrained and the more Socialist elements of AD's party doctrine were toned down. In the agrarian sector, a radical program of immediate large-scale expropriation and distribution of land was, on the whole, shelved in favor of a more "integral" program, stressing heavy capital investment and colonization, always less controversial than the expropriation of land already under cultivation. A clear indication of changing styles within AD is visible in the process followed in the preparation of a new Agrarian Reform Law. As with education, a law which in the trienio had been largely produced by one party now grew out of extended consultations among many groups.[28] Powell sums up the general issue well:

Should the leadership of the Peasant Federation, through land invasions and demonstrations, militate for a more rapid and drastic agrarian reform program, which might threaten the reformist government by strengthening the hand of its political opponents on the right, who opposed land reform? Or should the leadership use restraint in the pace of its demands and cooperate with the government in solving the administrative problems of the agrarian reform program, which might enhance the long-term probability of success and minimize political opposition to land reform, but at the same time might hazard the loyalty of the militant elements among the peasant masses? It was a replay of the tension from 1945 to 1948 between authority legitimation and interest articulation.[29]

The immediate result of these tensions was a major purge of radical leaders within the peasant movement, a purge conducted by AD party leadership and ratified by elections within the Peasant Federation and the general labor federation in late 1961 and 1962. Purges of radicals, combined with restraint in the tone and content of the agrarian reform program, clearly gained greater legitimacy for AD among traditional and competing elites. Traditional elites had less to fear, and competing electoral groups were able to survive within the unions, since after 1958 most unions and professional associations instituted a policy of proportional representation in order to eliminate the organizational parallelism characteristic of earlier periods.

In all these cases, legitimacy was won through restraint. Restraint, in turn, was achieved through open pressure by party elites on sectoral leadership to moderate demands in order to avoid arousing intense opposition and severe conflict. But why was a policy of restraint followed in the first place? First, AD leaders believed that more groups *should* be involved in the system (e.g., through coalitions), because it would strengthen the system and because it was right. This perspective was born of the experience of exile and reflection on the errors of the trienio. Second, leaders in AD and other democratic parties were afraid—they feared renewed conflict with the Right, and more importantly, they feared the extreme Left and the possibility of a Cuban-style revolution in Venezuela. Fear of the Left was widespread and was used by AD to keep the military, the church, and others lined up in support of the system. The threat of guerrilla warfare helped transform AD, in the eyes of others, from the Antichrist and extreme radical of the 1940s to a bulwark of moderation and stability in the 1960s.

Perhaps more than any other single factor, the development of a leftist strategy of insurrection in the early 1960s consolidated Venezuelan democracy, by unifying Center and Right around AD in response to a common threat. The alienation of the Left is so important that its origins deserve careful attention here. The decisions to reduce the scope and level of conflict after 1958 were made by top party leadership in exile and were later rejected by many who had led the underground struggle against military rule. This division, which often pitted younger leaders with experience underground against older exiles, was particularly notable in AD and URD. Young leaders saw the restoration of democracy in 1958 as an opportunity to push forward quickly with radical programs of change. Naturally, they rejected Betancourt's policy of coalitions and compromise with traditional elites, as these required the sacrifice of radical programs.

Moreover, during the resistance to military rule, AD and URD had cooperated as a matter of course with the Communists. Underground leaders saw no reason to exclude Communists from government and the administration of programs. The issue was joined from the very beginning, for the policy of coalition and compromise described above always excluded the Communist party, defined by Betancourt as a disloyal opposition.

The alienation of the Left took various forms. On the level of opinions and attitudes, the Left was isolated—Center and Right were close in attitudes, and both held positions far removed from those of the Left. In addition, the Left was much more divided internally than other opinion groups.[30] This division at the level of attitudes set the stage for AD's overall strategy—jettisoning the Left in order to reach compromise agreements with more conservative sectors. AD's leaders paid the price of their pursuit of compromise in a series of party divisions throughout the 1960s. In each case, more radical and Socialist elements split off after being expelled. The first and most serious split arose in April 1960, when the Movement of the Revolutionary Left (MIR) was formed. The MIR split was based on the generational-ideological cleavages already noted; and on formation, the new party took from AD its entire youth wing, some trade union groups, one senator, and seventeen deputies. The MIR immediately became a powerful force on the Left, posing a sharp, direct challenge to the legitimacy of AD's policies and procedures.

The first major clashes between the Left and the government arose over methods of political action. The government banned all unauthorized street demonstrations, and the Left replied by asserting that "the streets belong to the people," arguing that the regime should leave methods of popular struggle involving mass mobilization essentially untrammeled. President Betancourt rejected this position, arguing that the true reality of "the people" lay in their representative organizations:

The thesis that the streets belong to the people is false and demagogic . . . the people in the abstract does not exist . . . the people are the political parties, the unions, the organized economic sectors, professional societies, university groups. Whenever any of these groups seeks authorization for a peaceful demonstration, in a building or in the streets, there will be no difficulty in granting it. But as often as uncontrolled groups jump into the streets, under whatever pretext, they will be treated with neither softness nor lenience, for a country cannot live and work, acquire culture and forge riches, if it is always threatened by the surprise explosions of street violence, behind which the historical enemies of democracy, totalitarians of all names and colors, seek to engineer its discredit.[31]

In this speech, as often in action, Betancourt insisted on two central points: organizational concentration and the autonomy of politics. Limiting political methods by concentrating action in common organizational vehicles reflects a desire to avoid situations where conflict can get out of hand and to maintain a great deal of control over the consequences of action. Opposition and conflict are tolerated, and indeed built into the system, but are required to work within common forms and processes—parties, elections, congress, official agencies, and the like. Forms of action difficult to control, such as street demonstrations, land invasions, and private violence, are discouraged and suppressed. The autonomy of politics is affirmed by insisting that politics be left to professional politicians. Once leaders are elected by constitutional means, it was argued, they should be given considerable autonomy and not be subjected to a continuous barrage of demands. Betancourt's insistence on the concentration of political action in a limited range of organizations and arenas offers a clear alternative to "praetorian" politics, in which, according to Huntington, "social forces confront each other nakedly; no political institution, no corps of professional political leaders are recognized or accepted as the legitimate intermediaries to moderate group conflict. Equally important, no agreement exists among the groups as to the legitimate and authoritative methods for resolving conflicts."[32]

Conflict between the government and the Left escalated rapidly. Leftist parties were soon cornered and defeated on many fronts—their press was shut down, their labor leaders expelled from the trade union confederation, and their parliamentarians arrested. All this drove the Left to a strategy of insurrection, while poor economic conditions and apparent divisions within the government made them believe that any guerrilla war would be short and easy. The decision to launch an insurrection, taken in late 1961, represents the most basic challenge hitherto posed to the party system—a total rejection of its institutions as illegitimate, its methods as inefficient for identifying and resolving national problems, and its claims of democracy as a hollow shell for compromise with entrenched privilege.

The guerrilla movement failed. Although intense fighting continued into late 1964, the prospects for success were never very good, for the Left misjudged the nature of Venezuelan society. Their efforts to establish a base in the countryside were thwarted by previous organization and established loyalties. The untapped potential of the 1930s and 1940s was now occupied ground. For these reasons, the guerrilla movement was defeated politically before a shot was fired. It was isolated, unable to make alliances with other groups, and was gradually reduced to a shrinking core of die-hard militants.

The first to pull out were the Communists, who called a tacit truce in April 1965 and began to withdraw from armed struggle, opening renewed contacts with other political groups. Despite bitter criticism from the MIR, the Communist party Central Committee, meeting in 1968, concluded that the party should return to electoral politics. By this decision, the Communists implicitly accepted the rules of the game imposed by AD and its partners and began to seek reentry into national politics on their terms. This was accomplished by a front organization, Unión Para Avanzar (UPA), through which Communist candidates participated in the 1968 elections. The Communist party itself was legalized once again in 1969 by the new Christian Democratic regime. The changing position of the Left through the 1960s is very important for the political system. Insurrection was finally rejected by the Communists because it did not work. Furthermore, Communist leaders acknowledged that a strategy of armed struggle was inappropriate in Venezuela. To win power in a highly mobilized political order like Venezuela, it was necessary to organize masses and not to get mired down in vanguard strategies.[33]

The 1968 elections, while marking the reincorporation of the Left into the political system, were important in other ways as well. Power was turned over to an opposition party for the first time in Venezuelan history, as COPEI took office with only a slight plurality. In addition, by clarifying and reinforcing previous trends to a political system with a dual center (in AD and COPEI), these elections posed a potentially grave problem for the future. Given their key position in the political system, cooperation between AD and COPEI is clearly crucial to future stability. But direct, permanent coalition (on the model of the National Front between Liberals and Conservatives in Colombia) is difficult, if not impossible, given the need of both parties to maintain separate identities.[34] Rafael Caldera, the successful COPEI candidate for president in 1968, posed the issue this way:

... the union of Acción Democrática and COPEI would form an absolute majority in both Chambers. How could such a union be brought about? Could a governmental coalition really be established? On the one hand, Acción Democrática has as its immediate objectives internal reorganization and struggle for the conquest of power, which is its legitimate right within the law, and through the channels which the Constitution and our institutions have provided. This is probably incompatible, and they have expressed this to me, with participation in my government. On the other hand, I was elected as part of a national movement for change, and the nation would not understand my governing through a political coalition, which although perfectly respectable, has held power for ten years now.[35]

Although no formal coalition was put together during Caldera's administration, COPEI arranged a series of informal working agreements in the Congress with AD and other parties, ensuring sufficient cooperation to allow government to proceed. In this way, stability is guaranteed by continued moderation in the relations of government and opposition, without the need for institutionalization of such agreements in formal terms.

Conclusions: Norms and Structures

In analyzing the changing structure of conflict and its implications for political legitimacy and the survival of democracy in Venezuela, several factors might be emphasized. Consider first the role of prudent leadership.

From recent Venezuelan experience, it is clear that elites made conscious decisions to restrain and modify partisan conflict after 1958. This sort of decision, is, of course, rarely taken at any one time, but rather inferred, *post hoc,* from examination of events. In Venezuela, however, it is remarkable how easily one can pinpoint specific events in this pattern of decision: the Pact of Punto Fijo, formation of coalitions, negotiations with the church, restraint in programs, defeat of the Left, etc.

These decisions were part of the creation of a method for the institutionalization of conflict. Political elites in Venezuela did not set out to eliminate conflict. Rather, they recognized it as the legitimate expression of social diversity and invented means by which a variety of groups and interests could live together, without requiring the prior sacrifice of diversity as the price for stability. A central element of the method is its emphasis placed on common procedures, common forms of action, and mutual guarantees. In this context, "consensus" is a much more limited affair than is often implied by the use of that term—an operational code of coexistence, a delimitation of common ground, rather than an expression of identical substantive interests or beliefs.

The decision to accept and live with diversity deserves more extended comment. In studies of the breakdown of democracies, the argument is often encountered that democracy failed because traditional oppositions were not rooted out and a new social harmony instituted. It is similarly alleged that nations with patterns of cumulative cleavages, where social conflicts reinforce one another, are poor bets for survival, because of the nature of conflict itself. However, Venezuela, like many European cases, points up the potentially independent role of leadership decisions in counteracting social and political fragmentation or polarization.[36] In Venezuela, as we have seen, incentives to moderation and compromise, expressed through coalitions and a general reduction in partisan hostility, had a major, independent effect on the structure of conflict.

Venezuelan political leaders built a new political methodology, a set of procedures for handling conflict. The success of this method hinges on the central role of political parties. The great strength of party organization has provided elites with sufficient leverage to impose settlements on rank and file members. The role of leadership is reinforced by the fact that in Venezuela politics has clearly become a matter for specialists, a monopoly of the party organizations and their leaders. Parties play a key double-edged role in Venezuela. On the one hand, they manage the mobilization and incorporation of large masses of people into politics. On the other hand, by virtue of their broad and heterogeneous character, the parties per se have acquired an autonomous position with respect to any single sector. This development of a "public" perspective allows party leaders to aggregate many diverse interests, often restraining group demands in the name of overall political needs.

In normative terms, a profound learning experience occurred among Venezuelan leaders. Learning centered on the notion that politics really is what the cliché says: the art of the possible. Elites began to look at politics in terms of concession and compromise, and not merely as the all-out insistence on program and doctrine. Living in exile during the 1950s, AD leaders began to attribute their fall in 1948 to having pushed too many groups too far too fast. Thus, in marked contrast to their behavior during the trienio, political elites after 1958 exhibited several qualities essential to stability: restraint in goal-setting, restraint in the choice of means, and attention to intensities. Let us examine these points more closely.

Elsewhere in this series, Linz argues that what often seem to be unsolvable problems are not intrinsically so, but rather are produced by politicians who define problems in such a way as to create oppositions and conflicts that are themselves insoluble. In Venezuela, the devotion of leadership to redefining problems, methods of action, and relations among groups is very prominent. For example, the school issue, often a source of major conflict, has been resolved in Venezuela as a conflict over legitimacy.[37] The basic sense of guarantees between the Catholic sector and AD made possible lengthy negotiations over education. In this process, fundamental ideological differences were accepted and set aside, while talks concentrated on common ground. With agrarian reform, redefinition of the problem led to restraint in policy-making and implementation, concentrating on the search for less conflictive methods of agrarian reform. In the crucial area of methods of political action, the dominance of elections as a legitimate source of power is notable, as is the basic agreement among all groups to work within the commonly defined limits of the party system.

Structural and normative factors combined in Venezuela to favor what Etzioni has called the "encapsulation of conflict."[38] Encapsulation of conflict refers to the development of a self-enforcing set of rules and norms, whose constant use makes the system stronger by committing groups to act within already established processes. What were once innovations in intergroup relations become, through continuous, routine use, conventional expectations of common treatment. The successful implementation of these rules and norms rests, of course, on the viability of the structures through which they work. In Venezuela this means the political parties, whose deep social roots and powerful internal structure make the implementation of elite agreements possible.

The argument as presented to this point has an air of inevitability about it. But of course, no real social process ever proceeds quite as automatically as hindsight might lead one to believe. Rather, a wide range of situationally specific elements enters the process, and their impact must be taken into account. The key role of prudent leadership has already been emphasized. In addition, the structural and normative elements contributing to democratic stability received a powerful boost from the common threat posed from the Left. The exclusion of the Left from post-1958 political arrangements clearly helped legitimate AD in the eyes of its old enemies, making it a stable bulwark against repetition of the Cuban Revolution in Venezuela.

In this context, it is instructive to compare the evolution of the Catholic sector after 1958 with the fate of the Left. The Catholic sector was incorporated into the system. It accommodated itself to the system, acknowledged the legitimacy of political processes, and offered, sought, and accepted mutual guarantees of survival. The regime abandoned more radical elements in its program in order to secure the loyalty of Catholic groups, while the church, in turn, refrained from raising basic challenges and buried the hatchet of religious-political conflict. For the Left, however, already organized along mass lines, alienation from the regime resulted from precisely the kinds of bargains through which Catholics and others were incorporated into the system. But with the Left, no compromises were made until defeat was ensured. The extension of mutual guarantees was contingent on the abandonment of legitimacy conflicts in both cases, but the procedures differed notably: concession and compromise with the Catholics; and defeat and acquiescence in the system for the Left.

The difference between these cases deserves further reflection, because it contains, in microcosm, much of the explanation for the survival and stabilization of Venezuelan democracy. So far I have emphasized legitimacy conflicts and their resolution. But legitimacy conflicts are not all the same, and their resolution has different consequences for different groups. In Venezuela the regime incorporated traditional and established groups through compromise, convincing them of the benefits of organization and action according to the new system's rules. In this process, the system's rules do not change: rather, they are frozen, and the substantive limits of action are set in such a way as to avoid fundamental conflict. The incorporation of radical challenging groups, however, was contingent not on negotiation and mutual benefits, but rather on defeat. Here, incentives to compromise were rare, for radical challengers have little to gain from mere incorporation into the system. To achieve their goals, they must expand the system, broaden its scope, and mobilize new and hitherto excluded groups. But the bargains struck with traditional sectors exclude just this kind of strategy, ruling out immediate revolutionary change.

In cold strategic terms, then, it may be easier for democracies to incorporate traditional oppositions than radical ones. The Venezuelan experience presents a strategy of incorporating conservative groups first, and then defeating and reincorporating (on modified terms) the radical opposition. To those who decry such a strategy as a betrayal of the goals for which democracy was established in the first place, Venezuelan leaders might reply that it is better to reduce immediate demands and concentrate on establishing institutional continuity. In this way, the possibility of future change remains open, as institutions survive and acquire broadly based legitimacy. Immediate pressure for radical change might stimulate powerful opposition leading to a reactionary coup and the liquidation of all reform. In other words, half a loaf is better than none.

While, in strategic terms, this approach may pay off in consolidation of the system, it is important to realize that such results have a price—programs shelved, alternatives excluded, and change postponed. In closing I would like to consider some of the costs and consequences of the pattern of change in Venezuela in the 1960s and speculate briefly on the future.

Conclusions: Costs and Benefits

In the terms employed in these pages, Venezuela is clearly a "success." Democracy was consolidated in the face of determined opposition from both Right and Left. Mass participation has been maintained and combined with competition and stability, legitimate political institutions were built, and social progress has been achieved. But because Venezuela opted for success in the form described here, it represents to many not success, but rather an example of all that is wrong with Latin American development—increasing gaps between rich and poor, continued dependence on foreign economic control, and a reformist orientation which sidesteps basic issues of change. The costs of stabilization are alleged to be too great—the success of elites is viewed as a failure to implement "real change."[39]

Let us consider the costs of stability in Venezuela. A striking feature of Venezuelan politics is what might be called a structural coercion, operating at all levels of the political system. This coercion requires all groups and interests to work through the matrix of party if they are to be effective. A major factor preventing complete ossification has been party competition. The need to compete for support, and the increased balance among major parties, has helped avoid some of the dangers common to more hegemonic systems, such as riding roughshod over minorities.

Nevertheless, the current evolution of the system toward a dual center, shared between AD and COPEI, raises important questions about the fate of weaker groups. AD has convinced others of the benefits of working within the system. But if instead of a one-party hegemony, minor groups face a permanent duopoly, may they not feel equally frustrated? With little chance of ever achieving power or seeing their programs translated into action, will they feel the temptation of conspiracy or insurrection?

Furthermore, one important sustaining aspect of the system has been weakened. A major source of strength has been the ability of party leaders to control sectoral groups. But group interests are not infinitely malleable, and the long history of party splits in Venezuela bears witness to the rejection by some groups of these attempts at restraint. The tight linkage of party to sector remains, but multiple party splits have produced a division of control in trade unions, peasant syndicates, and other party-related groups. Instead of two or three major party lines, many sectors are divided into six or seven groups. This multiplication of divisions makes reliable and predictable coordination between levels of action less certain, and reduces the ability of government to control sectoral action.

A final problem for the future of the party system is perhaps a tribute to its own success. Since 1958, social change has proceeded apace, and Venezuela has developed an infrastructure of roads, transport, and electricity, while extending health and educational services in the nation. Population has grown, particularly in the cities, and the development of a national highway network has reduced the isolation of previously peripheral areas. But political parties remain closely tied to the geographical-demographic patterns of previous years. AD and COPEI are still largely based on the periphery of Venezuela, with most of their support in small towns and rural areas.[40] Despite tremendous migration to the cities (about one-fifth of the population now lives in Caracas), these parties have so far failed to organize support in the cities; urban voters have chosen instead to support nonparty, personalistic appeals.[41] In the long run, then, the key elements in the system may be based on a permanently declining share of the population.

The first version of this chapter was completed in September 1973, shortly after the overthrow and death of Salvador Allende in Chile. In conclusion, it is worth considering Chile and Venezuela together. Chilean politics from 1970 to 1973 bears a sharp resemblance to the trienio in Venezuela. Issues were increasingly defined in all-or-nothing terms, and many came to see their very survival threatened by the continued existence of the regime. All kinds of social groups were polarized and split apart, and the nation was engulfed in a rising tide of private and public violence. As a result, military action in both nations came in response to the calls of many political actors caught up in struggles which made the system seem illegitimate.

The experience of Chile is a sobering one and makes the costs and sacrifices entailed in the stabilization of Venezuelan democracy perhaps more acceptable.[42] For elites clearly saw these as necessary to ensure stability. Political leaders in Venezuela sought to build institutions first, believing that only with firm, legitimate institutions, and a broad commitment of diverse groups to their existence, could any reform policies be implemented. A set of authentic political traditions and the expectations created by action within common democratic processes had to be established first.

Perhaps Venezuela represents a middle ground. Since 1958, politics has been marked by the caution, prudence, and care appropriate to a period of transition and institution-building. The danger in such an approach is that decisions taken in response to the problems of a given situation may be transformed into permanent limits to change, and it becomes difficult for policy-makers in one period to break free of the restraints imposed in another. Perhaps now, with twenty years of experience in democracy, with a stable and skilled set of leaders occupying the Center, and the defeat of Right and Left alike, the scope of policy in Venezuela can be expanded to deal more directly with the pressing challenges and problems visible in the nation today.[43]

NOTES

1. This paper draws heavily on the ideas and data presented in my book, *Conflict and Political Change in Venezuela* (Princeton, N.J.: Princeton University Press, 1973). Given this general debt, no further reference will be made to the book, except to indicate the location of more extended discussions of particular points raised below.
2. A useful discussion of legitimacy in these terms is Charles W. Anderson, *Politics and Economic Change in Latin America* (Princeton, N.J.: Van Nostrand, 1967), pp. 90ff.
3. A useful discussion of the proportional representation system employed in Venezuela is David J. Myers, *Democratic Campaigning in Venezuela: Caldera's Victory* (Caracas: Editorial Natura, 1973), pp. 72–77.
4. The role of changing leadership norms in altering mass behavior is examined for Cuba by Richard Fagen in his *The Transformation of Political Culture in Cuba* (Stanford, Ca.: Stanford University Press, 1969), p. 150. For a general analysis of the role of leaders in shaping the political world of followers, see Murray Edelman, *The Symbolic Uses of Politics* (Urbana: University of Illinois Press, 1967), esp. chap. 1.
5. See Robert L. Gilmore, *Caudillism and Militarism in Venezuela, 1810–1910* (Athens, Ohio: Ohio University Press, 1964), for a study of regionalism and civil war in nineteenth-century Venezuela. A very good account of the transition to a new system at the turn of the century is Ramón J. Velásquez, *La caída del liberalismo amarillo*, 2d ed. (Caracas, 1973).
6. Velásquez, *La caída*, gives a brilliant account of the social basis of nineteenth-century militarism.
7. See A. Arellano Moreno, *Mirador de la historia política de Venezuela* (Caracas: Ediciones Edime, 1967), esp. pp. 19–21. In *La caída*, pp. xix–xx, Velásquez notes that "By 1935, younger generations doubted if struggle between parties had ever existed in Venezuela, in any stage of her history.... The regime founded by Cipriano Castro in 1899 and consolidated by Juan Vicente Gómez in his 27 years of absolute power had cut down the century-old trees of the political parties, and not even the memory remained of that political landscape. Venezuela was like ploughed land, waiting for the seed."
8. A useful account of the impact of nineteenth-century civil wars on the aristocracy is Domingo A. Rangel, *Los andinos en el poder* (Caracas: Talleres Gráficos Universitarios, 1964) esp. chaps. 1–4.
9. The best source on the peasant movement is John D. Powell, *Political Mobilization of the Venezuelan Peasant* (Cambridge, Mass.: Harvard University Press, 1971). Data on the decline of traditional agricultures are drawn from Powell, pp. 15–27, and María De Lourdes Acedo de Sucre and Carmen M. Nones Mendoza, *La generación venezolana de 1928: Estudio de una élite política* (Caracas: Ediciones Ariel, 1967), pp. 54–55.
10. José Silva Michelena, *The Politics of Change in Venezuela*, vol. 3, *The Illusion of Democracy in Dependent Nations* (Cambridge, Mass.: MIT Press, 1971), p. 79.
11. Silva Michelena, *Politics of Change*, p. 55, table 3.1.
12. This point is discussed in general terms in Samuel Huntington, *Political Order in Changing Societies* (New Haven: Yale University Press, 1968), p. 407.
13. The many roles of party organization in urban *barrios* are discussed in Talton F. Ray, *The Politics of the Barrios of Venezuela* (Berkeley and Los Angeles: University of California Press, 1969), p. 103.

108　DANIEL H. LEVINE

14. AD's initial attempts at organization are described in Rómulo Betancourt, *Venezuela: Política y petróleo,* rev. ed. (Caracas: Editorial Senderos, 1967), esp. chap. 3.
15. This is a common pattern in the traditional Latin American church. See Ivan Vallier, *Catholicism, Social Control, and Modernization in Latin America* (Englewood Cliffs, N.J.: Prentice-Hall, 1970), pp. 25–28.
16. Powell, *Political Mobilization,* p. 68.
17. Data on the growth of the Peasant Federation are provided in Powell, *Political Mobilization,* p. 79. The growth of the trade union confederation is reviewed in John D. Martz, *Acción Democrática: Evolution of a Modern Political Party in Venezuela* (Princeton, N.J.: Princeton University Press, 1966), p. 260.
18. For a general discussion, see James S. Coleman, *Community Conflict* (New York: The Free Press, 1957).
19. Powell, *Political Mobilization,* pp. 83 ff.
20. AD's attitude toward other parties during the trienio is discussed in Martz, *Acción Democrática,* pp. 321–22.
21. Speech by Betancourt on 12 June 1946, reprinted in *Trayectoria democrática de una revolución: Discursos y conferencias,* 2 vols. (Caracas: Imprenta Nacional, 1948), vol. 2, p. 22.
22. A Jesuit magazine greeted the fall of AD with an editorial entitled "God Has Saved Us." See *SIC (Revista de Orientación),* no. 110 (December 1948).
23. Changes in education in this period are discussed in Levine, *Conflict,* pp. 94–98. On the agrarian situation, see Powell, *Political Mobilization,* pp. 87–94. A general account of military repression is José V. Abreu, *Se Llamaba SN,* 2d ed. (Caracas: Editor, José Agustín Catalá, 1964).
24. Rómulo Betancourt, *Tres años de gobierno democrático,* 2 vols. (Caracas: Imprenta Nacional, 1962), vol. 1, p. 13.
25. This process works at several levels. Speaking of lower class urban groups, Talton Ray points out that "The proportionate size of the minority can grow, of course, as a result of a coalition arrangement which allows persons affiliated with the coalition parties to identify with the in group and therefore to share, in spirit if not in fact, the benefits of government attention. As more persons are brought under the coalition's umbrella, the ranks of malcontents are weakened and partisan contention eases off" (Ray, *Politics of the Barrios,* p. 167).
26. Two very useful general discussions are Arend Lijphart, "Consociational Democracy," *World Politics* 21, no. 2 (January 1969): 207–23; and Val Lorwin, "Segmented Pluralism: Ideological Cleavages and Political Cohesion in the Smaller European Democracies," *Comparative Politics* 3, no. 2 (January 1971): 141–76.
27. Betancourt's relations with the military are discussed in Robert J. Alexander, *The Venezuelan Democratic Revolution: A Profile of the Regime of Rómulo Betancourt* (New Brunswick, N.J.: Rutgers University Press, 1964), pp. 105–17, and Edwin Lieuwin, *Generals vs. Presidents: Neomilitarism in Latin America* (New York: Praeger, 1964), pp. 86–91.
28. The politics surrounding the Agrarian Reform Law of 1960 are described in Powell, *Political Mobilization,* pp. 106–12.
29. Ibid., p. 105.
30. For data on this point, see José Silva Michelena, "Desarrollo cultural y heterogeneidad cultural en Venezuela," *Revista Latinoamericana de Sociología* 3, no. 2 (July 1967), especially pp. 191–93.
31. Betancourt, *Tres años,* vol. 1, p. 245.
32. Huntington, *Political Order,* p. 196.
33. It is interesting to note that since 1968, the Communists themselves have suffered a major division. Younger and more radical elements were expelled and formed a new party. Here, as previously with AD and the MIR, conflict centered on the insistence of top leadership on hierarchy, discipline, and the need to save the party organization, even at the cost of sacrificing more direct and immediate revolutionary goals. Despite the nature of their critique, this group, now organized as the Movement to Socialism (MAS), also operates according to the rules of the game—actively building a trade union base while conducting a vigorous campaign for the presidency and other offices in the 1973 elections.
34. There is some evidence that President Betancourt wanted to explore the possibility of AD

and COPEI backing one presidential candidate in the 1963 elections. His initial efforts were rejected by his party. See Powell, *Political Mobilization,* pp. 196–97.

35. Quoted in Juan C. Rey, "El sistema de partidos venezolano," *Politea* 1 (1975): 225.

36. See Lijphart, "Consociational Democracy," and Lijphart, *The Politics of Accommodation Pluralism and Democracy in the Netherlands* (Berkeley and Los Angeles: University of California Press, 1968).

37. The school issue as a persistent conflict in Western European development is discussed by Seymour Martin Lipset and Stein Rokkan in the Introduction to their *Party Systems and Voter Alignments* (New York: The Free Press, 1968). See also Kalman H. Silvert, "Conclusions," in *Churches and States: The Religious Institution and Modernization,* ed. Kalman H. Silvert (New York: American Universities Field Staff, 1967), esp. pp. 216–17.

38. See Amitai Etzioni, "On Self-Encapsulating Conflicts," *Journal of Conflict Resolution* 8, no. 3 (September 1964): 242–55.

39. A sharply critical perspective is visible in Silva Michelena, *Politics of Change,* and also in Frank Bonilla, *The Politics of Change in Venezuela,* vol. 2, *The Failure of Elites* (Cambridge, Mass.: MIT Press, 1970).

40. See David Myers, "Urban Voting, Structural Cleavage, and Party System Evolution: The Case of Venezuela," *Comparative Politics* 8, no. 1 (October 1975): 119–51, for detailed ecological data which support this analysis.

41. A recent study of urban voting patterns in Venezuela is John D. Martz and Peter B. Harkins, "Urban Electoral Behavior in Latin America: The Case of Metropolitan Caracas, 1958–1968," *Comparative Politics* 5, no. 4 (July 1973): 523–50.

42. The late President Allende defined his differences with parties like AD and leaders like Betancourt in a revealing interview with Regis Debray. See Debray, *The Chilean Revolution: Conversations with Allende* (New York: Vintage Books, 1971), p. 70. As Arturo Valenzuela points out in his essay, the economic straits of the Allende regime made political solutions more difficult. (See Arturo Valenzuela, *The Breakdown of Democratic Regimes: Chile* [Baltimore: The Johns Hopkins University Press, 1978].) It is often argued that the great wealth of Venezuela is really what made political reconciliation possible—everyone could be paid off. But the Venezuelan state has enjoyed great wealth for many years, years which have seen bloody dictatorship and attempts at mutual extermination by political groups, as well as democratic reconciliation. Certainly wealth helps. But in Venezuela, it is clear that the political choices which made for democratic consolidation were *prior to and independent from* the use of money as a tool of reconciliation. The Venezuelan case makes a strong argument for the relative autonomy of political leadership, institutions, and choices—an argument all too visible, with different consequences, in the other cases considered in this volume.

43. I have speculated at length on the likely future prospects of Venezuelan democracy. See my "Venezuelan Politics: Past and Future," in *Contemporary Venezuela and Its Role in International Affairs,* ed. Robert Bond (New York: New York University Press for The Council on Foreign Relations, 1977), pp. 7–44.

4.
Political Leadership and Regime Breakdown: Brazil

Alfred Stepan*

On 31 March 1964 the Brazilian military overthrew the president of the country, João Goulart, and after assuming power themselves began to construct an authoritarian political regime.[1] Until that time, by almost any criteria, Brazil had not experienced a fully functioning democratic regime. However, from 1945 to 1963 electoral participation had become freer and had greatly expanded. Four presidential elections had been held on schedule in this period, and in each case the electoral victor had been installed in office. Though military intromission in politics was high throughout the period—a military overthrow of the elected president in 1954, a military coup in favor of the newly elected president in 1955, and an abortive coup attempt in 1961— the military nonetheless had not violated until this time a twentieth-century tradition that had kept them from assuming office themselves.

After the coup of 1964, however, despite frequent assertions by successive military governments of their intention to prepare the way for a return to civilian rule (as well as initially high civilian expectation that this would occur), military authoritarian control of Brazilian society steadily widened. Thus the acts of 1964 by which the military came to power saw the end of a quasi-democratic political system, and 1964 can be characterized as not merely a coup against a government but a breakdown of regime.

This breakdown was the end result of a long and complex process in which many factors played a part, a process whose complete treatment is beyond the scope or intention of this chapter.[2] In order to fit this study within the framework of the wider comparative study of the breakdown of regimes, the case of Brazil will be approached here from two levels. The first is the "macro-political" level, which examines strains within the political system of a social, economic, and ideological kind predisposing the regime to breakdown. However, it is clear that in Brazil these generalized strains in the

*An earlier version of this paper was first presented as part of the project on the Breakdown of Democratic Regimes at Varna, Bulgaria, in 1970. Because I found the approach useful I subsequently developed the argument in much greater detail in part 3 of my *The Military in Politics: Changing Patterns in Brazil* (Princeton, N.J.: Princeton University Press, 1971). I wish to thank Princeton University Press for permission to borrow heavily from that book for this chapter.

regime were not sufficient cause for its actual breakdown. Specific political strategies and acts, many of them the result of decisions or nondecisions by the chief executive, João Goulart, were also determinants in the final outcome of the crisis. The second level of analysis is thus the "micro-political" level, which takes us into a study of the quality and style of political leadership, especially in the crucial period immediately before the final breakdown of the regime. This area of inquiry allows us to get close to some of the most important variables in the breakdown of regimes, such as the ability or inability of a president to capitalize on existing supports and to avoid contributing to the consolidation of effective opposition.

The first part of this chapter, in accordance with the above schema, analyzes the changing social and economic context in which a sense of crisis arose in Brazil before 1964 and examines the ways in which this sense of crisis contributed to a belief among important military and civilian elites that the regime possessed neither legitimacy nor the internal ingredients for survival. The second part argues, however, that these broad political and social changes, and the declining value attached to the quasi-democratic regime in Brazil, did not in themselves bring about a breakdown of the regime. Many factors tended, until the very last days before the final coup of 1964, to support a continuation. What brought the regime to the breaking point was the quality of the political leadership of President Goulart, whose acts in the last months of the regime crucially undermined existing supports. The critical role that the sequence of political events and the quality of the individual political leader can play in shaping political outcomes has been relatively neglected in recent studies in comparative politics. In regard to the functioning of democracies, works such as Dankwart Rustow's on the emergence of democratic regimes, Juan Linz's on the breakdown of democratic regimes, and the writings of Arend Lijphart and Eric Nordlinger on conflict regulation in democracies redirect attention to the role of political choices and the sequence of political events in the formation, breakdown, or consociational consolidation of democratic regimes.[3] Brazil provides an interesting case study of the specifically political aspects of regime breakdown.

Social and Economic Loads on the Brazilian Regime

The strategies and actions of President Goulart can only be understood within the wider context of broad changes occurring within Brazil that contributed to a heightened sense of regime crisis. At the broadest level we can categorize the changes in the Brazilian political system in the years before the regime breakdown and especially between 1961 and 1964 in the following manner: (1) an increasing rate of political and economic demands made on the government, (2) a decreasing extractive capability due to the decline in the growth of the economy, (3) a decreasing political capability to convert demands into concrete policy because of fragmentation of support, and (4) an increasing withdrawal of commitment to the political regime itself.[4]

Some of these trends may in fact have been "cyclical" rather than "secular." Politically, however, the important fact is that in the crisis atmosphere that dominated Brazil from 1961 to 1964 these trends were perceived by much of the political elite as evidence of a structural crisis.

Social Mobilization and Economic Decline

One of the factors putting new loads on the political system was the rate and composition of population growth. Brazil's population doubled in the twenty-five years preceding the breakdown of the regime. Brazil had an average annual population increase of 3.0 percent, one of the highest in the world. In terms of comparative "loads" on the different economic systems, it compared with 2.4 percent for India, 1.2 percent for France and West Germany, 1.0 percent for Japan, and less than 1.0 percent for Bulgaria, Denmark, and England.[5]

The growth of the politically relevant population capable of making demands on the output functions of the government increased at an even faster rate than the population growth rate indicates. In the decade 1950 to 1960, Brazil's rural population grew from 33 million to 39 million, while the urban population grew much more rapidly, from 19 million to 32 million.[6] This new, rapidly expanding urban population created a whole series of increased requirements for transportation, jobs, and distribution of food and housing.

In the atmosphere of increasing social mobilization and inflation, growing demands were made on the regulative and distributive capabilities of the government. Strikes increased sharply and the government became more and more involved in strike arbitration. In 1959, for instance, government labor tribunals were involved in 524 labor conflicts; by 1963 this figure had risen to 1,069.[7]

In addition to the rapid escalation of demands from the urban sector of the political system, significant elements of the rural population itself shifted in the early 1950s from "parochial" status to "subject" status, or even "participant" status.[8] In March 1963 rural workers were granted the right to form rural unions and for the first time came under the protection of the minimum wage laws.[9] These laws hastened the competition between individual political leaders, the Catholic church, and the government's highly political land reform agency (SUPRA) to organize the peasants into cooperatives, peasant leagues, and rural unions. It is true that the revolutionary nature and class consciousness of Francisco Julião and the peasant leagues were overrated and overpublicized.[10] Nonetheless, viewed historically, a major change was occurring in the quality and quantity of political demands that the peasants and their political mentors were making on the political system.[11]

A final indicator of increasing social mobilization is the electoral system. The total number of voters increased sharply from 6,200,805 in the 1945 presidential election to 14,747,321 in the 1962 congressional and gubernatorial elections.[12] More importantly, the political intensity and ideological polarization in the 1962 elections was much greater than in previous elections, as numerous leftists staged vigorous campaigns and were opposed by militant free enterprise and anti-Communist business groups.[13] This increasing political competition both reflected and created a rising level of demands upon the political system.

At the same time, the political system showed a decreasing extractive capacity. In part this was due to a decline in the rate of growth of the Brazilian economy. Many of the demands in the 1950s had been satisfied by the rate of growth in the per capita gross national product (GNP), which for most of the decade was one of the highest in the world. In 1962, however, the growth rate began to decline sharply, and in 1963 there was an actual decline in the per capita GNP (see figure 1).

In terms of political capability, the increasing social mobilization and later the downturn in economic growth increased the demands made on the "dis-

Figure 1.   Percentage Change in Real Per Capita GNP, 1957–63

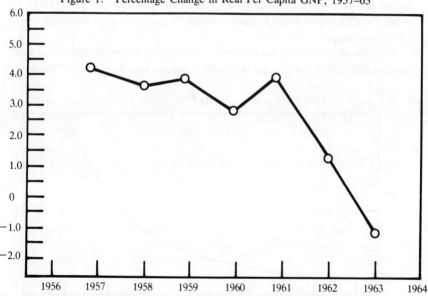

SOURCE: International Monetary Fund, *International Financial Statistics: Supplement to 1966/67 Issues*, p. 28.

tributive'' ability of the government in regard to goods, services, and payments. In response to these demands and in a populist effort to generate greater support, the Goulart government (in office between 1961 and 1964) increased government expenditure. The percent of gross domestic product (GDP) allocated to current account expenditure of the federal government—operational costs of the bureaucracy, subsidies, and transfers—rose from 10.9 in 1959 to 14.4 in 1963. At the same time, however, government tax receipts, which had risen from 17 to 23 percent of the GDP from 1955 to 1959, fell to 20 percent by 1963.[14] Thus in Almond and Powell's vocabulary of governmental capability we can characterize the Brazilian situation in 1962–64 as one in which the government's ability to extract resources such as revenue was declining while the loads on its distributive capability were increasing.[15]

One result was a rapid increase in the government's budget deficit, which accelerated the inflation. Brazilian inflation, always chronic, became acute after 1961 as prices rose by over 50 percent in 1962, 75 percent in 1963, and at a rate of over 140 percent in the three-month period before the collapse of the Goulart government (see figure 2).

The sense of crisis in the economic system was intensified by some indications that the industrialization process was not merely temporarily slowing but facing possible secular decline. The argument was raised that the import substitutions that had been a vital ingredient of Brazil's rapid industrialization in the 1950s were approaching the exhaustion point by the early 1960s.[16] Also, Brazil's export stagnation contributed to serious foreign exchange difficulties and import constraints.

The pressure on Brazil's economy was intensified because it coincided with a declining capacity to extract resources from the international environment.

Figure 2.   Cost of Living Price Index, 1957–63

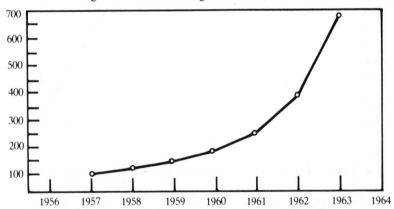

Source: International Monetary Fund, *International Financial Statistics: Supplement to 1966–67 Issues*, p. 27.

Both private and public resources were drying up, due to fears of (and reprisals for) Brazil's inflation, economic nationalism, and political radicalization.[17] By mid-1963, the U.S. government had begun to curtail new development aid contracts with the Brazilian central government. In 1963, debt repayment obligations were so staggering that the finance minister reported to the cabinet that amortization and interest payments already scheduled for the years 1963–65 would amount to $1.8 billion, or about 43 percent of the expected export revenues for that period.[18]

Decreasing Capacity to Convert Demands into Policy: Fragmenting Patterns of Support

In the early 1960s, Brazilian politicians spoke increasingly of the systemic crisis facing the country because of the increased level of demands and the decreased capacity of the economic system to satisfy them. From the early 1950s on, each president had attempted to formulate a coherent development plan, but in each case the plans were abandoned because the president was unable to aggregate political support and because Congress either vetoed the plan or was so divided that it was incapable of allocating resources according to any development priorities. The period before the breakdown of the regime in 1964 was one of increasing fragmentation of the political party system. No single party since 1945 had significantly increased its percentage of nonalliance votes. In fact, the percentage of party alliance votes had been growing at every congressional election (see table 1). The growth of short-term alliances had a disaggregating effect on any program the parties may have stood for at the national level, because the alliances were normally local or state alliances entered into only for the purpose of winning a seat in the federal Congress. Parties standing for different policies in the Congress formed temporary alliances at the local level.[19] The alliances normally disappeared after the election and were unrelated to sustained aggregated support for any program. For example, none of the twenty-six alliances made for the 1958 elections were among the thirty-two formed for the 1962 elections.[20] This steady growth of temporary alliances made it increasingly difficult to make the representatives responsible either to the party or to the wishes of the electorate and has been characterized as a process of "progressive unauthentication."[21]

Within the party system the major source of aggregation under the Vargas and Kubitschek governments in the 1950s was the uneasy coalition between the rural bosses and nationalist entrepreneurs of the PSD party (Partido Social Democrático) and the urban labor leaders of the PTB (Partido Trabalhista Brasileiro). The Brazilian political scientist Hélio Jaguaribe, in his formulation of various possible models of Brazilian growth, termed this coalition "a party of development" and implied that it was an intrinsic part of the success

Table 1. Growth of Electoral Alliances in
Congressional Elections, Percentage of Party Vote; 1945–62

Year	PSD	UDN	PTB	Party Alliances
1945	42.3	26.3	10.1	—[a]
1950	22.2	14.0	13.6	16.7
1954	22.0	13.6	14.9	25.7
1958	18.4	13.2	14.7	33.3
1962	15.6	11.2	12.1	41.0

SOURCE: Ronald Schneider, "Election Analysis," in Charles
Daugherty, James Rowe, and Ronald Schneider, *Brazil Election
Factbook: Number 2, September 1965* (Washington, D.C.: Institute
for the Comparative Study of Political Systems, 1965), p. 60.

[a] In 1945, no party alliances were allowed.

of the pragmatic "neo-Bismarckian model" he considered the most appropriate for Brazil's development.[22] The growing radicalization (both Left and
Right) within the Brazilian polity, the differential attitudes of the PTB and
PSD toward industrial strikes and especially agrarian reform—with its emotional side issues such as rural unionization, land invasion, and constitutional
change allowing for expropriation of land without prior payment of cash—
increasingly fragmented this major source of aggregation. In 1960, these two
parties had allied in eight out of eleven states in which gubernatorial elections
were held. In 1962, they were not allied in any of the eleven gubernatorial
races.[23]

Withdrawal of Civilian Commitment to the Political Regime

One of the purposes of this volume is to redirect attention to the attitudes
and beliefs of the loyal opposition and the defenders of the regime in accord
with our premise that these groups are often more important for the survival of
democracy than the beliefs and actions of the disloyal opposition which have
received so much more attention in social science literature.[24] Significantly,
those most empowered to defend the regime, the last two presidents in power
before the breakdown in 1964, Quadros and Goulart, were both pessimistic
about the chances of the political system working effectively, and it could be
argued that they both worked harder at attempting to change the regime than at
achieving more limited goals within the existing framework.[25] Quadros in fact
resigned in the hopes of being given a Gaullist mandate to rule and implement
changes without the normal constitutional constrictions. His successor,
Goulart, frequently talked of his powerlessness to govern the country and
indeed appeared to allow some problems to worsen in order to strengthen his
claim that the system required basic change.[26]

In addition to presidential ambiguity over the effectiveness of the political system, the near civil war that occurred after Quadros's resignation in 1961 and Goulart's assumption of the presidency greatly increased the mobilization of forces within Brazil on both the Left and the Right. In both groups the resignation strengthened the feeling that Brazil was entering a revolutionary stage that called for a new political order. Politicians from the Left and the Right made attempts to resolve the political crisis by extraparliamentary means. The curtailment of the powers of the office of the president before Vice-President Goulart was allowed to assume the presidency in 1961 was in essence an attack on the regime by centrist and conservative civilians and military officers. Many frustrated democratic leftist reformers who had been proregime became antiregime and argued that reform could only come through massive pressure and plebiscitary democracy, or even revolution. President Goulart's adviser, Leonel Brizola, spoke of the need to form "Grupos de Onze" (clandestine groups of eleven armed revolutionaries). Conservatives prepared to defend themselves by force. In the countryside, landowners armed themselves in preparation for civil war. In the cities, especially São Paulo, right-wing vigilante units proliferated.[27]

This sense that the regime was doomed and that Brazil was at the threshold of revolution dominated much of the political dialogue in the period from 1961 to 1964. A few months before the coup of 1964 the right-wing authoritarian nationalist Oliveiros S. Ferreira, a leading columnist for *O Estado de São Paulo,* argued characteristically:

With the renunciation of President Jânio Quadros there opened a crisis of regime—perhaps the most grave in the entire history of the Republic—a power vacuum which must be filled or we will be plunged into the chaos of a civil war. The question that was placed before all lucid men after the renunciation was how to surmount the crisis; that is, what conception of historical process, which types of organizations, and what forms of popular associations should replace the conceptions, parties and regime which have demonstrated themselves incapable of resolving . . . the great national problems.[28]

Celso Furtado, a prominent member of the reformist democratic Left, the first director of SUDENE (Superintendency for the Development of the Northeast), and the chief designer of the Three-Year Development Plan formulated in 1963 for Goulart, writing before the breakdown of 1964 also described the situation as a crisis of regime:

The country's economy, at the mercy of a series of structural constrictions, is by the very nature of its problems in an unstable situation. The primary forces of development—population growth, urbanization, desire for improved living conditions . . . are piling up like political energy in the waters of a river that has been dammed. The disturbing action of these pressing forces tends to increase with the reduction of the economy's rate of growth. We have seen that this reduction led to an aggravation of the inflationary process, which indicates that these forces are increasingly sterile. However, the tension created by these dammed-up forces has led to the awakening of a wide number of groups who have become aware that development is threatened by structural obstacles that are beyond the capacity for action by the present ruling groups. . . . Situations of this kind lead, almost inevitably, to the disruption of the existing balance of forces and the abandonment of conventional political methods.[29]

An analysis of newspaper editorials in the period preceding the coup of 1964 reveals that the crisis was essentially one of regime, in contrast to the preceding crises of 1954, 1955, and 1961, which all essentially concerned individual governments. Before these latter crises, in each of which the military executed or attempted coups, the major theme of newspaper editorials in Brazil was the illegitimacy of the chief executive. This element was of course present in the crisis of 1964. But the editorials in 1964 even more emphatically voiced fear of social disintegration and political "subversion." There was an overtone of elite panic that was absent in editorials relating to the crises in the earlier period.

The *Jornal do Brasil,* for example, believed "the state of law has been submerged in Brazil" and stressed that it was in such situations that "revolutions like that of Russia in 1917" emerged.[30] The *Diário de Pernambuco* ran an editorial entitled "Fruits of Generalized Madness" and warned readers that Brazil faced an hour of "desolation" unless the situation was basically altered.[31] Even the normally moderate *Correio da Manhã* feared that with each incident "indiscipline was getting uncontrollable" and apocalyptically concluded that it was impossible "to continue in this chaos in all areas."[32]

A number of other indicators reveal the atmosphere of regime crisis. The level of civilian arming on the Right and Left was unquestionably much higher than in the periods before the other coups between 1945 and 1964. (The only comparable civilian arming was that in anticipation of the crisis of regime at the end of the Old Republic in 1930.) The coup of 1964 was also preceded by unprecedented crises of authority within the army and by mutinies among the enlisted men.

Another symptom was the quickened pace of elections, plebiscites, and extraparliamentary attempts to change the political rules of the game.[33] Normally in Brazil the presidential election, held every five years, is the only political contest in which national power is perceived to be in the balance. In the three and one-half years between October 1960 and March 1964, however, the country experienced the turmoil of six major political contests, all relatively inconclusive. These contests began with the presidential election in October 1960 and subsequent resignation of Quadros in August 1961; this was followed by a near civil war which was resolved only when Goulart accepted the presidency under a new prime-ministerial form of government. Then came the fiercely contested congressional and gubernatorial elections of 1962, President Goulart's bitter campaign to hold a plebiscite to regain former presidential powers, and the plebiscite itself in January 1963. In October of that year

President Goulart requested Congress to rule by state of siege. Finally, there was the March 1964 drive for "Basic Reforms" with the implicit threat to close Congress and hold a new plebiscite.

The Impact of Political and Economic Crises on the Military: The Growth of Institutional Fears and New Military Ideologies

The military atmosphere leading up to the civil-military crisis of 1964 was in a fundamental way unlike that before the crises of 1945, 1954, 1955, and 1961. One of the key aspects of civil-military relations as they existed before 1964 was that influential civilians and military officers believed that civilian political groups as a whole could rule within the parliamentary constitutional framework and that the political demands emerging from social and economic changes could be transformed into acceptable outputs by the political system. This was an essential element in the return of executive power to civilians following the military coups in Brazil in 1945, 1954, and 1955. Belief in civilian capacity to rule was also instrumental in maintaining a boundary or restraint on the extent of military activity in politics. It was generally understood in the traditional "moderator pattern" of civil-military relations that existed prior to 1964 that the military in times of temporary crises could overthrow a government but would restrain from assuming power and destroying the democratic regime itself.[34] However, in the generalized political and economic crises between 1961 and 1964, numerous factors tended to weaken military perception of the desirability of maintaining this traditional boundary to their political activity.

Especially significant was the development among groups of military officers of a fear that politics was at such a radicalized stage, and the existing political parties and groups so fragmented, that no single group within the polity was competent to rule the country. The rhetoric of mobilization and radicalization, coming in the wake of the Cuban Revolution, was feared by many officers as the prelude to the destruction of the traditional army. The increasing politicization of the enlisted ranks, most marked in the sergeants' revolt in Brasília in September 1963, intensified this fear among officers and was seen to threaten military discipline. Finally, the growing use of political criteria for promotions in the army in order to create an armed force loyal to the president (always a factor in the Brazilian military) was perceived by many officers to have reached alarming proportions.[35] Many felt it not only endangered the hierarchical structure of the military and the personal career expectations of the officers but was also destructive to the nonpartisan role of the military institution itself.

All these factors contributed to the development of attitudes within the officer corps that were no longer consistent with the traditional role of the military, in which the military "moderated" the political system during times of crisis but never actually assumed governmental power itself. At the military's Superior War College (*Escola Superior de Guerra,* ESG), an ideology developed that both questioned basic structural features of the political system and implicitly envisaged a new political role for the military, in which the military would become the "director" and not merely the "moderator" of the entire political system. The fact that the military developed such an ideology, at a formal level, was a factor in the crisis of regime in Brazil, just as the military development of revolutionary warfare doctrines in France, Indonesia, and Peru was an intrinsic part of the crisis of regime in those countries.[36]

Thus by early 1964 important elements within the Brazilian military were becoming increasingly apprehensive about the threats to the military institution, while at the same time groups within the military began to feel that the military possessed, through the work of the Superior War College, the development doctrines, as well as the personal and organizational strengths to rule Brazil. It is not surprising then that numerous small civil-military groups throughout Brazil were openly discussing the overthrow of President Goulart and even the possibility of establishing a new regime in Brazil long before March 1964.

Political Leadership and Regime Breakdown in Brazil: The Realm of the Noninevitable

A working hypothesis that this chapter brings to the analysis is one also stressed by Linz, namely that while powerful economic, political, and ideological strains normally contribute to the breakdown of a regime, these macrosociological factors do not in themselves lead inevitably to its fall. The diffuse generalized factors that are placing a strain on the system have to be brought to a crisis point by the interaction of actors and issues at the micropolitical level.

In fact, there were many factors tending to support the regime as it existed under President Goulart, or at least to inhibit any coup initiatives by military officers. It was in the erosion of existing regime supportive factors that the quality of individual leadership, problem-solving behavior, and political strategies of the chief executive played an extremely important role. Indeed, the analysis of democratic regimes that survive severe crises may well demonstrate that the political leaders paid close attention to reinforcing and relying upon the regime supportive factors.[37] Alternatively, in the case of breakdown, political leaders all too often, wittingly or unwittingly, contribute to the unnecessary erosion of regime support.

There were a number of factors that as late as the beginning of March 1964 tended to support the survival of the Goulart government and to inhibit military attempts to overthrow the regime. First was the vested interest of numerous politicians—Center, Right, and Left—in the maintenance of the regime in order to continue their careers. Many of the most important civilian governors, who had traditionally played a key role in central power decisions, had a stake in the continuation of the formal functioning of the political system because they were themselves prominent candidates for presidential elections slated for October 1965. Adhemar de Barros, governor of the most powerful state of the union, São Paulo, with a state militia of over thirty thousand men at his command, was an active candidate of the Populist PSP party. Carlos Lacerda, governor of Guanabara state, and Magalhães Pinto, governor of Minas Gerais, were not only men with strong state militias but also contenders for the presidential nomination of the UDN party. On the Left, President Goulart could not, by the terms of the Constitution of 1946, succeed himself, and since a relative of the president was also constitutionally barred from running, Leonel Brizola, former governor of Rio Grande do Sul, was also denied the opportunity to run. This meant that the most powerful governor of the Left, Miguel Arraes of Pernambuco, also had a strong vested interest in Goulart's remaining in office and the election being held on schedule. Lacerda, Magalhães Pinto, and de Barros all knew of the formulation of a plan to overthrow Goulart in case Goulart attempted a coup to extend his own powers, but none of these governors committed themselves to this plan until late March 1964. The antiregime plotters felt that without the support of these key governors, however, Goulart could not be overthrown.[38]

Another factor inhibiting the overthrow of President Goulart was that regardless of the distrust in which he was held by many people, he was nonetheless the constitutionally elected president of Brazil. From this fact flowed both the legalistic support acquired from his mere occupancy of this office and the power to appoint civilians and military officers most loyal to him to positions of importance. Here was another source of regime support which had to be taken into account in any political strategy.

From the military viewpoint, there were also several reasons why the emergence of new attitudes—such as institutional fear, declining confidence in civilians, and increased confidence in the military's own abilities to rule—were nonetheless insufficient reasons for assuming power. While small groups of military officers formed, in Linz's terms, a "disloyal opposition" after 1961 and were looking for an excuse to overthrow Goulart and the regime, the military institution as a whole had been badly divided by the abortive attempt to block Goulart from assuming the presidency in 1961. The fear of splitting the military again acted as a major inhibition to any attempt to overthrow Goulart without unanimous military support. In an interview with General Golbery do Couto e Silva, a major participant in the military movement to overthrow Goulart, Golbery noted that "1961 was a disaster for the Army. We decided that we would attempt to overthrow Goulart only if public opinion was in our favor."[39] Speaking of the obstacles to a military coup, Golbery also argued that in 1963 the activists in the military planning a revolution represented only 10 percent of the higher officer corps, while another 70 percent to 80 percent were "legalists" or simply nonactivists. While many of this latter group were becoming increasingly apprehensive about the state of affairs in Brazil, and especially about the question of military discipline and unity, nonetheless they would follow the president in his formal capacity as commander in chief of the army. The other 10 to 20 percent of the officer corps were pro-Goulart activists, many of whom Goulart had appointed to key troop commands and administrative posts.

As late as February 1964 there was widespread fear that Goulart still had sufficient active support that an attempt to overthrow him could lead to civil war lasting two or even three months.[40] As long as Goulart was acting constitutionally there was no loud demand by civilians for the military to intervene. Without this demand, the military activists could not get a "winning coalition" together to take an aggressive first step against Goulart.

Given these various inhibiting factors, a strong case could be made that President Goulart could have completed his term of office without being displaced by the military and without the complete breakdown of the political regime. It is difficult to speculate on the course of events if a military coup had not occurred in April 1964. One possibility is that the widespread consciousness of governmental powerlessness and the need for structural reform could have been capitalized on in the presidential elections scheduled for October 1965, and a victorious candidate for the Left, or a victory by the still enormously popular ex-president Kubitschek, could have mobilized a mandate for democratic reform. Another option was that the more radical forces in such groups as AP, MEB, peasant leagues, and some trade unions could have had more time to develop into a genuine national force. But 1964 was too soon for them. Both of these options have been completely foreclosed for the last fourteen years by the events that Goulart himself helped set in motion. Let us turn to these events.

If we accept that, as late as February 1964, there were powerful inhibitions to the overthrow of Goulart, why then was Goulart actually overthrown, and with such relative ease? Clearly the economic and political crisis had generated, for the military and for many national and international elite groups, the "chemical reagents" capable of producing a breakdown of the regime: the necessary components existed well before 31 March 1964. But they were not sufficient cause for a regime change: the reagents had to be brought to a critical "temperature" and "pressure" for reaction actually to occur.[41] Here the question of the quality and style of Goulart's political leadership became critical, for it was in the strategies and tactics he used in his efforts to "reequilibrate the political system" that in fact crucial support was eroded and a crisis situation brought to the breakdown point.

Goulart's Strategies—Crisis Intensification

In mid-March of 1964 Goulart came to a decision to resolve the political crisis by attempting to change the balance of power in his favor. This decision was to alter profoundly the future of Brazilian politics. It is thus legitimate to analyze his action as a strategy and, since Goulart was deposed a little more than three weeks later, to look for weak points in it. A step-by-step account will show the crisis moving toward resolution.

The final stages of the crisis began on 13 March with a massive rally held in Rio de Janeiro. The president and his trade union supporters had organized the rally knowingly, in the sense that they considered it the first step toward resolving a crisis. On the morning of the rally, Goulart told an interviewer:

Today I am going to run all the risks. The most that can happen to me is that I will be deposed. I will not renounce or commit suicide.[42]

The interviewer remarked that the situation in Brazil did not call for either renunciation or suicide. Goulart replied:

I know. I am only imagining the worst that could happen, following my decision to push reforms and obtain greater powers from Congress. But nothing will happen because my military support [*dispositivo militar*] is excellent. Assis Brasil has guaranteed me that at my command, the army will follow. . . . From here on forward, I am only going to govern with the support of the people. And what everyone is going to see today [at the rally] is that the people have changed. They are awakened, they are ready for the grand problems of the country.[43]

Goulart was counting on mobilizing the political power of the masses and demanding reforms by plebiscite, by decree, or by pressuring, or even closing, Congress. To do this he implicitly recognized his need for not merely the passive support of the army but the active, aggressive support of key Goulart-appointed generals. The strategy, to be effective, would have required that federal army troops give protection and backing to the mass demonstrations and strikes Goulart was planning throughout the country. It would also probably have involved key army leaders threatening Congress in order to pass the "Basic Reforms." If Congress refused, the army would be the essential factor in any attempt by Goulart to insist on a national plebiscite for these reforms. Likewise, active support of the three service chiefs would be required if Goulart was to attempt to declare a state of siege.[44]

This strong reliance by Goulart on the loyal military activists he had appointed to important positions is consistent with the "moderating pattern" of civil-military relations until 1964. In this system, a weak executive ruling a divided country will attempt to use the military to augment his power. One of Goulart's close associates described the president's attitude toward the military as he entered the crisis period: "Goulart felt he had good relations with the army. . . . He wanted to put the military in as many key positions as possible. It was a form of power and had to be used. . . . He felt he had to pressure Congress by mobilizing mass opinion and by use of the military."[45] This approach is consistent with Goulart's behavior as president in the period from 1961 to 1963, in regard to his use of the military to force an early holding of the plebiscite, to request a state of siege, and to keep opponents in check.[46]

Thus, Goulart's assumption that he could use the military was not without precedent. However, his tactic of appointing new service chiefs when the old ones did not agree with him—he had had four such chiefs since assuming the presidency—cut him off from accurate feedback about military feeling. Officers closest to him, who urged him forward on his course of increasing pressure on Congress, were more and more out of touch with the bulk of military sentiment. Moreover, his strategy of mobilizing the masses by using leftist activists in the country, while expecting to balance the Left with the military who would also help push the reforms through, had inherent points of tension and weakness.

The inherent danger in regard to military support was that a diffuse, personalist mobilization of the masses, if it were to succeed in pressuring Congress, could go beyond most military officers' tolerance of internal disorder. Also, Goulart's attempts to use the Communist organization ran the risk of diminishing the intensity of support of those officers who endorsed his reforms on nationalist and leftist grounds but who disliked the institutional connection with the Brazilian Communist party.

A serious weakness of Goulart's strategy in regard to the Left was that the Left was too fragmented and too unmobilized to support it; moreover, Goulart himself was unable to lead the Left effectively because, in the past, he had made ambiguous turns both to the Left and the Right. Goulart was not trusted by a number of the most prominent figures of the left. Miguel Arraes, the most important leftist candidate for the upcoming presidential elections, feared that Goulart might upset the election schedule. Arraes also knew that Goulart had always attempted to keep him under control by appointing strong, anti-Communist generals to command the Fourth Army, based in his state capital of Recife. In addition, Arraes was aware that Goulart had attempted to depose both him, the major leftist governor, and Lacerda, the major rightist governor, in 1963 in order to solidify his position. Arraes told various people that he feared that if Goulart executed a coup, Arraes himself would be one of the first to suffer.[47]

The leader of the Communist party, Luís Carlos Prestes, was also deeply ambivalent about Goulart. Prestes wanted to use Goulart to mobilize the country, but he feared that a premature attempt to radicalize the country and eliminate the bourgeoisie from a reform coalition would precipitate a counter-coup in which the Communists would be destroyed.[48] Prestes also feared that if Goulart in fact carried off a leftist coup, Goulart might very possibly not keep his promise to make the Communist party legal.[49]

Francisco Julião, the most famous leader of the peasant leagues in the northeast, was hostile to Goulart, whom he accused of trying to turn him into a rural trade union boss, controlled by the Ministry of Labor. Julião felt that Goulart had not backed him in his last election campaign.[50]

Brizola, the most volatile member of the Left, was constantly charging Goulart with being a bourgeois and an opportunist. Brizola's mouthpiece, *Panfleto,* published in February and March of 1964, often criticized Goulart's policies. In early March, Brizola went so far as to say that he would never stand on the platform with Goulart again, because Goulart had so many conservatives in his cabinet.[51]

Finally, the basic ambivalence of the trade unions toward Goulart was illustrated by their refusal to back his request for the state of siege in September of 1963.

The Goulart strategy of forcing the system to a crisis resolution was successful in that it intensified the crisis. Within nineteen days of the rally on 13 March the Brazilian political system had been fundamentally transformed. The results, however, were the opposite of what Goulart had intended. Let us analyze why.

The 13 March Rally and Civil-Military Aftermaths

The two decisive steps for civil-military relations that precipitated the 1964 breakdown were the rally on 13 March and a mutiny of sailors on 27–29 March.

At the 13 March mass rally, widely televised and broadcast, Goulart launched a campaign for broad structural and political reforms that came to be known as the "Basic Reforms." He announced he had just signed a land reform decree which declared subject to expropriation all underutilized properties of over 1,200 acres situated within six miles of federal highways or railways, and lands of 70 acres located within six miles of federal dams or drainage projects. He also nationalized all remaining private oil refineries in Brazil and outlined future plans to enfranchise illiterates (by which means he would almost double the electorate) and legalize the Communist party.

He demanded that the Constitution be reformed because it was obsolete, since it "legalized an unjust and inhuman economic structure." His brother-in-law, Leonel Brizola, went further and declared that Congress had lost "all identification with the people"; he urged the establishment of a "Congress composed of peasants, workers, sergeants, and nationalist officers." Both Brizola and Goulart posed the threat of a plebiscite, using the enlarged electorate to bypass Congress if Congress posed an obstacle to these plans.

Goulart followed up the promise of his rally by presenting his Basic Reforms to Congress on 15 March with a pointed reminder that the three armed services ministers had seen and approved the program. It was announced that a series of mass demonstrations would be held throughout the country. The legally unrecognized high command of labor, the CGT (*Comando Geral dos Trabalhadores*), threatened a general strike if Congress did not approve the constitutional changes by 20 April and also recommended that Goulart declare a unilateral moratorium on the repayment of the foreign debts. May Day loomed as the day of resolution if the political elites remained intransigent.[52]

In terms of strategy and the tactics of political leadership and political survival, what can be said about the effectiveness of Goulart and his allies? Without attempting to discuss the merits of the goals themselves, it can be argued convincingly that Goulart's tactics diminished his support and tended to increase the possibility of a military coup backed by strong civilian opinion.[53]

First, in the euphoric atmosphere that pervaded the Left after the 13 March rally, great hope was placed on the mobilization of groups that had previously been marginal to the political process. Despite the fact that Goulart launched a major attack on existing power-holders, he had not first organized sufficient support to make such an attack feasible. As even one of his own staff acknowledged, "Goulart wanted to make more reforms than he really had the strength to do. He had no organized support for the big reforms he announced."[54] Almost no effort was made to retain as allies the moderate Left and Center, who had in the past cooperated on some reform issues. For Goulart, as well as for a number of other rhetorical nationalists such as Sukarno and Nkrumah, the emotional power of revolutionary symbols and the physical presence of the masses appears to have had a debilitating effect on the capacity to make the normal "political survival calculation," i.e. judging actions in terms of strategically located allies gained versus strategically located enemies created. One of Goulart's closest allies in this crisis period later commented that the mass rally had disoriented Goulart's political perceptions: "Friday, the thirteenth, was the beginning of the President's drive for power. It carried him to a delirium of ephemeral glory . . . [in which] he underestimated his adversaries and overestimated the strength of the masses."[55]

A characteristic example of the almost willful disregard for winning or retaining potential allies was the frequent utterances by major leftist activists that the composition of a future strong reforming government (which the new power of the masses was "certain" to generate shortly) should not include any "bourgeois reformers," such as San Tiago Dantas, a widely respected and influential politician of the moderate Left. Even a newspaper such as *Diário Carioca*, which had strongly supported the programmatic reforms demanded by Goulart, was offended by such tactics.[56]

In addition to alienating potential allies, it is clear that the 13 March rally, by simultaneously raising numerous fundamental problems to crisis level, tended to maximize the number of Goulart's opponents among those strategically located in the power structure. Between 13 March and 15 March, Goulart's demands for fundamental reforms threatened elements among the landowners, military officers, congressmen, foreign capitalists, anti-

Communists, and industrialists. The rhetoric of revolution, coupled with the soaring inflation, created increasing fear and insecurity among the middle classes. On many issues the above groups were hostile to one another, but the Goulart offensive brought them together and minimized their differences.[57] Many people who were "progovernment" shifted to a position we previously referred to as "proregime but antigovernment." "Antigovernment" groups increasingly became "antiregime."

The justice minister later wrote from exile about this counterproductive aspect of the massive rally for the Goulart government. He acknowledged reluctantly that the March 13 rally "came to be the touchstone of the opposition in combating the government. The rally created the expectation of a crisis, of a 'coup,' raids, riots, mutiny, or general subversion in the country. . . . After 13 March, the opposition was galvanized."[58] Indicative of this galvanization of the opposition was the even larger rally of many middle-class people in São Paulo on 19 March to demonstrate against Goulart and in favor of legality.[59] The rhetoric of "resentment politics" gained Goulart a few supporters but also won him some powerful and strategically located enemies. An example is Brizola's calling General Muricy a "gorilla" to his face on a public platform. General Muricy, a commanding general in the north, was one of the first to go into armed revolt against Goulart. Frequent ridicule of Congress was another tactic that was not conducive to getting Congress to cooperate in passing the basic reforms that the Goulart government needed.

A more general example of Brizola's attempts to win marginal additional support at the cost of creating powerful enemies in the center of the political system was his repeated call for the formation of "Grupos de Onze." Private appeals might have been just as effective and would not have created fear among the landowners and the middle class—nor have caused some military officers to shift from a position of neutrality to active conspiracy against Goulart.

Reaction to 13 March—Erosive Effects on Factors Impeding a Coup

Goulart's attack, during the 13 March rally, on the Constitution as archaic and obsolete weakened his own claim, as the constitutional president, to obedience from the military. This point was made a number of times in public statements and newspaper editorials. The *Diário de Notícias* editorialized:

It is undeniable that subversive forces exist clearly aimed at making an attempt to overthrow the regime and existing institutions. . . . These forces seem to have coopted the President himself and have placed him for the first time in the forefront of the subversive process of opposition to the law, to the regime and to the Constitution.

If the Supreme Executive authority is opposed to the Constitution, condemns the regime, and refuses to obey the laws, he automatically loses the right to be obeyed . . . because this right emanates from the Constitution. The armed forces, by Article 177 of the Constitution, are obliged to "defend the country, and to guarantee the Constitutional power, law and order."... If the Constitution is "useless"... how can the President still command the armed forces?[60]

The 13 March rally also generated for the first time a widespread fear that the drive of the Goulart government might result in postponement of national elections, scheduled for October 1965, or a sharp change in the electoral rules (such as making Goulart, or his relative Brizola, eligible). This had an important impact on civilian-military opinion toward displacing Goulart. The military had been badly divided in their 1961 attempt to displace Goulart unilaterally without prior civilian sanction or support. A number of the key conspirators against Goulart decided that any attempt to oust him had to be initiated by the governor of a major state who had the backing of his own state militia.[61] The two most likely states were São Paulo and Minas Gerais. Both were governed by men who were suspicious of Goulart yet nonetheless had a vested interest in his remaining in office and elections being held on schedule. However, when it appeared that Goulart was trying to restructure the political system, an attempt which might preclude their attempts at the presidency, the two governors began to plot actively against Goulart.

Governor Magalhães Pinto reacted quickly, issuing a manifesto on 20 March on national television that promised Minas Gerais would resist any "revolution commandeered from above." The next day he made arrangements with the governor of the neighboring state of Espírito Santo to use the port of Vitória and railroads to get supplies into Minas in the event of a civil war in which Minas Gerais stood armed against the federal troops of Goulart.[62] Such a war, the governor felt, might last as long as three months. He is reported to have felt that any discussion of the presidential elections was by this time "surrealistic."[63]

The governor of São Paulo, Adhemar de Barros, went on television the night of 20 March to make an impassioned, three-hour address condemning the Goulart government for fomenting revolution. He emphasized his willingness to resist by force and said the São Paulo state militia had 30,000 troops, as well as airplanes to transport them. He pointed out that this force was twice as large as the federal army garrisoned in São Paulo, in which there were a number of pro-Goulart generals.[64]

The armed forces were deeply affected by the rally of 13 March, and their internal divisions over whether they should attempt to displace Goulart began to be reduced. The change of position of the governors of Minas Gerais and São Paulo greatly strengthened the military conspirators.

The rally also resulted in a changed atmosphere in the press. Before 13 March, no editorials directly charged the military with the responsibility for resolving the crisis. The rally, however, raised such issues as changing the Constitution, holding a constituent assembly, and closing Congress. After 13 March appeals began to be made to the constitutional role of the military to guarantee all three branches of government—the legislative and the judicial as well as the executive. Editorials requested the military not to give protective backing to government-sponsored threats to order. This loud public response to the rally of 13 March facilitated the role of the conspirators within the military.

An editorial in *O Jornal,* entitled "Defense of Illegality," appearing two days after the rally, illustrates the new mood of open condemnation of the military for continuing to obey the "illegal" order of the president: "The armed forces say they participated in the illegal and revolutionary rally . . . in obedience to the order of the President! No one is obliged to accept and obey an abusive order!"[65]

In addition to these specific reactions, the rally had more general effects on civil-military relations. Implicit in Goulart's appeal for settlement of the crisis outside traditional political channels was the threat of force. Many different groups began to arm themselves. More importantly, from a political standpoint, it was widely believed by key civilian and military officers that the nation was taking to arms. To this extent, the arena was rapidly becoming one in which the dominant idiom was one of violence, rather than politics. Since the military considered itself to have a monopoly on the legitimate use of arms, and perceived maintenance of internal order as one of its primary functions, it began to move to the center of the arena and assume a dominant position within the political system, thus underlining the relevance of Lasswell and Kaplan's dictum: "The balancing of power is particularly affected by the expectations that prevail about the probable mode by which conflicts will be settled. . . . An arena is *military* when the expectation of violence is high; *civic* when the expectation is low."[66]

The rally greatly increased expectations of force and preparations for a showdown by the forces of the Left and Right. On both sides there were multiple movements, with no central organization. Anti-Goulart factions in the military were getting a more receptive hearing for their articulation of the need for preparation for a countercoup, but they were still far from unified over the necessity of backing a coup of their own. For many military men, a coup attempt still spelled civil war—disaster for the country and for the military as an institution.

The Resolution of the Crisis—The Enlisted Men's Naval Mutiny

It was at this point that the next decisive step in the breakdown process occurred. Despite the build-up of pressure by the active anti-Goulart civilians and military forces, as late as twelve days after the 13 March rally no "winning coalition" existed to overthrow Goulart. Goulart had a number of strategically located officers who both favored the reform program and stood by him. The bulk of the remainder of the officers were legalistic, in the sense of being nonactivists. But arguments expressed in a letter by General Castello Branco were beginning to make a powerful impression on these men, as they began to ask themselves whether their "legalism" entailed loyalty and obedience to the president, and whether obedience to him was still an obedience "within the limits of the law."

Given this lack of unity among the opposition forces, an attempted coup by one sector of the military would have risked splitting the military at this time. The active plotters within the military were convinced that Goulart was intent on becoming a dictator but felt they must wait until he made such a blatant move that they could mobilize support against him easily.

The probable intention of Goulart's strategy was to build up pressure among the masses for reform without losing the passive obedience of the legalistic officers and the active support of key military officers, supporters Goulart needed if he were to bypass Congress and rule by decree. Holding these forces together was made especially difficult because to a great extent Goulart was spurred on by the highly emotional and often contradictory forces of the Left, which he found difficult to unify and direct. The movement was at an explosive point. There was risk of its getting out of control as an effective tactical instrument. The risk lay in the loss of a delicate balance between the increasingly radical civilians and the increasingly threatened officer corps.[67]

The naval mutiny of 26 March occurred against this background. More than one thousand sailors and marines barricaded themselves in an armory in Rio de Janeiro. The naval minister attempted to quell the mutiny. Goulart, instead of backing the minister, in effect dismissed him and allowed the trade unions to participate in the choice of a new minister in his place.

At the time of the mutiny, Goulart was extremely indecisive about his course of action. The mutiny made him face a decision he did not want to make—to punish the enlisted men for the mutiny and risk losing their active support or to treat the mutineers lightly and greatly risk increasing fears among those officers who saw leniency as a threat to the principle of military discipline. Goulart's minister of justice, Abelardo Jurema, wrote that most of the advice that the Goulart government received from civilian activists was to side with the sailors, since Goulart did not have much support to lose among naval officers in any case.[68] Their argument overlooked the crucial factor of the *intensity* of the opposition to Goulart, which was greatly increased by Goulart's action and by the symbolic impact it had on all three services, each of which felt threatened.

In the last moments Goulart vacillated and, according to his chief army aide, General Assis Brasil, abdicated the decision, saying to the new naval minister: "The problem is yours, Admiral. You have a blank check with which to resolve it. If you wish to punish or expel [the mutineers], the decision is yours." The admiral reportedly replied, "I intend, President, to grant an amnesty."[69]

Repercussions within the officer corps were profound. The issue of institutional self-preservation by means of control over military discipline was one over which ideologically divided military officers had the highest internal agreement. The naval mutiny caused a shift in position that hurt Goulart among all three major groups within the military—the active plotters, the legalist uncommitted officers, and the pro-Goulart officers.[70]

The naval mutiny galvanized the active plotters, both civilian and military, into action against Goulart. The operations order issued on the night of 31 March 1964 by General Guedes, commander of the infantry division that first moved against Goulart in the effort to remove him from the presidency, clearly indicates the way in which Goulart's handling of the mutiny acted as a catalyst in the revolutionary drama. The general's order explained to his division that he and Governor Magalhães Pinto had decided it would be a mistake to move against Goulart without profound provocation. In his opinion, and the governor's, any attempt to displace Goulart before Goulart expressly challenged the law would have given Goulart an air of legality and would have been counterproductive. "It would have attracted to his side a forceful sector of the armed forces who lack confidence in politics and are committed to legal formalism." It was necessary to assemble a defensive conspiracy and wait until Goulart stepped beyond the bounds of the law. His slogan, the general explained, was: "He who breaks the law first is lost!" What happened in the mutiny, he felt, showed that he was correct. With the naval mutiny the military had "arrived at the moment for action, and had to act quickly lest it be too late."[71]

Among the legalistic officers, who comprised the majority of the military officers and who were reluctant to take a bold step against the constitutionally elected president, Goulart's sanctioning of indiscipline and disorder allowed the question of legalism to be reformulated. Obedience was owed to the president "within the limits of the law." To many officers, the president's actions now seemed to lie outside the law.

The impact of the naval mutiny of 26 March upon the strong Goulart supporters was powerful. Juan Linz has correctly noted in his introductory essay that the intensity of the belief in the legitimacy of a government is most important for those who participate in a crisis from within the authority structure. Their passive support is not enough; they must feel that the government is so legitimate that it commands their *active* support.

For Goulart, his staff was his *"dispositivo militar,"* his hand-picked men in key locations throughout the country, who in the past had been his active supporters in crises. Goulart's minister of justice, Abelardo Jurema, described, however, an angry meeting between himself and a military officer, Colonel Lino Teixeira, following the mutiny, which illustrates how seriously the issue of military discipline had weakened active support for Goulart:

I was eating in a restaurant in the city . . . when I was approached by Colonel Lino Teixeira. He was furious. . . . He did not understand the situation. He passionately declared his feelings of revolt, anger, and surprise, feelings he said that the pro-Jangistas [military favorable to Goulart] shared. He stressed that the government had lost substantially all of its military *dispositivo*. . . . He, who only yesterday had been fighting on the side of the President and the reforms, was now ready to fight alongside Carlos Lacerda [a chief plotter against Goulart] to maintain military discipline, which in his view had been irreparably wounded.[72]

A member of the general staff of the army, who did not join the conspiracy against Goulart and who was subsequently purged from the army commented: "The thing that finally was most important in moving military opinion against him [Goulart] was the 'inversion of hierarchy'! Even strong 'Jangistas' broke with him after the mutiny and his speech to the sergeants."[73]

Most of the strong Goulart supporters in the military did not actively join the opposition, but what was crucial was that when the government was actively challenged by the plotters, the intensity of military support for Goulart was not sufficient to prevent Goulart's displacement. Not one officer died defending the Goulart government.

Conclusion

Obviously, this paper cannot cover all the important factors influencing the course of events that led to the regime's breakdown in Brazil in 1964. I have barely touched on the growth of military ideology and education, via the Superior War College, which contributed greatly to military confidence to assume full political power in 1964. Another important factor was the role played by the United States in contributing to the destabilization of the Goulart government and to the shoring up of the military coup. The U.S. government cut back economic and other aid to the Goulart government, moved a task force in the direction of Brazil that could have been ready in case the anti-Goulart coup force encountered heavy resistance, and extended strong political and economic support to the military government after the coup.[74]

Nonetheless, this study of the micro-political events as they took place within the broad context of changing social, economic, and ideological conditions tending to lead to a generalized expectation that the regime was at a critical turning point does illuminate, I believe, the special role that a political leader can play in bringing a regime to a final breakdown point. A number of interesting questions about Goulart's political style and his fall from power remain for further analysis and research. Why, for instance, did Goulart overestimate his political strength? I have already mentioned as one element of his misreading of this strength the exhilaration and consequent disorientation he experienced after speaking to large crowds. Another clue to the extent of Goulart's estrangement from the realities of politics lay in the nature of his political advisers. Goulart had surrounded himself with men who identified with him so personally that they were unrepresentative of the institutions they came from and uninfluential within them. General Assis Brasil, chief of the Casa Militar and therefore one of the key liaisons between the government and the military, is a classic example of a military man who urged Goulart forward to action even though he himself had lost touch with the military institutions he supposedly represented.

A more difficult field of inquiry concerns Goulart's *style* of politics. Goulart talked of the need for revolution, but in the early moments of the coup against him, when it was still by no means certain that he would be overthrown, he personally cautioned his own military commanders to avoid bloodshed. His ambiguity and indecisiveness enraged and demoralized his military supporters.

One other area needs examination—the area of political personality. Goulart had always been the subject of a "whispering campaign" of innuendo, even among his own associates. It was often hinted he was personally and politically ineffectual. Undoubtedly his bravado leadership of the masses filled some personal need. The pattern of confrontation and capitulation that characterized his career suggests that a psychological analysis would be valuable for a fuller understanding of Goulart's political performance.

At the political level, the outcome of his political acts, strategies, and style of politics was to finally erode existing supports to the regime. Combined with structural weaknesses in the regime, Goulart helped pave the way for the final breakdown of the Brazilian regime in 1964.

Indeed, this analysis confirms the conclusion of Alberto Guerreiro Ramos, a leading politician on the Left at the time of the breakdown of the regime, and a distinguished social scientist, who described Goulart's actions in the following terms:

In 1964 he seemed to lose his sense of reality.... To a certain extent, one could say that Goulart's fall occurred on March 31, 1964, because he *wanted* it so. He deposed himself by letting himself be deposed. It is clear that Goulart had ways of stabilizing his power, but it appears that he behaved as if he preferred the actions which led to his downfall.... Goulart could have finished his presidential period had he decided to behave according to its objective possibilities; Goulart's downfall was not inevitable.[75]

NOTES

1. This regime is analyzed in Alfred Stepan, ed., *Authoritarian Brazil: Origins, Policies, and Future* (New Haven: Yale University Press, 1973).
2. The Brazilian case has been examined from a number of different perspectives. Philippe C. Schmitter, in his *Interest Conflict and Political Change in Brazil* (Stanford, Ca.: Stanford University Press, 1971), argues that the coup was in part a restoration movement endeavoring to reestablish the semicorporatist structure that was being challenged in the years leading

up to 1964. His emphasis thus is not on "breakdown" but rather on "continuity." Fernando Henrique Cardoso in his "Associated-Dependent Development: Theoretical and Practical Implications," in Stepan, *Authoritarian Brazil*, pp. 142–76, argues that the coup brought the political system into alignment with the new economic changes induced by the associated-dependent development process. For a seminal effort to place the 1964 breakdown in Brazil and the 1966 breakdown in Argentina in an analytic framework in which competitive political populism, within the confines of dependent import-substitution industrialization, precipitates a ceiling effect crisis, which in turn contributes to the emergence of a bureaucratic-authoritarian coalition that endeavors to impose a new development model, see Guillermo O'Donnell, *Modernization and Bureaucratic-Authoritarianism: Studies in South American Politics,* Institute of International Studies, University of California, Politics of Modernization Series, no. 9 (Berkeley: 1973). With some qualifications and modifications, I use a variant of this framework to analyze the background to the "exclusionary installation attempts" that began in Brazil in 1964, Argentina in 1966, and Chile in 1973 in chap. 3 of my *The State and Society: Peru in Comparative Perspective* (Princeton, N.J.: Princeton University Press, 1978). Both the "corporatist continuity" and the "structural crisis" arguments are useful: corporatist elements were indeed very strong throughout the 1945–64 semidemocratic interregnum, and the breakdown has in fact facilitated the repression that has played such an important part in the current economic model. Nonetheless I do not feel that either the corporatist continuity or the new repression was inevitable. There remained a small margin of maneuverability within which the process of increasing democratization and participation could have been expanded. How the leaders of the electoral regime contributed to the elimination of this margin remains an important topic and is the subject of this chapter.

3. See Dankwart Rustow, "Transitions to Democracy: Toward a Dynamic Model," *Comparative Politics* 2, no. 3 (April 1970): 337–64; Arend Lijphart, "Consociational Democracy," *World Politics* 21, no. 2 (January 1969): 207–25; Eric A. Nordlinger, *Conflict Regulation in Divided Societies*, Harvard University Center for International Affairs, Occasional Papers in International Affairs, no. 29 (Cambridge: 1972); and the introductory essay by Juan J. Linz.

4. This framework owes much to the suggestive analysis of the capabilities of political systems in Gabriel A. Almond and G. Bingham Powell, Jr., *Comparative Politics: A Developmental Approach* (Boston: Little, Brown, 1966), especially pp. 190–212; and in Gabriel A. Almond, "Political Development: Analytical and Normative Perspectives," *Comparative Political Studies* 1, no. 4 (January 1969): 447–70.

5. All growth rates are for the years 1958 to 1966, as cited in United Nations, *Demographic Yearbook 1966*, pp. 104–111.

6. Brasil, *Anuário estatístico do Brasil—1962*, p. 27. Figures are rounded off to the nearest million.

7. See the section on "Conflitos do trabalho" in ibid., p. 271, and the 1966 edition, p. 339. While a four-year time span is too short to assert that this was a secular trend, the dominant impression in Brazil was clearly one of spiraling labor conflict.

8. For the political differences between parochial, subject, and participant status, see Gabriel Almond and Sidney Verba, *The Civic Culture* (Princeton, N.J.: Princeton University Press, 1963), chap. 1.

9. For a discussion of the law, see Caio Prado Júnior, "O estatuto do trabalhador rural," *Revista Brasiliense*, no. 47 (May-June 1963): 1–13.

10. For an analysis of the nonrevolutionary aspects of Julião, see Anthony Leeds, "Brazil and the Myth of Francisco Julião," in *Politics of Change in Latin America*, ed. Joseph Maier and Richard W. Weatherhead (New York: Praeger, 1964), pp. 190–204. Benno Galjart, in "Class and 'Following' in Rural Brazil," *America Latina*, no. 7 (July-September 1964); pp. 3–24, emphasizes the traditional and mutually competitive aspects of the peasant leagues.

11. The most extensive treatment of the overall growth of rural activism is Neale Pearson, "Small Farmer and Rural Worker Pressure Groups in Brazil" (Ph.D. diss., University of Florida, 1967).

12. *Anuário estatístico do Brasil—1966*, p. 535. For a general discussion of the expansion of voter participation in Brazil, see Joseph L. Love, "Political Participation in Brazil, 1881–1969," *Luso-Brazilian Review* 7, no. 2 (December 1970): 3–24.

13. Two collections of articles concerning the 1962 elections at the local, state, and national

levels are the issue of *Revista Brasileira de Estudos Políticos,* no. 16 (January 1964), and Themistocles Cavalcanti and Reisky Dubnic, eds. *Comportamento eleitoral no Brasil* (Rio de Janeiro: Fundação Getúlio Vargas, January 1964).

14. See Joel Bergsman, *Brazil: Industrialization and Trade Policies* (London: Oxford University Press, 1970).

15. For their definitions of "extractive capability" and "distributive capability," see Almond and Powell, *Comparative Politics,* pp. 195–98.

16. An influential article advancing this thesis was Maria Conceição Tavares et al., "The Growth and Decline of Import Substitution in Brazil," *Economic Bulletin for Latin America* 9, no. 1 (March 1964): 1–59. A variant of this theme also runs through O'Donnell, *Modernization and Bureaucratic-Authoritarianism,* chap. 2.

17. Private capital also reacted negatively to the 1962 profit remittance law. Werner Baer estimates that the inflow of private foreign capital declined from 108 million U.S. dollars in 1961 to 71 million in 1962 to 31 million in 1963. See Werner Baer, *Industrialization and Economic Development in Brazil* (Homewood, Ill.: Richard D. Irwin, 1965), p. 200.

18. The finance minister's report is reprinted in *Correio da Manhã,* 5 July 1963, cited in Thomas Skidmore, *Politics in Brazil, 1930–1964* (New York: Oxford University Press, 1967), p. 257.

19. See Ronald Schneider, "Election Analysis," in Charles Daugherty, James Rowe, and Ronald Schneider, *Brazil Election Factbook: Number 2, September 1965* (Washington, D.C.: Institute for the Comparative Study of Political Systems, 1965), p. 64.

20. Pompeu de Souza, "Eleições de 1962: Decomposição partidária e caminhos da reforma," *Revista Brasileira de Estudos Políticos,* no. 16 (January 1964); pp. 10–11.

21. Ibid., p. 7.

22. Hélio Juaguaribe, *Desenvolvimento econômico e desenvolvimento político* (Rio de Janeiro: Editôra Fundo de Cultura, 1962), pp. 83–84, 101.

23. Schneider, "Election Analysis." See also Skidmore, *Politics in Brazil, 1930–1964,* pp. 229–33.

24. This argument is developed more fully in the introductory essay by Linz.

25. The almost universal reaction of Quadros's close advisers to his sudden resignation was a bitter fury that measures they felt could have been taken within the limits of the existing political framework were aborted; talk and interview with Cândido Mendes, New York, spring 1965. (Cândido Mendes had been an adviser to President Quadros.) Likewise, Goulart abandoned the Furtado Plan of development and various other policies shortly after the attempt to implement them began.

26. For a particularly striking case of Goulart's emphasis on his helplessness, see the interview he gave to *Manchete,* 30 November 1963.

27. In an interview with former officials of a São Paulo vigilante unit, they asserted that as early as June 1963 they had held massive private meetings and were arming themselves.

28. Oliveiros S. Ferreira, *As fôrças armadas e o desafio da revolução* (Rio de Janeiro: Edições GRD, 1964), pp. 13–14. Ferreira himself was active in a civil-military group attempting to overthrow Goulart and impose an authoritarian nationalist solution to the Brazilian impasse.

29. Celso Furtado, *Dialéctica do desenvolvimento* (Rio de Janeiro: Editôra Fundo de Cultura, 1964), p. 134.

30. Front page editorial in large type, 29 March 1964.

31. Editorial, 31 March 1964.

32. Editorial, 31 March 1964.

33. In his introductory essay Linz argues that this is a characteristic feature of the breakdown process.

34. I develop the theoretical and empirical aspects of the "moderator model" of civil-military relations in my *The Military in Politics: Changing Patterns in Brazil;* see especially pp. 62–66.

35. A study of the *Almanaque do Exército* for 1964 reveals that of the line officers promoted to general grade during President Goulart's tenure, only five out of twenty-nine (17.2 percent) had graduated first in their class in any of the three major service schools. This contrasts with the thirty-four out of seventy-three (46.5 percent) of those officers promoted to general before Goulart came to the presidency.

36. This argument is more extensively developed and documented in my "The New Professionalism of Internal Warfare and Military Role Expansion" in Stepan, *Authoritarian Brazil*, pp. 47–65.

37. As the chapter in this volume by Daniel Levine documents, this was a central part of President Betancourt's strategy in Venezuela during the critical years of 1958–63.

38. A number of key coup organizers stressed this point in interviews with the author.

39. Interview with General Golbery do Couto e Silva, Brasília, 18 September 1967.

40. Numerous military men I talked to mentioned this.

41. Chalmers Johnson, *Revolutionary Change* (Boston: Little, Brown, 1966), pp. 90–94, makes a similar distinction between the necessary revolutionary preconditions and final causes of a revolution, which he calls the "accelerator." I prefer not to use this term because it (although not the body of Johnson's analysis) implies that we are only concerned with the speeding up of the "inevitable" breakdown.

42. Quoted in Antônio Callado, "Jango ou o suicídio sem sangue," in Alberto Dines et al., *Os idos de Março* (Rio de Janeiro: José Alvaro, 1964), p. 256. The reference to resignation is to the renunciation of President Jânio Quadros in August 1961; the reference to suicide refers to the suicide of President Vargas in August 1954.

43. Ibid., pp. 256–57. "Dispositivo," as used in the Goulart period, meant more than "support" (*apoio*). It meant senior officers who were personally loyal and actively committed to implementing the president's policies. The "dispositivo" in theory included all the military officers and troops under the command of these key senior officers.

   General Assis Brasil was the chief of the president's military household and, as such, one of the president's chief liaison officers with the military.

44. Since Goulart was overthrown by elements of the military shortly after the 13 March rally that began the deliberate intensification of the crisis, this scenario was never put into effect. Nonetheless, for even the outside observer, the broad outlines of the government's attempt to move the political system toward resolution were clear. The author was in Brazil in this period and wrote an article a week before the coup entitled, "Brazil: Mend or End," *Economist*, 4 April 1964, p. 31, that reflected this sense of imminent crisis.

45. Interview, 11 October 1968, Rio de Janeiro, with Raúl Riff, President Goulart's press secretary, who later had his political rights cancelled by the military government.

46. This is discussed in greater detail in my *The Military in Politics*, pp. 67–72.

47. See Fernando Pedreira, *Março 31: Civis e militares no processo da crise brasileira* (Rio de Janeiro: José Alvaro, 1964), p. 13; also Dines, *Os idos de Março*, pp. 31, 83.

48. See Skidmore, *Politics in Brazil*, p. 278, and his long bibliographic footnote on p. 414. Since the coup, the Communist party has published several reevaluations, in which they are critical of the "immature strategy" that precipitated the counterrevolution.

49. Dines, *Os idos de Março*, p. 30.

50. See Julião's interview with Antônio Callado, in *Tempo de Arraes: Padres e comunistas na revolução sem violência* (Rio de Janeiro: José Alvaro, 1965), pp. 59–60.

51. Dines, *Os idos de Março*, p. 19.

52. For the 13 March rally, and its immediate aftermath, see the author's "Brazil: Mend or End," p. 31. For a description written by the justice minister of the Goulart government, see Abelardo Jurema, *Sexta-Feira, 13: Os últimos dias do Govêrno João Goulart* (Rio de Janeiro: Edições O Cruzeiro, 1964), pp. 139–49. Also, Dines, *Os idos de Março*, pp. 195–219, 249–62.

53. I personally feel that most of the goals were desirable in some form.

54. Interview with Raúl Riff.

55. Jurema, *Sexta-Feira*, p. 149.

56. See their angry editorial, "Frente ampla ou frente estreita?" *Diário Carioca*, 24 March 1964.

57. Given the widespread feeling that Brazil was in need of fundamental reforms, and the lack of unity among the elites, a potentially more fruitful reform strategy could have been to reform sequentially, attempting to build the biggest possible constituency for each reform, each time reconstituting coalitions for new reforms. For a discussion of this reform strategy, see the last two chapters in Albert Hirschman, *Journeys toward Progress* (New York: Twentieth Century Fund, 1963); see especially his "Model 1: Engineering Reform with the Help of the Perspective of Revolution," pp. 277–85.

58. Jurema, *Sexta-Feira,* pp. 144–45.
59. A detailed study of this counter-rally does not yet exist and would be worthwhile.
60. Front page editorial, *Diário de Notícias,* 23 March 1964.
61. For example, General Mourão Filho, the general who finally initiated the coup, has written that he would have attempted a coup earlier if he had received a manifesto to the nation from four major governors. See his official account, published as an army order, "Relatório de revolução democrática iniciada pela 4a RME, 4a DI em 31 de Março de 1964." *Commando de 4a Região Militar, 4a Divisão de Infantaria e Guarnição de Juiz de Fora* (9 May 1964).
62. See the extremely interesting chapter by Pedro Gomes on the role of Minas Gerais in the coup, "Minas: Do diálogo ao 'front,'" in Dines, *Os idos de Março,* pp. 87–89.
63. Ibid., p. 91.
64. See the chapter on the role of São Paulo in the coup by Eurilo Duarte, "32 mais 32, Igual a 64," in Dines, *Os idos de Março,* pp. 125–60.
65. "Defesa da ilegalidade," *O Jornal,* 15 March 1964. Complete text reproduced in Dines, *Os idos de Março,* pp. 392–93. Original order is in the *Arquivo do Marechal H. A. Castello Branco,* located in the library of the General Staff School (ECEME) in Rio de Janeiro.
66. Harold D. Lasswell and Abraham Kaplan, *Power and Society: A Framework for Political Inquiry* (New Haven: Yale University Press, 1950), p. 252.
67. An example of the lack of governmental discretion or control over the left that was endangering this balance was the ministry of education's deliberate showing to a militant sailors' organization the Russian film *The Battleship Potemkin,* in which the parallel between the role of the Russian sailors in the Russian revolution and the possible role of sailors in Brazil was made in a complementary running commentary. See "Provocações," *O Jornal,* 24 March 1964, p. 4. Two days after the article was published, the sailors rebelled and presented Goulart with an undesired crisis of military discipline.
68. See Jurema, *Sexta-Feira,* pp. 151–58. For a detailed account of the mutiny, see Mario Victor, *Cinco anos que abalaram o Brasil* (Rio de Janeiro: Editôra Civilização Brasileira, 1965), pp. 493–514.
69. See the testimony of General Assis Brasil at a military investigating tribunal after the coup, reprinted in *O Estado de São Paulo,* 2 and 3 July 1964.
70. The naval mutiny was so obviously counterproductive that two generals who were later purged from the military even argue that it must have been deliberately instigated by right-wing officers. Interview with General Luiz Tavares da Cunha Mello and General Nicolau Fico, 10 October 1968, Rio de Janeiro.
71. General Bda Carlos Luiz Guedes, *Boletim da Infantaria Divisionária/4 NR 58,* 31 March 1964, p. 2 (copy in possession of author). For a similar account by General Maurão Filho, another key military officer, see *Relatório da revolução democrática iniciada pela 4a RM E 4a DI em 31 de Março de 1964,* p. 3.
72. Jurema, *Sexta-Feira,* pp. 162–63.
73. Interview with General George Rocha, 5 October 1968, Rio de Janeiro.
74. On the role of the United States, see my *The Military in Politics,* pp. 123–33, and my commentary to the article "From Counterinsurgency to Counterintelligence," in Julio Cotler and Richard Fagen, eds., *Latin America and the United States: The Changing Political Realities* (Stanford, Ca.: Stanford University Press, 1974), pp. 361–67. Documentation concerning the ordering on 31 March 1964 of U.S. naval, air munitions, and fuel support to the coast off São Paulo is contained in recently declassified material in the Lyndon B. Johnson Library in Austin, Texas. For a brief discussion of this material, see Jan Knippers Black, *United States Penetration of Brazil* (Philadelphia: University of Pennsylvania Press, 1977), pp. xi–xii. These archives represent a major new source of material on U.S. involvement in Brazil and still await serious scholarly research. Detailed selections from the archives were printed in the *Jornal do Brasil* in December 1976. For U.S. involvement in Brazil in this period also see Moniz Bandeira, *Presença dos Estados Unidos no Brasil* (Rio de Janeiro: Editôra Civilização Brasilera, 1973).
75. From his "Nationalism in Brazil: A Case of Political Breakdown" (unpublished manuscript, 1969, pp. 32–33, 35). In a book written before the breakdown of the regime, he cautioned that the revolutionary Left was dealing with intellectual abstractions rather than actual reality and might endanger the possibility of a fundamental revolution from developing. See Guerreiro Ramos, *Mito e verdade da revolução brasileira* (Rio de Janeiro: Zahar Editôres, 1963).

5.

Permanent Crisis and the Failure to Create a Democratic Regime: Argentina, 1955-66

Guillermo O'Donnell*

On 28 June 1966, military officers "acting as representatives of the armed forces" ousted Arturo Illía, the constitutionally elected president of Argentina. They did not bother to take the usual steps for prevention of popular disorder—which did not occur. Foreign correspondents reported a surprising lack of opposition from the public at large.[1] Their impression was confirmed by survey data, which showed that 66 percent of the respondents approved of the coup and only 6 percent disapproved.[2] All major groups (except the ousted political party and a few minor parties, as well as university students) expressed support for the coup and for the new military government. The Junta Revolucionaria, formed by the chiefs of staff of the army, navy, and air force, ousted the president and the governors of the states, dissolved Parliament, dismissed the judges of the Supreme Court, and enacted an Estatuto Revolucionario whose regulations prevailed over the national constitution. All political activities were banned, political parties were dissolved, and elections were postponed *sine die*. The junta appointed retired general Juan Carlos Onganía as president. Communiqués from the junta and the new president stated the reasons for the coup. The most important of these were: (1) the lack of harmony and solidarity in and among the major social groups, which had led to anarchy, subversion, and neglect of the public interest; (2) the inability of previous civilian governments to solve the national problems of economic stagnation, inflation, lack of authority, widespread social unrest, and loss of international prestige; (3) the unrepresentativeness of the leadership of the political parties and of most organized groups; (4) the irresponsible behavior

*An earlier version of this chapter appeared in my *Modernization and Bureaucratic-Authoritarianism: Studies in South American Politics* (Berkeley: Institute of International Studies, University of California, Berkeley, 1973). I wish to thank the Institute of International Studies for permission to use that material.

138

of political parties, which had led to the polarization of public opinion and inefficient governmental performance; and (5) the danger of a breakdown of the cohesion of the armed forces, the only solid institutions remaining after a long period of national crisis.[3]

This was certainly not the first coup in Argentine history.[4] But it differed from all the others in that it was the first time that the armed forces, with a high degree of internal cohesion, had decided to take political power directly into their own hands for a long and indefinite period, with no intention of convoking elections or returning government to political parties in the foreseeable future. The preceding period, 1955–66, had been punctuated by numerous attempts (successful and unsuccessful) at military coups, but none had changed the existing political system. Rather, the continued political instability of that period was a characteristic feature of the workings of a pseudo-political democracy that denied electoral access to the first plurality (i.e., the largest single political party in a multiparty system) of the electorate.[5] The importance of the June 1966 coup is that it was a conscious effort to change the existing political system by the inauguration of a bureaucratic-authoritarian regime. This "culminating" event ("culminating" in terms of the focus of this chapter) was the result of manifold factors, among them the recurrent political instability of the years between 1955 and 1966.

It is important to bear in mind here certain important distinctions. This chapter is intended to contribute to the explanation of the 1966 change in the Argentine political system by analyzing the crucial step that brought about that change. Thus it is not focused on the examination of the political instability that prevailed between 1955 and 1966, except insofar as this seems to have contributed to the final breakdown.

It is always difficult to decide how far back one should go in examining the factors that seem to have effected the event or phenomenon being analyzed. In the present case it is evident that limiting the examination to the factors that were immediately related to the 1966 coup, such as the military's decision to intervene, the high degree of cohesion among the coup leaders, and the goal of inaugurating a different type of political system, would be too restrictive. Consideration of these factors immediately raises questions concerning the reasons for the military decisions and the lack of public opposition to the coup.

In this way the focus of analysis is broadened; but such a broadened perspective involves problems. First, the conceptual neatness of an explanation centered on only the most immediate factors is sacrificed. Second, it is impossible to avoid simplifying the broad historical and social factors that are thought to have exerted an important influence on factors more immediate to the coup. Why did the military change the goals of its intervention in 1966? Why was this coup decided upon by military officers who had shortly before taken a very explicit *legalista* (i.e., anti-coup) stand? Why was the 1966 coup executed with such an unusual degree of cohesion among the armed forces? Why did most organized groups in Argentine society hasten to express support for the coup and the military government? And in what ways did these circumstances relate to the attempt to inaugurate and consolidate a new type of political system in Argentina?

However, even with its pitfalls, a broad analytical perspective is desirable because it alone will allow a search for answers to these questions. The strategy I intend to follow here will begin with a brief examination of some aspects of Argentine history. Next, I shall study aspects of the general social context of the 1955–66 period. The first phase will provide the main outlines of a "longitudinal" perspective, while the second will give a detailed picture of Argentina immediately before the 1966 coup. These two sections will establish the coordinates within which the factors most directly related to the coup will be studied, which will be done in the final section of the chapter.

Some Aspects of Argentina's Historical Legacy

The analysis here of the historical aspects that preceded the 1966 coup (some of them by many years) will of necessity be very selective. There is no pretense here to write history. The aim is to identify some social problems that emerged during certain historical periods and have remained as "constants" in Argentine society. The historical discussion will be limited strictly to those developments which seem indispensable for this purpose.[6]

"Constants," as used here, are characteristics of Argentine society that have remained as persistent problems or constraints, limiting the possibilities of political action. The persistence of certain historical constants and the emergence of new ones is, during each historical period, a major part of the constellation of problems that must be faced. Each such constellation is made up of the constants and the cluster of more specific problems that confront the political actors in each particular period. These constants could have been eliminated by previous governments, but the fact that they have not has—to borrow Weber's analogy—loaded the dice more and more against formation of an effective political system in Argentina. This failure has in turn fostered the persistence and accumulation of an increasing number of constants.

National Unification and the Landed Oligarchy

Two constants have persisted from a very early period. The first is a high degree of incongruence between actual political behavior and political behavior as prescribed by formal institutions and dominant ideologies.[7] The second is a strong disaffection of vast sectors of the population vis-à-vis the existing political system and the holders of political power, based on salient cleavages around important issues and on an unequal distribution of political resources.[8]

During Spanish colonial rule two very different patterns of settlement prevailed in what would later be Argentina. The central and northern regions were economically part of the Peruvian Viceroyalty, and the conquistadors established a patriarchal rule over largely self-sufficient societies, which they found fit quite well with the hierarchical world-view they had brought from Spain. In contrast, Buenos Aires was very much a secondary settlement; the lands around it were sparsely populated by nomadic Indians and lacked any economic value. The village, although a port, was too distant to benefit from the more affluent Peruvian region, and it had been prohibited by Spain from engaging in international trade. But the expansion of British commerce brought Buenos Aires into conflict with Spain, and soon it became a major center for smuggling. The legislation that the Spanish enacted to prohibit commerce and smuggling in Buenos Aires was utterly ineffective (as was the legislation to protect the Indians of the Peruvian regions). The famous dictum that "the will of the King is obeyed but not executed" accurately reflected the reality.

The movement toward independence from Spain, which originated in Buenos Aires, triggered sixty years of convulsion and anarchy. The civil wars of independence were almost a continuous civil war. On one side of the struggle were the *unitarios*, based in Buenos Aires and heavily involved in international trade. Eager to absorb all European ideological trends, they drafted laws and constitutions for a nation that did not yet exist and that would successfully resist their claims to rule. Their opponents, based in the central and northern regions, sought to preserve their patriarchal, precapitalist way of life. At stake were two very different ideologies and economic interests: the philosphy of the Enlightenment as opposed to that of late Spanish scholasticism, and the incorporation of Argentina into the world market as opposed to the persistence of the closed, subsistence economies of the interior. After they gained independence, the Spanish colonies were, as Richard Morse puts it, "a decapitated patrimonial state" in quest of a legitimacy formula.[9] For the unitarios, outwardly oriented and without traditional legitimation, "government" meant some form of constitutional government in the fashion of Western Europe or the United States. The obvious difficulty was that the context in which the newly independent Spanish colonials operated was not at all the type of society presupposed by those models, and the difference between the two was too great to be ignored. One possibility would have been to try to establish institutions better adapted to the actual conditions, but many unitarios believed that imposing the forms of constitutional government, for the sake of "progress" and at any cost, would necessarily push social reality toward a resemblance to the model societies. Transplanted institutions would shape a social reality that would be compatible with them. After many failures, a constitution was enacted in 1852 that has endured (at least nominally) until the present. The representative who formally proposed the text to the constitutional convention said:

There are only two ways of building a nation: to take her behavior, her character and her habits as they are, or to give her the code that must create the proper behavior, character and habits if the country does not have them. Since this is the case, since the country is in chaos, this constitutional project is the only way to save her.[10]

During the civil wars the words "constitution," "liberalism," and later on, "democracy," *belonged* to the unitarios; but the incongruence between institutional and formal prescriptions of behavior and the actual performance of government was as great as it had been under Spanish rule. In addition, these terms became the symbols of a minority that denied the traditional culture and destroyed the social structures and forms of government of a large proportion of the population.[11] The privileged location of Buenos Aires as a port meant that its inhabitants could act as middlemen for the introduction of European (mainly English) manufactured goods. Because the craft industries of the interior could not compete with these imports, the territorial expansion of the hegemony of Buenos Aires resulted in the extinction of many domestic economic activities. This helps to explain the stern resistance of the interior against Buenos Aires.

When the pace of the industrial revolution accelerated in England during the second half of the nineteenth century, Buenos Aires was able to acquire economic resources and warfare technology that firmly established its hegemony over the interior. But even after 1870, when the country was relatively peaceful, the transplantation of democratic political institutions continued to create major problems. In particular, maintenance of these institutions required that elections be held, when the supporters of the central government were frequently in a minority. Since there was no possibility of allowing the *barbares* to rule, electoral fraud, as well as violence and openly arbitrary exercise of the central government's powers, became a frequent occurrence.

At this point a third Argentine constant became clearly evident. The democratic "rules of the game" were to be given only limited and conditional adherence by the ruling sectors; the application of these rules was subject to the proviso that it produce the "correct" government.[12] If this requirement were not met, the rules were suspended to the extent and for the period necessary to assure that the "correct" government would attain power. As would happen in succeeding periods, since "playing democratically" endangered democracy (as defined by the ruling sectors), the only solution was to act in a blatantly undemocratic fashion while asserting that such action was necessary "for the sake of democracy." Given the consistently high level of popular disaffection toward rulers and institutions, it is not difficult to understand how this constant bred cynicism, instead of helping to establish the legitimacy of the system and its institutions.[13]

At the end of the nineteenth century the ruling sectors eagerly adopted the new ideas emanating from Europe, mixing positivism with Darwinian and Spencerian concepts. The struggle previously defined as "civilization against barbarism" could now be "scientifically" interpreted. Ruling sectors maintained that there was no hope until the remnants of Spanish culture and the "degraded races" were replaced by European immigration.[14] At the turn of the century, during a period of rapidly growing need for labor because of export expansion, the national government actively encouraged Europeans to immigrate.[15]

Another constant, which initially had favorable consequences, manifested itself in this period—i.e., the dependence of the Argentine economy on international trade and capital movements, with limited capabilities for domestic control of their effects. Since the end of the eighteenth century, a basic tenet of the unitarios had been free trade, under which Argentina would export agrarian goods and import most of the industrial products it needed. When British industry expanded rapidly around 1870, so did its need for the exports that Argentina was in a particularly good position to provide. The vast pampas around Buenos Aires, which could provide the cereals (and later, the beef) for export, became essential in the new international trade situation; the economic center in Argentina shifted decisively from the central and northern regions to Buenos Aires. Great efforts were exerted to establish the financial and transport structure required to open the pampas to capitalist exploitation. The extent and rapidity of this expansion into the pampean land can be seen in the data presented in table 1.

Under this external inducement the Argentine economy grew rapidly in the years between 1870 and 1914. The country won an international reputation for prosperity. The standard of living—at least in the Buenos Aires area—was

Table 1. Selected Economic Indicators: Argentina, 1870–1914

	1865–69	1890–94	1910–14
Total length of railroad track (kilometers)	503	—	31,104
Total merchandise exports (millions of gold pesos)	38	—	410
Total area sown with crops (millions of hectares)	0.58	—	20.62
Total wheat exports (annual averages, millions of gold pesos at 1910–14 values)	0.2	28.1	78.1
Total corn exports (same measure as wheat)	0.3	6.0	72.4
Total frozen beef exports (same measure as wheat)	0.0	0.1	49.7

Sources: Carlos Díaz Alejandro, *Essays on the Economic History of the Argentine Republic* (New Haven: Yale University Press, 1970), pp. 2–5; and Ernesto Tornquist and Co., *The Economic Development of the Argentine Republic in the Last Fifty Years* (Buenos Aires, 1919), pp. 26, 116–17, 139–40.

high as a result of the advantages that Argentina enjoyed in the international market for the exportation of cereals and beef. But the rest of the country lagged far behind Buenos Aires and the surrounding pampas region. Furthermore, millions of hectares of the best pampean land were appropriated by a tiny sector of the population: Argentina never had an open frontier.[16] The resources from which Argentine prosperity derived were monopolized by the very few, the beneficiaries taking for granted that this was the only road to progress. As one president of the period, Juárez Celman, stated: "With *latifundio* we have achieved the present progress and our outstanding economic and productive capacity. The system of big property has made us rich."[17] Perhaps more important, this privileged stratum consisted, by and large, of less-than-efficient entrepreneurs who showed very little interest in industrial activities.[18] These factors combined to restrict what would otherwise have been an unusual opportunity for building a solid economy and a more open society.

The Middle Class

By the end of the nineteenth century (especially in Buenos Aires), the expanding economy had created an important middle sector, formed by merchants, professionals, civil servants, and owners of the primitive industries that typically appear in the large export-sites of agrarian-export economies. Recent investigations have shown that sheer distance from central, industrial-good exporting economies and some tariff protection for certain products stimulated the growth of some industry, but such industry was owned largely by foreign nationals. This, combined with a preference on the part of the government and ruling sectors for open trade policies, prevented the emergence of a numerically important and politically active national industrial bourgeoisie. Instead, within the middle class the salaried, nonentrepreneurial sectors prevailed overwhelmingly. This middle class fully accepted the existing socioeconomic policies and, if anything, were more anti-industry and more pro–free trade than the oligarchy. Their political demands were limited to fair elections and open access to high-ranking national government positions.[19] However, their road to political power was not easy. Only after three unsuccessful civil-military revolts was a law passed providing for honest electoral registrations, secret ballots, and custody by the military of the urns in which the ballots were deposited.

This long delay in the admission of the middle class into the political arena reflects another constant: the strong resistance by established political actors to the expansion of political participation to include new actors, even when favorable economic circumstances and almost total policy consensus minimized the "risks" of such expansion. When these favorable circumstances later changed, and new political actors disagreed sharply on policy matters, outright opposition to further expansion became the rule.

As Peter Smith argues elsewhere in this volume, neither the oligarchy's concession to the claim for clean elections nor the election in 1916 of the Partido Radical leader, Hipólito Yrigoyen, meant genuine commitment of the oligarchy to democratic rules of the game. The new government operated under conditions of "uncertain legitimacy,"[20] subject to a satisfactory (as defined by the old rulers) handling of national affairs. The oligarchy retained control of crucial political resources—social prestige, economic power, influence on the army, control of the press and the university. Throughout the *Radicales* period the old rulers demonstrated contempt toward the parvenus, whom they saw as inefficient and unreliable people who, after all, were only following the old socioeconomic policies of the ruling sectors.[21]

The Radicales governments were not entirely free of fraud and arbitrary interventions of the central government into the affairs of the states, but on the whole they made remarkable progress in electoral practices and in extending the rule of law. It was particularly unfortunate for Argentina that the British economy began to decline after 1914. Because of this decline and less than skillful government policies, economic growth slowed. Finally, with the impact of the world crisis that began in 1929, the economic situation became very serious. The oligarchy saw in these conditions a confirmation of their belief that only they could govern. In 1930 an oligarchy-backed military coup ousted the Radicales government.

The old oligarchy, then generally called the *Conservadores,* attempted to govern in the midst of the economic crisis. They undertook a program of industrialization designed to save badly needed international currency and provide an internal market for agrarian production.[22] The severe impact of the crisis in the interior of the country, combined with governmental efforts to industrialize in Buenos Aires, drew large numbers of people into urban life.[23] These new migrants were to form the basis of a large urban proletariat, remaining close to their agrarian origins and bringing with them a long record of grievances against the central government. The Conservadores were faced with the old predicament: since they were "democratic," sooner or later they had to call elections. They first tried a gubernatorial election in Buenos Aires State in 1931, which resulted in a Radicales victory. Since the "correct" candidate had not won, the election was annulled, and a federal delegate appointed in place of the elected governor. Later, when former Radical president Marcelo de Alvear tried to run in presidential elections, his candidacy was vetoed by a decree. As a result, under the motto of "Intransigence," the Radicales abstained from electoral participation and organized several unsuccessful civil-military rebellions. Even with the abstention of the Radicales, the Conservadores could not risk honest elections. Systematic "patriotic fraud" was practiced, on the grounds that it was the only way to avoid the disasters that would follow if a majoritarian government were elected.[24] To quote Whitaker:

As the Presidential election of 1937 approached, the rising Radical tide made Justo [the president, elected by fraud in 1932] himself uneasy over the chance of passing electoral control to the right people. Accordingly, he and his followers simply stole the elections by fraud and force. . . . For the political health of the country the effect was disastrous. Coming on top of all that had gone before it seemed to confirm what non-conformists had been saying for years past: that in Argentina democracy was only a snare to facilitate dominion and exploitation of the nation by a privileged few.[25]

For the Radicales and for the still inarticulated groups that rapid industrialization and urbanization had given rise to, this was the "infamous decade." This label reflected, among other things, the outrage produced by the huge concessions that the Conservadores, attempting to preserve part of the original export market, made to British interests. Nationalist sentiment against both Conservadores and British influence increased.

The 1930s saw sweeping political and social changes. The new import-substituting industrialists sought to increase their sway over government decisions. The military saw industrialization as the path to international power and British influence as the major obstacle to industrialization. Ideological alternatives to democracy were being tried in Europe in the 1930s with apparent success. Moreover, the church, particularly after the beginning of the Spanish civil war, was ready to grant ideological legitimacy to antidemocratic movements. From all these elements a nationalist-industrialist ideology with strong authoritarian components began to develop. It had a wide appeal against which the old ruling sectors could oppose only a mockery of democracy and a dependent association with England.[26]

The Urban Popular Sector

During the 1930s the urban popular sector (i.e., the working class and segments of the lower middle class) went through a process of rapid political activation. But none of the existing political parties was willing to absorb a sector formed largely of recent rural migrants—not even the Socialists and Communists, whose basic constituencies were skilled workers and European migrants.[27] World War II further complicated the domestic political situation. The demands for autarchy and industrialization, as well as the diffusion of pro-Axis ideologies, clashed with British interests and with the pro-Allied international policies that most of the ruling sectors favored. Like the rural migrants, the new industrialists and many military officers could find no political parties through which to channel their preferences. The new issues and ideologies had a profound impact on the military, and for the first time the oligarchy could not count on its firm allegiance. In 1943, when it became evident that the 1944 elections were to be decided by "patriotic fraud," the military ousted the Conservadores government. In the resulting military government, Colonel Perón emerged as the leader best able to pull together all the dissident elements that the Conservadores period had generated.[28] Against this coalition, the Radicales, Conservadores, Socialists, and Communists formed a "Democratic Union," but they were defeated (in honest elections) by Perón in 1946.[29]

This is not the place for a study of *Peronismo*.[30] It included authoritarian components which were a blend of the ideologies of the 1930s with a traditional (for Argentina) style of leadership.[31] Perón's policies of income distribution in favor of industry and the popular sector, the enactment of comprehensive labor and welfare legislation, and the introduction of numerous economic controls gained an enthusiastic response from the popular sector, but were very much at odds with the preferences of the recently displaced ruling sectors. As a consequence, and for the sake of "defending democracy," very early in Perón's government the old parties engaged in "disloyal opposition," reinforcing the authoritarian tendencies inherent in Peronismo.[32] The personalities of Perón and his wife appealed to the masses, particularly urban and rural workers. In addition, during Perón's government the standard of living of these sectors rose significantly, many of the rights of labor were effectively protected, and workers could feel that they had gained some influence in national affairs. When attacked, Perón did not miss an opportunity to emphasize his opponents' past behavior as a support for his argument that the "return to democracy" they advocated was a trick for establishing a dictatorship to oppress the people. To say the least, Perón had a strong argument when he observed that his opponents had never practiced the liberal advice they were now giving.

The effect of these developments was to increase the conflict between Peronistas and anti-Peronistas, and to decrease the chances that the formally democratic institutional framework could operate. Both sides helped to create a situation that is well summarized by Floria:

Perón's period was not only the period of Peronismo; it was also the period of anti-Peronismo. This polarization, as it was afterwards called, was the result of the articulation of power and opposition according to rules that were not shared. There were not two parties; there were "two countries": one whose inhabitants could only conceive of Argentina with Perón, and another that could only accept Argentina without Perón and, in terms of power, without Peronismo.[33]

By 1950 the broad coalition that Perón had formed began to disintegrate. Crop failures, misallocation of resources, unfavorable trends in international trade, and the increasing need for foreign currency to sustain advancing industrialization led to an economic crisis. Simultaneously, the authoritarian and repressive components of Peronismo were significantly reinforced. Though unwilling to oppose agrarian interests by pursuing a program of land reform, and unwilling to force industry to absorb the costs of the economic crisis, Perón's government had to protect the gains achieved by the urban workers, its staunchest supporters. After 1949 the industrialists started to withdraw their support and align themselves with the opposition, and in 1954 Perón became involved in a serious conflict with the Catholic church. The armed forces also began to waver in their support, and when, after two abortive attempts to stage coups in 1951 and June 1955, they found that the only remaining solid support for Perón came from the popular sector, they finally ousted him in September 1955.

During the provisional government of General Eugenio Aramburu (1955–58), with the support of the now bitterly anti-Peronista armed forces, the old leaders of the old parties returned to power. The point to be emphasized here is that by 1955 two fundamental and overwhelmingly salient cleavages had coincided: the political division of Peronistas and anti-Peronistas, and the socioeconomic division of the popular sector (constituted largely of the working class) and the labor unions against the rest of society. The result was intense and cumulative polarization.[34]

After 1955 a program of "democratization" was undertaken which resulted in a drastic decrease in the share of wage income in the GNP, numerous attempts to weaken labor unions, and the electoral proscription of the Peronista party. If to these are added the effects of economic stagnation and inflation, it is hardly surprising that the Peronistas maintained their allegiance to Peronismo.[35] The fact that the legal road to political power was closed to them, memories of recent times in which they had been much better off, the need to fight constantly for their shares of income, the vengefulness of the provisional government's policies—all of this hardened the Peronistas' opposition. Widespread social unrest followed.[36]

For anti-Peronistas any return to the pre-1955 political situation was totally out of the question. This view was shared by the armed forces, from which all officers suspected of Peronista leanings had been purged. The military leaders had not forgotten that shortly before being ousted, Perón had seemed determined to organize workers' militias. When a rebellion by Peronistas failed in 1956, the anti-Peronista military officers, breaking an unwritten rule, ordered the leaders of the rebellion shot, thereby increasing the existing polarization.

All the constants described above were still very much a factor in Argentine life. The Peronistas had been removed from government in the name of "democracy." This meant elections would be necessary, but the "wrong" party—the *Peronista* bloc—controlled the largest share of electors. Under these circumstances, political activity was severely constrained: it could serve neither as a means for the return of Peronistas to government, nor as a channel for the implementation of socioeconomic policies favored by Peronistas and the labor unions.[37] The discrepancy between the outwardly expressed democratic beliefs of the ruling sectors and the actual workings of the political system was almost beyond measure. In addition, the severe socioeconomic crisis (which will be analyzed further below) had accentuated the rigidities in the social structure and was creating new patterns of stagnation and dependence. Finally, no matter how great the economic, social, and political costs, the ruling sectors were determined to close any significant political access to the politically activated urban popular sector.

Here I have tried merely to underline political and social constants "extracted" from historical sequence, without attempting the task, impossible here, of explaining their emergence. Despite the pitfalls inherent in a highly condensed description, it was essential to discuss these constants. They refer to historical factors whose more immediate effects, whether on the social processes studied in the section immediately following or on those connected with the 1966 coup that are the subject of the final section of this chapter, are difficult to measure. But insofar as they determine a persistent and pervasive political climate, these constants form the broad base of reference without which it seems impossible to achieve an understanding of more specific factors.

The focus of this chapter turns now toward a more "horizontal" perspective: an analysis of the social context of the 1955–66 period. This analysis is provided on the assumption that this context, to a large extent influenced by the historical constants, exerted a direct influence on the military intervention of June 1966.

The Social Setting of the 1966 Coup

In 1966 the average per capita income in Argentina was $818 (in 1966 U.S. dollars).[38] In 1960 unionized workers numbered around 2,600,000.[39] Agriculture and industry contributed 16.6 and 34.0 percent respectively, to the GNP while 21.4 percent of the working age population was employed in agriculture and 28.0 in industry.[40] Clearly, Argentina was far from being an underdeveloped "traditional" agrarian society. But these data must be considered from the perspective of a long period of slow growth.[41] In 1929 the average per capita income in Argentina was about $700 (1960 U.S. dollars).[42] At that time the Argentine per capita income was slightly below that of Australia, a country remarkably similar to Argentina in terms of production and relations with the world market. Today, Australia's per capita income is almost twice that of Argentina.

From 1925–29 to 1961–65, the average per capita growth rate in Argentina has been 0.8 percent yearly. Díaz Alejandro offers this description of the situation:

Since 1930 . . . the growth rate has been so small, the cyclical fluctuations so violent, and the swings in income distribution so pronounced that it is easy to believe that during some years several groups have been worse off than they, or their parents, were during 1925-1929. Furthermore, in some public services (e.g., telephones, railroads, the post office, statistical services) and in some import-substituting manufactures, quality has deteriorated so that a quality-corrected growth rate would be even smaller. . . .Although time-series for the Argentine terms of trade are of doubtful reliability, it is likely that they declined between 1925-1929 and recent years; correcting the growth rate for this decline would further shave it.[43]

If we take the Perón period (1946-55) as the baseline, the per capita income reached in 1947 was not surpassed until 1965, and the per capita real wages of 1947 were surpassed only in 1958 and in 1965, to fall below the 1947 level in the following years.[44] The characteristics of this arrested development require closer examination:

(1) When the GNP time-series since 1946 are considered, it can be seen that within the average low growth rate, wild fluctuations have taken place from year to year. As column 1 of table 2 shows, in the years 1948, 1949, 1950, 1952, 1956, 1959, 1962, 1963, and 1966 net losses in per capita income were registered, and in some cases losses were substantial.

(2) The average rate of inflation has been 26.5 percent annually between 1946 and 1966, but it was substantially higher in the 1955-66 period *and* in the years of negative growth (see column 2 of table 2).

(3) After reaching a maximum of 46.9 percent in 1952, the salary and wage share in the GNP declined to 39.8 percent in 1965 (see column 3 in table 2), even though the productivity per worker in 1961 was 23 percent above the 1953 level.[45]

(4) During the 1949-66 period Argentina suffered a chronic foreign exchange shortage (see column 4 of table 2), which was aggravated in the years of economic recovery.

Many economists agree that the foreign exchange shortage has been the single most important factor in retarding economic growth in Argentina. This shortage has been closely related to other factors. First, as table 3 shows, the quantum index of Argentine exports declined from 1925-29 to 1960-64 not only in per capita but also in *absolute* terms, reflecting lagging agricultural productivity (see column 2 of table 3). During most of this period the domestic terms of trade discriminated against agrarian products (see column 3 of table 3). In addition, of the net increase in national capital stock between 1929 and 1955, only 1.0 percent went to the rural sector.[46]

Second, from the 1930s nearly until the end of Perón's government, Argentine industry expanded "horizontally" by putting heavy emphasis on consumer goods import substitution. But the exhaustion of these "easy" stages of import substitution placed serious strains on Argentina's declining import

Table 2. Annual Measures of Various Key Economic Indicators, 1946–66

Year	1 Annual Changes in GDP per Capita (percent of previous year's level in constant pesos)	2 Yearly Inflation	3 Wages and Salaries as Percentage of GNP	4 Change in Net Foreign Exchange Reserves (in millions of current U.S. dollars)
Perón's government				
1946	6.4%	17.7%	38.7%	—
1947	11.9	13.5	37.3	—
1948	−0.7	13.1	40.6	—
1949	−6.5	31.1	45.7	−269
1950	−0.3	25.5	45.9	166
1951	2.1	36.7	43.0	−333
1952	−8.2	38.7	46.9	−173
1953	5.1	4.0	44.8	279
1954	1.9	3.8	45.6	−33
1955	5.0	12.3	43.0	−175
1955–66 period				
1956	−0.2	13.4	42.6	−19
1957	3.6	24.7	41.4	−60
1958	5.3	31.6	43.3	−217
1959	−7.7	113.7	37.8	113
1960	6.1	27.3	38.4	161
1961	5.1	13.5	39.9	−57
1962	−3.7	28.1	39.1	−234
1963	−5.5	24.1	39.1	202
1964	6.2	22.1	38.2	−11
1965	6.7	28.6	39.1	139
1966	−2.4	32.3	39.8	53

SOURCES: Column 1: Banco Central de la República Argentina, *Origen del producto y composición del gasto nacional: Suplemento del Boletín Estadístico, n. 6* (Buenos Aires: Banco Central, 1966), p. 18, and Díaz Alejandro, *Essays*, p. 352. Column 2: Díaz Alejandro, *Essays*, p. 528 (Buenos Aires cost of living). Column 3: UN-ECLA and CONADE, *El desarrollo económico y la distribución del ingreso en la Argentina* (New York: United Nations, 1968), p. 164. Column 4: Díaz Alejandro, *Essays*, p. 353.

Table 3. Economic Indices, 1925–64

	1	2	3
Years	Quantum Indices of Merchandise Exports (1951– 54 = 100)	Index of Agrarian Production (1960 = 100)	Internal Terms of Trade (ratio of rural prices to industrial prices) (1935–39 = 100)
1925–29	179	—	100 (1935–39)
1930–39	167	—	72 (1940–45)
1940–44	135	86	77 (1945–49)
1945–49	133	85	83 (1950–55)
1950–54	106	87	93 (1956–58)
1955–59	124	99	96 (1959–61)
1960–64	160	102	103 (1962–64)

SOURCES: Column 1: Díaz Alejandro, *Essays*, p. 76. Column 2: Banco Central, *Origen del producto*, p. 36. Column 3: Díaz Alejandro, *Essays*, p. 89.

capacity. Domestic industrial expansion was hindered by problems of high costs and distorted schedules of supply, as well as severe financial, technological, and managerial limitations. Under such conditions, the need for critical inputs of intermediate and raw materials, as well as of capital goods, grew at a time when exports were lagging. There were growing demands for capital and technology transfers from abroad, indicating a need for (as well as the great difficulties to be faced in) making significant advances toward more mature industrialization; i.e., a more vertically integrated industrialization, with a better structure of costs and supply. Furthermore, increases in the domestic fabrication of capital goods were almost entirely at the level of relatively simple equipment, and Argentine production was not able to satisfy the growing demand for more complex equipment. The yearly average of machinery imports was 198 million U.S. dollars in 1951–55, 352 million in 1956–60, and 498 million in 1961–65.[47] An observation made by Díaz Alejandro neatly summarizes this situation: the income elasticity of Argentine demands for imports was 2.6, which meant that, when and if national income grew by one unit, it generated a demand for 2.6 units of imported goods; therefore, the foreign exchange positions of the country was worsened by positive rates of growth.[48]

The effects of the factors cited—particularly the pressure of the growth years on the foreign exchange position of Argentina—led to drastic devaluations of the peso, usually combined with programs aimed at restricting internal demand and eliminating "marginal" industrial producers. By making imports and exportable agrarian goods more expensive, devaluations fed inflation at the same time that the effects of internal policies drastically decreased output and demand. As can be seen in table 1, the years of negative growth were usually also those of higher inflation and negative income redistributions. One major goal of the devaluations was to increase, by the restriction of domestic demand and income transfers, short-run available exports and, in the long run, to improve agrarian productivity. These effects were supposed to be produced by improving the domestic agrarian terms of trade and the dollar value of rural exportable commodities. But these policies meant severe income losses for the urban-industrial sector, which led to the intense social conflict that marked the 1955–66 period. As a consequence of this conflict, the redistributive policies were soon relaxed, and the presumably beneficial consequences that would have followed from them were never realized.[49]

An important effect of inflation and devaluations has been a wild fluctuation in income shares. As a UN-ECLA and CONADE study says:

The effect of these devaluations on income distribution occurs in two stages. In the first, a horizontal distribution takes place when relative prices change in favor of agriculture, consisting of inter-sectoral income changes from the urban sectors to the agrarian sector or, more specifically, to agrarian producers. But since the effect of devaluation on relative prices is combined with policies of salary restriction or increased unemployment, to some extent the horizontal redistribution is transformed into a vertical redistribution. This means that, in the final analysis, the main income changes (produced by devaluations) are harmful to urban workers and beneficial to agrarian producers, while the relative position of urban entrepreneurs is damaged only to the extent that the effects of devaluation are more intense than the effects of salary (restriction) policies.[50]

In short, devaluations benefit the agrarian sector, but as inflation proceeds and no new devaluation takes place, the urban sector (however its share is allocated between workers and entrepreneurs) recovers its losses. At some point, the effects of devaluation are annulled or even reversed, domestic economic activity increases again, a new foreign exchange crisis is produced, and a new devaluation is made. The magnitude of the shifts of income for several Argentine sectors during 1958–65 can be seen in table 4.

It is difficult to exaggerate the political consequences of this turbulent economic situation, particularly in a setting combining a low level of political legitimacy and a high degree of popular disaffection. Note that the combination of constantly high inflation (aggravated in negative growth years) with drastic devaluations and slow growth meant that to remain at the same level of monetary income would have involved heavy losses in real income. Thus, gains made by all sectors were extremely unstable, and the situation created by slow and erratic economic growth served to raise the stakes of the conflict.

Before going any further, let us look at some more disaggregated data. As previously noted, the real wage income in 1965 was about the same as in 1945. However, as table 2 showed, the share of salaries and wages in the GNP decreased during the 1955–66 period. This apparent discrepancy disappears at the level of more disaggregated data. First, the recurrent attempts to eliminate "marginal" industrial producers, combined with the introduction of more

Table 4. Intersectoral Income Variations Expressed as Percentage of Income Participation of Each Sector, 1958–65

	Average of Absolute Variations	Maximum Yearly Positive Variation	Maximum Yearly Negative Variation
Rural			
Agrarian	12.1%	34.8%	−20.8%
Urban			
Industry	4.8	10.1	−8.5
Construction	7.8	37.5	−11.1
Commerce	6.2	7.8	−22.0
Transport and communications	4.4	12.7	−6.7
General government	8.1	14.3	−17.0
Electricity, gas, and water	10.1	37.5	−20.0

SOURCE: UN-ECLA and CONADE, *El desarrollo económico*, p. 217.

capital-intensive techniques, produced a large pool of urban unemployed, especially in the early 1960s.[51] Since real wage data reflect only the incomes of those lucky enough to find work, they give only a partial picture of the income position of the popular sector. Second, among those employed, there were wide differences in the real income positions of those workers who were well organized and those who, as members of the less dynamic sectors of the economy, lacked the degree of organization necessary to obtain satisfaction of their economic demands.

The source of data for table 5 does not discriminate between wage and salary earners, but census data show that an important proportion of the "Industry and Mining" and "Construction" categories consists of blue-collar workers. The "Commerce and Finance" category is formed largely by white-collar workers, while "Services" (which includes government workers) is a very mixed category. It is important to note that while industrial workers fared relatively well, other blue-collar and apparently most white-collar employees did not. This circumstance surely underlay the disaffection shown by these latter groups during the 1955–66 period, their initial willingness to support the military government, and their responsiveness to a "law and order" appeal. However, no matter how badly they fared, the nonindustrial workers did better than those sectors even less capable of exerting effective pressure on the national government. As table 5 shows, pensioners and *rentistas* in particular were heavy losers.[52]

In other words, at the national level the economic "game" was quite close to zero-sum, and the better organized (and perhaps in the short-run, economically more indispensable) sectors of urban entrepreneurs, agrarian entrepreneurs, and industrial workers could increase their shares of real income at the expense of other, less organized, politically weaker sectors and regions.

The government as an institution was another loser. In terms of gov-

Table 5. Average Real Income of Families in Selected Years (1953 = 100)

	1946	1949	1953	1959	1961	1965
Salary and wage earners						
Industry and mining	88	119	100	90	115	**146**[a]
Construction	106	**137**	100	98	108	118
Transport and communication	106	**128**	100	95	106	110
Commerce and finance	85	**111**	100	94	**111**	112
Services	84	**113**	100	91	103	109
Entrepreneurs						
Agriculture	111	82	100	**143**	89	117
Industry, mining, and construction	115	**148**	100	124	135	143
Commerce	162	**175**	100	161	169	155
Transport	86	104	100	150	143	**170**
Services	109	**132**	100	98	105	109
Social security pensioners	105	130	100	79	96	97
Rentistas	**150**	122	100	56	49	39
TOTAL	103	116	100	108	112	124

Source: UN-ECLA and CONADE, *El desarrollo económico*, p. 130.

[a] Year of maximum real income in boldface throughout.

ernmental resources (i.e., the pool of human and economic means at its disposal for the making and implementation of policies), there was a steady deterioration in the 1955–66 period. In Lasswell's terminology, poor governmental performance and diminished resources resulted in a serious "power dis-accumulation" that hampered governmental problem-solving capabilities.[53] This reduced capability reflected the general social situation but also contributed significantly to its worsening and to the final breakdown in 1966.

In 1965 the tax revenues of the national government amounted to 13.2 percent of the GNP, which decreased to 11.9 percent in 1960 and to 10.9 percent in 1965. The income of the social security system amounted in the same years to 5.0, 3.5, and 4.8 percent of the GNP.[54] (The deterioration of governmental income can be seen clearly in table 6, where comparable data for other countries have been included.) The substantial decline in personal income taxes (see table 7) was partially compensated for by increases in indirect taxes but the impact on income distribution was regressive. The drop in governmental income generated huge budget deficits, which were met by highly inflationary increases in the money supply.[55] The proportion of government expenditures allocated to public works dropped from 20.9 percent of the national budget in 1955–59 to 14.5 percent in 1965.[56] A partially overlapping category—public capital investments—declined by 8.6 percent between 1955–60 and 1960–65.[57] Although the data are incomplete, it is very probable that real salaries of government employees declined throughout this period, partially recovering during 1964–66, but never returning to the 1949 level. Perpetual political crisis resulted in a constant turnover of cabinet members

Table 6. Taxation Data for Argentina and Selected Other Countries

	Percentage of Working Age Population Filing Income Tax Returns	Declared Taxable Income as a Percentage of Total Personal Income
Argentina		
1953	10%	18%
1959	9	10
1961	5	9
Other countries		
United States (1950)	89	77
England (1952–53)	90	80
Australia (1958–59)	80	68

SOURCE: UN-ECLA, *Economic Bulletin for Latin America* 9, no. 1 (April 1966).

and high-ranking civil servants, and in the few government activities which can be measured for productivity, a decline is evident.[58]

The general process can be summarized as follows: devaluations benefited agrarian producers and were paid for by the urban sector. This situation was reversed by-the inflation and economic reactivation that took place between devaluations. Within the urban sector another game was played for the allocation of gains and losses among different categories of entrepreneurs and workers: the gains that could be appropriated by some of the organized categories were paid for by other less organized sectors and areas. Inflation meant that anyone could lose, on the average, one-fourth of his real income in a year.[59] As a consequence of this situation a "catching-up game" developed, in which only a few sectors were able to influence public policies in order to stay ahead in the constantly changing distribution of income shares. In this sense, a "powerful sector" was one that was able to maintain or improve its real-income position by ensuring the implementation of favorable government

Table 7. Direct Taxes as Percentage of Total Government Income in Argentina, 1946–64

Perón Government		1956-64	
1946	38.5%	1956	34.1%
1947	46.3	1957	37.9
1948	49.8	1958	39.3
1949	46.9	1959	29.1
1950	47.3	1960	32.8
1951	43.0	1961	33.0
1952	47.3	1962	30.6
1953	45.0	1963	30.6
1954	41.7	1964	28.3
1955	41.8		

SOURCE: *Panorama de la Economía Argentina*, no. 3, 1967, pp. 23–24.

policies—such as urban and rural entrepreneurs or industrial workers. (In this sense not even the government could be considered powerful.)

An important part of this game consisted of determining strategies that would enable sectors to gain power. First, since rapid inflation continued, a sector that was trying to catch up had to do so in a relatively short time. Second, the focus of demands for policies that would permit "catch-up" was not on institutions such as Parliament, the political parties, and state governments, which played at best a marginal role in the reallocation of economic resources. These demands were concentrated on the presidency, with the result that it became increasingly unlikely that other political institutions could play a meaningful role. Third, the focus on the presidency increased the importance of channels of access that enabled actors to exercise power over the president.[60] Thus, the military became the most effective channel for the satisfaction of sectoral demands; civilian groups sought to influence military factions which could exercise power over the presidency. This fractionalized the military and resulted in more and more numerous and changing demands being channeled through them.

The channeling of demands through the military involved a very real threat of ouster to the government.[61] This danger was evident in the numerous *planteos* (demands from the military backed by the threat of force if they were denied), as well as in the many coups and attempted coups between 1955–66. Those sectors that could induce threats of coups from the military had a definite advantage in playing the catching-up game. These inducements could be obtained through direct access, as in the case of the urban and rural entrepreneurs. For the better-organized urban workers, indirect strategies could produce similar results. By promoting social unrest, as well as by paralyzing production through strikes and the occupation of factories, they could make a government appear unable to maintain even minimal levels of law and order, and thus put it in immediate danger of being ousted. That is, the situation benefited those workers in the better-organized and wealthier unions that could threaten governments with sustained disruptions. (This is reflected in the income figures in table 5.)

It should be borne in mind that the legitimacy of the governments of this period was widely questioned, and that there was generalized political disaffection. Under these conditions threats were very real, and any government that valued survival in office could not ignore them. Hence the governments tended to adopt whatever policies best satisfied the sector that was most threatening at a given time. But the zero-sum conditions meant that each such policy decision raised new threats from other powerful sectors. Frequent policy changes resulted from each governmental decision to placate one sector and the new threats that each such decision generated. (The fluctuations in the preceding tables reflect this pattern)

The resulting situation is well characterized by Huntington's concept of mass praetorianism.[62] In a situation where the primary political aim was control of the means for threatening the survival of the government, political institutions designed for more consensual problem-solving could hardly survive. And where the "threat" strategy prevailed, the most effective way for a sector to have its demands met was to be more threatening than the other sectors. Thus, there was a tendency to escalate the levels of threats. The only effective strategy for each sector was to play according to the actual rather than the institutionally prescribed rules. An "idealistic" sector would have lost heavily in a struggle in which, because of stagnation and inflation, the stakes were very high. A dynamic process had begun that would be very difficult to stop: praetorianism breeds more praetorianism until the conditions for systemic breakdown are reached.

Praetorian politics at high modernization become very complex in two ways. First, social differentiation leads to a greater number of highly activated political actors playing—at several levels simultaneously—a catching-up game based on threats to the government. Second, the combination of high stakes and weak constraints means that formally prescribed patterns become very poor indicators of actual political behavior. The influence of the constants identified earlier in the chapter created the initial conditions of dubious legitimacy, a high degree of popular disaffection, and intense rigidity of the established sectors. The Peronista period accelerated social differentiation and political demands well beyond social integration and social performance. Developmental bottlenecks diminished possible payoffs and made the competition for the allocation of social resources close to a zero-sum game. Under these conditions, government personnel had little opportunity for effective decision-making and policy implementation beyond what was demanded by the more threatening political actors. The steady deterioration of government strength aggravated the social situation. In the catching-up game, most political actors and sectors pursued the vitally important goal of at least keeping pace with inflation, using whatever strategies were most effective. Unfortunately, the most effective strategies for the individual actors were also the most damaging to overall social performance. Each actor was trapped in a situation he could not attempt to change by his own actions without losing heavily and was forced to act in ways that led to even further deterioration of the social context upon which the satisfaction of his demands largely depended. Given the historical heritage and the intensity of social conflict, it was very unlikely that these actors could have reached agreements among themselves that would have channeled their competition into less damaging patterns. This should have been accomplished by governmental action, but the government's low level of legitimacy and limited resources prevented any serious efforts in this direction. This situation fits perfectly the general framework proposed by Juan Linz in his introductory essay: the decaying legitimacy of the regime is compounded by its increasing inefficacy in deciding and implementing policies that can satisfy a significant part of the politically relevant population.

The continued crises generated by this situation annul most individual and sectoral gains. But since there is no way for individuals or sectors to change the institutional parameters (the rules of the game), the only course is to continue along the same lines, hoping in each case that the social deterioration can be minimized. Slowly the possibility of another course emerges. After they have played a "loser's game" for some time, it becomes evident to most actors that the majority lose consistently while a few gain, only to have most of their gains annulled shortly thereafter. Once this pattern is recognized, the parameters of the situation are widely questioned. It is concluded that the rules of the game ought to be changed, and with them the political institutions that have been unable to conduct the game in ways more beneficial to the participants. When this assessment becomes general, what might be termed a "ceiling consensus" is reached, and most sectors agree that the political system should be changed and new parameters for competition established. Of course, such a "consensus" is limited strictly to this point: the actors disagree as much as ever about what the new rules should be. Given a previous history of mass praetorianism, it is likely—when the political system changes—that there will be an authoritarian imposition of new "rules" by whatever coalition succeeds in gaining the governmental power.

This is the "power vacuum" described in the Bracher-Linz model of breakdown of political regimes. Authorities have evidently failed to overcome praetorianism in a way that would have supported their legitimacy and even minimally enhanced the efficacy of their rule. From that point on, the only unknown factor is a matter of how long it will take for a winning coalition to emerge from the set of political actors that have reached the "ceiling consensus."

Political Opinions and Attitudes

Observers see many so-called paradoxes in Argentine politics. For example, Kalman Silvert finds the following paradoxical attitudes: (1) "zero-sum mentality" and "lack of responsible entrepreneurship"; (2) "the almost universal view . . . that no public measure can be good for almost everybody"; (3) "the narrowness of loyalty horizons . . . [and] the failure to accept the state as the ultimate arbiter of secular disputes."[63] I would argue that while Silvert is correct in his perception of attitudes, he is wrong in believing that these attitudes are paradoxical. They may be so from the point of view of Argentina's relatively high level of development (gauged by static criteria that do not allow for consideration of the circumstances and processes analyzed in the preceding pages), but these attitudes are hardly surprising given the social context from which they stem.

Table 8. Positive Response to the Survey Question, "Does the Government Have a Great Effect on Your Daily Life?"

United States	41.0%
Germany	38.0
England	33.0
Italy	23.0
Mexico	7.0
Argentina	41.0
Upper class (N = 157)	52.2
Middle class (N = 960)	40.3
Lower class (N = 721)	39.9

SOURCES: For Argentina: Jeane Kirkpatrick, *Leader and Vanguard in Mass Society: A Study of Peronist Argentina* (Cambridge, Mass.: M.I.T. Press, 1971), p. 159. For other countries: Gabriel Almond and Sidney Verba, *The Civil Culture* (Princeton, N.J.: Princeton University Press, 1963).

NOTE: For Argentina, N = 2,000.

Survey data, unfortunately scant, provide support for Silvert's perceptions. In a nationally representative sample (which did not include the sparsely populated Patagonian states) taken three months before the 1966 coup, respondents were asked several of the questions used by Almond and Verba in *The Civic Culture*.[64] Table 8 shows the measure of one important component of political activation—political awareness—indicating that the impact of government on daily life, as perceived by the Argentine respondents, was very high. Only 20 percent of the respondents declared themselves supporters of a political party; 54 percent did not even lean toward any party.[65] In another survey taken shortly before the 1966 coup, to the question "Do you think that Argentine politics needs new men?" 83 percent answered "Yes," and only 4 percent, "No."[66] In Kirkpatrick's survey 42 percent agreed with the statement "A few leaders would do more for the country than all the laws and talk."[67] A similar percentage expressed the belief that the government is controlled by influential people and groups who do not care at all about people's needs—an attitude reflected in perceptions of the social structure, as shown in table 9. The sectors perceived as most influential are the least "acceptable" groups—i.e., 71.6 percent of the respondents would not back a military supported party, 58.4 percent a church supported party, and 89.7 percent a landowner supported party.[68]

As these data indicate, economic concerns are by far the most salient. The answers to the question "What do you consider the most important problems this country is facing at present?" reported in table 10, clearly reflects this primacy.

The relationship of the concerns reported in table 10 to political opinions is evidenced by the 96 percent positive answers given to a question asking if respondents would support a party that "promised to stamp out corruption and inefficiency from government"; further documentation of this relationship is

Table 9. Response to the Survey Question, "Who Has the Greatest Influence over Government?"

Military	33.8%
Church	14.6
Landowners	10.0
Peronistas	8.3
Labor unions	8.3
Entrepreneurs	4.5
Other, Don't know	20.5

SOURCE: Kirkpatrick, *Leader and Vanguard in Mass Society,* p. 161.

NOTE: N = 2,000.

Table 10. Responses to a Survey Question Concerning Argentina's Most Important Problems

	Income Groups			
	All	Low	Medium	High
Socioeconomic concerns				
High cost of living	35%	32%	38%	10%
Inflation, general economic situation	27	22	27	60
Housing shortage	7	6	7	10
Various social and economic problems	7	8	7	4
Wages (low, inadequate)	3	5	2	—
Pensions	3	5	2	—
Unemployment	7	12	4	—
Political concerns				
Bad government, corruption in politics	7	8	7	4
Trade union, corporation problems	2	1	2	6
Other				
Other answers	3	3	2	17
No problems	2	2	2	—
Don't know, No answer	8	9	8	2

SOURCE: Gallup Survey, *Polls* 2, no. 3 (Spring 1967).

NOTE: N = 1,000 residents of the Buenos Aires area. Questions were open ended; multiple answers were permitted.

found in the answers given to the question "What classes, in your opinion, profit most from the government of President Illía—laborers, middle classes, or upper classes?" (see table 11). If one considers as "favorable" those responses that indicate that the respondent's own sector plus "All" benefit from the Illía government, less than 15 percent of the low and middle income respondents express favorable opinions. Even high income respondents are far less satisfied than would be expected. (Note the sharp rise of "No one" answers among high income respondents.)

With respect to the economic situation, there was broad recognition of the zero-sum conditions (see table 12). As may be obvious, a prediction that the

Table 11. Response to the Survey Question "Who Profits Most from the Illia Government?"

	All Respondents	Income Group of Respondent		
		Low	Middle	High
Laborers	3%	4%	2%	4%
Middle classes	6	4	8	4
Upper classes	53	63	50	27
All, everyone	7	5	7	15
No one	17	9	19	35
Don't know	14	16	13	14

SOURCE: Gallup Survey, *Polls.*

NOTE: N = 1,000 residents of the Buenos Aires area.

Table 12. Response to the Survey Question "Do You Think That Argentina's Economic Situation Will Improve, Remain the Same, or Deteriorate in the Next Months?"

Improve	24%
Remain the same	19
Deteriorate	48
Don't know	9

SOURCE: Kirkpatrick, *Leader and Vanguard in Mass Society,* p. 181.

NOTE: N = 2,000 residents of Argentina.

Argentine economy would remain the same is a pessimistic view. The responses reported in tables 13 and 14 are a good indication of the perceived efficiency of the government for coping with major problems.

The data in tables 9–14 reflect a politically informed population, conscious of the inefficiency of government, skeptical about political parties, hostile in their intersectional perceptions, and aware of the zero-sum character of the national wealth. A very weak commitment to the survival of the existing political system—even when menaced by unpopular sectors—is indicated by the large segments of the population that agree on the desirability of "throwing the rascals out" and the need for a "strong man." Even though the military is unpopular, by 1966 the way was paved for a military takeover that would not meet popular resistance.

Unhappily, interview data are almost totally lacking for other social sectors and groups. Except for entrepreneurs, there are no interview data on the elite's political opinions and attitudes.[69] Not surprisingly, entrepreneurs show hostility toward labor and its leaders, fears of labor's eventual access to political power, and receptivity to "law and order" appeals.[70] Government is per-

Table 13. Response to the Survey Question, "Do You Think the Government Will Be Able to Check Inflation?"

Yes	20%
No	67
No opinion	13

SOURCE: Gallup Survey, *Polls* 2, no. 3 (Spring 1967).

NOTE: The sample consisted of 1,000 residents of the Buenos Aires area.

ceived by them as the epitome of red tape and inefficiency, and the major business organizations openly welcomed the ouster of presidents Perón (1955), Frondizi (1962), and Illía (1966).

As has been suggested earlier in this chapter, discussion of the politics of labor unions is, to a very large extent, discussion of Peronismo. The events of 1955–66 could hardly inspire labor union allegiance to government, and—in agreement for the first time with the ruling sectors (but for different reasons and with very different expectations)—the unions and Peronista leaders welcomed the 1966 coup.[71]

Very little is known about the underpaid and overstaffed government bureaucracy, but it seems evident that low salaries, widespread patronage, and the lack of a civil service career prevented the emergence of a public service that, in the midst of crisis, could have maintained a reasonably high level of problem-solving.

A general, socially diffuse factor which provides a common basis for the different attitudes of the various sectors should be mentioned. In contrast to what might be expected in a so-called developing country, contemporary Argentina has lacked a feeling of "emergence"—a sense that the present, whatever its shortcomings, is better and more promising than anything that has gone before. Argentina's history and literature and, more generally, its intellectual climate are pervaded by the memory (or imagination) of lost opportunities and of periods in which the country is seen to have been better off than it is today. There is also a pervasive search for a historical

Table 14. Response to the Survey Question, "According to the Government, the Recently Authorized Rise in Prices Will Raise the Cost of Living Only Some Two Percent. Do You Think This Is Correct or That It Will Be More?"

Correct	4%
More	86
No opinion	10

SOURCE: Gallup Survey, *Polls* 2, no. 3 (Spring 1967).

NOTE: N = 1,000 residents of the Buenos Aires area.

scapegoat—for the identification of actors and sectors to whom the responsibility may be attributed for a history perceived largely as failure. Even today, the nineteenth-century struggles between unitarios and federales are recalled with bitterness. The failure to achieve a more congenial social context has led to the cynical belief that political and sectoral competition takes place in a Hobbesian world. This view was confirmed for Argentine intellectuals, on both the right and the left, by the problems described in the preceding sections, and what they had to say about the political and social situation made the final breakdown of the pre-1966 political system even more likely.

Due to the linearity of language, I have been able to provide only a very limited account of the highly complex interactions among the political history, the socioeconomic context, and the attitudinal dimensions of pre-1966 Argentina, but what has been presented should suffice to indicate the general setting within which the factors immediately connected to the 1966 coup should be examined.

The Coup of 1966

As one Argentine sociologist has observed, at one time or another "Argentine politicians have all gone 'to knock on the door of the barracks.'"[72] Between the overthrow of Perón (in 1955) and 1962, the armed forces were controlled by gorila military officers, with various factions alternating in control, in different moments and in different services, reflecting the high degree of fractionalization of Argentine politics.[73] From these circumstances grew shifting alignments and intense internal conflict in the armed forces. When there is conflict inside the military, it is essential to study the internal alignments, their origins, their connections with other political forces, and their political consequences. Only in this way is it possible to examine the military as a political actor, subject to various inducements but responding to these inducements in special ways that depend to an important extent on factors relating to military organization. This means looking behind public statements and into details of organization virtually inaccessible to empirical research. I cannot claim any substantial advantages over others in this matter, but on the basis of informal interviews I had with leading military officers during the 1955–66 period, as well as published evidence, I propose the preliminary analysis that follows.[74]

By ousting Perón, undoubtedly a majoritarian dictator, the armed forces made an appeal to the need for restoration and preservation of political democracy. Subsequently, their anti-Peronista stand was strongly reinforced by a climate of great social unrest and the effects of the cold war and the Cuban Revolution. Peronista unions and the armed forces came to personify the opposite poles of an intense social conflict. The poor performance of civilian governments created much dissatisfaction among military officers. The army chief of staff, General Toranzo Montero, said that the armed forces were "the guardians of the republican way of life against any extremism or totalitarianism" and were ultimately responsible, due to the "failure of civilian authorities," for solving the problems allegedly caused by Peronismo and "subversion" and for "restoring the values of national unity and public order."[75] This assumption of the role of custodian of basic values opened wide the door for a long series of planteos and coups, especially after President Frondizi came to power in 1958 by means of an electoral "covenant" with Perón. The military's definition of its own role made it the interpreter of the content of the basic values it had been assigned to protect, as well as the interpreter of when and how the basic values were being threatened—paving the way for the electoral proscription of Peronismo and the political parties suspected of being façades for it. Since it could be argued that the basic values were involved in practically all governmental decisions, the military became the most effective channel through which various sectors could have their demands satisfied by the government. Thus, the military became a reflection of all the anti-Peronista sectors of Argentine society. This direct involvement in partisan and sectoral issues destroyed vertical patterns of military authority, led to numerous internal putsches, and shortened the careers of many officers.

By supporting the traditional political parties while remaining verbally committed to what they considered to be democracy, the military officers found themselves in the old predicament: the "correct" parties and candidates could not win fair elections.[76] When they ousted President Frondizi in 1962, the military officers made it clear that they intended to establish a long-term dictatorship, which they presumed to be what was needed to restore "order and authentic democracy" to Argentina. But within the army and the air force a strong reaction had taken place. Many officers protested against the deleterious effects on careers and military organization of the high fractionalization caused by direct political involvement. They proposed that military men should withdraw from politics and "return to their specific duties." In retrospect, it is clear that this was an argument for organizational survival.[77] The suspension of direct political involvement would necessarily mean rejecting military plans to eliminating political parties and elections. The argument for organizational survival and career preservation had wide appeal within the military; in addition, its "back to the barracks" implication evoked immediate support from many civilian sectors alarmed by the prospect of a military dictatorship. The intramilitary conflict was perceived as one between the dictatorial gorilas and the more democratic, professionalist military officers.[78] The factions clashed twice (September 1962 and April 1963), and the upshot was a decisive legalista victory. During the short frays, the legalistas issued persuasive communiqués stating that they were fighting for democracy, for a professionalist, apolitical army, and for the right of the people to cast their ballots "without exclusions" (which necessarily meant lifting the electoral ban on Peronistas). After their victory, however, the legalistas found that despite agreement on the professionalism issue, they were as divided as ever concerning the question of whether or not to allow Peronistas to run (and very likely win) in the next elections. After some internal debate the opinion that "totalitarian parties could not be granted the benefits of democracy" prevailed—i.e., the electoral arena remained closed to Peronistas. The legalistas presided over the messy presidential elections of 1963 in which Illía, the candidate of the old Radicales, was elected by less than one-fourth of the total vote.[79]

After the legalistas won control of the armed forces in 1963, important organizational changes took place. The navy, stronghold of the gorilas, had been decisively defeated, and the army established its clear hegemony over the navy and the small air force. The armed forces, under the strong leadership of General Onganía, the army chief of staff, and aided by U.S. advisory missions, were able to reestablish vertical authority and to foster professionalization markedly. This resulted in restoration of more normal authority and career patterns, increased organizational capabilities, new modes of military training that emphasized both the study of modern technology and of "contemporary problems," steady absorption of U.S. and French "antisubversive" and "civic action" doctrines, a marked decline in personal contacts with political party personnel, and a corresponding increase in personal contacts with those I have called "incumbents of technocratic roles."[80] The resulting feeling of achievement within the military contrasted sharply with the general social situation described earlier in this chapter.

The high organizational costs of fractionalization were fresh in the military memory, and the officers were determined to avoid situations that might risk reintroducing it. As a consequence, the channeling of sectoral demands, and planteos in particular, were explicitly rejected by the new military leadership (and the 1963–66 period was by and large free of them).[81] Professionalism entailed redefining the role of the armed forces as "above politics." As General Onganía repeatedly observed, the armed forces should abstain from political intervention except "under extreme circumstances." (The definition of "extreme circumstances" was of course left to the armed forces.) First, military disengagement from direct political involvement would not only facilitate professionalism but also make possible a much more general and severe condemnation of civilian authorities: their failures could no longer be attributed to military intervention. Second, a role that was above politics would mean a refusal to take sides in purely "civilian" conflicts, but not a loss of interest in whatever national affairs the military deemed deserving of its attention. This was clearly indicated in a speech in which General Onganía stated his conception of the military role:

[The armed forces exist] to guarantee the sovereignty and the territorial integrity of the state, to preserve the moral and spiritual values of Western civilization, to ensure public order and internal peace, to promote general welfare, and to sustain the Constitution, its essential rights and guarantees, and the republican institutions it has established. . . .[In order to achieve those goals] two fundamental premises must hold: the need [of the armed forces] to maintain its aptitude and capability for the custody of the highest interest of the nation, and the economic and social development of the country.[82]

The functions of the armed forces, according to this conception, are even broader than those envisioned by the gorila leaders. It was quite clear that the main practical difference between the two factions consisted in the legalistas' refusal to engage in planteos and direct partisan involvement.

But perhaps of greater significance were the requirements referred to by General Onganía as "fundamental premises." If the armed forces were to perform their functions properly both their organizational strength and the steady socioeconomic development of the country were necessary conditions. Consequently, anything that menaced or hindered the achievement of either condition could be construed as impeding the fulfillment of military functions. Since the performance of these functions was so essential, anything that threatened their necessary conditions was a threat to the most fundamental interest of the nation. Since governments could jeopardize, by action or by omission, these necessary conditions, it was obvious—given this conception of the military role—that government personnel could not receive the allegiance of the military. In the same speech, General Onganía went on to say:

Obedience is due, in the last analysis, to the Constitution and its laws, never to men and political parties that may eventually hold power. If this were not the case, the fundamental mission of the armed forces would be subverted. They would not be apolitical any more; they would become a praetorian guard at the service of some persons or groups.

The fact that the Radicales had supported the defeated military faction tended to increase the likelihood of systemic breakdown. In addition, the persistence of the socioeconomic problems described earlier in this chapter could be interpreted as an indication that the "basic premise" of socioeconomic development was not being met. This, combined with the consistently high degree of social unrest, contributed to fears of the spread and final victory of "subversion," which would implant "totalitarian extremism" and eliminate the armed forces. Government inefficiency and a low rate of socioeconomic development interacted to generate this so-called subversion. The elimination of subversion was part of the "specific duties" of the military (the custody of "national security"), and according to this interpretation, it was at the socioeconomic and governmental levels that the fundamental causes of subversion could best be attacked and eliminated. Thus the military saw the whole set of social problems (everything that could be subsumed under "achieving socioeconomic development" and "ensuring governmental efficiency") as within the range of its responsibility to maintain national security.[83] The scope of these social problems suggested that their solution could only be achieved by direct control of government, and since their existence was interpreted as a threat to national security, it followed that the armed forces would not have fulfilled their duties until the problems had been "solved."[84] Hence direct control of the government by the military would be necessary for the indefinite period required for achieving these solutions.[85]

These conclusions were based on the military's conviction of its own superior capacity to deal with the problems of a slow rate of socioeconomic development and government inefficiency. This conviction stemmed in part from the poor performance of government authorities and the deteriorating social conditions under continued conditions of mass praetorianism that obtained after the legalistas won control of the armed forces, but it was probably mainly the result of the successful professionalist drive. Through professionalization, the military had established clearly defined authority patterns, and military training had greatly improved. The armed forces had been able to solve their problems while civilian sectors continued in a situation of crisis, which could not help but greatly enhance the military's perception of its own superior ability for dealing with problems.[86] The ultimate conviction on the part of the military of the legitimacy of its rule would derive from the anticipated historical demonstration of its superior capacity to govern (as compared with previous civilian governments).[87]

Of course, the military's concern for the state of the society included more direct organizational considerations. The aggravation (or even the persistence) of the social conditions prevailing under mass praetorianism might reintroduce fractionalization within the military, whatever the effects of its efforts at professionalization. Since, according to the legalista conception, fractionalization would hinder the fulfillment of essential military functions, any risk in this respect would also be interpreted as a threat to the highest interests of the nation. Thus military intervention to eliminate threats to its internal cohesion would be justified to whatever extent might seem necessary to the military itself.[88]

Local elections held in 1965 showed that the Peronistas retained the first plurality of the electorate. Aside from the formerly overthrown Peronistas and Frondizistas, the governing Radicales were the only party that could attract more than 10 percent of the total vote. By this time there were abundant indications that a "ceiling consensus" had been reached by most of the civilian sectors, and consequently the inducements for a new military intervention became very strong. Social unrest was high, with numerous strikes, occupations of factories, and manifold acts of less organized violence. President Illía had acquired the reputation of being a slow and ineffective decision-maker, while Parliament seemed to have been reduced to a forum for personal quarrels which produced no legislation. Meanwhile the military had greatly enhanced its own abilities (and even more greatly enhanced its assessment of those abilities).

In short, the conditions for a final systemic breakdown had reached a critical stage when, in 1965–66, the organizational evolution of the military gave it the internal cohesion and sense of its own ability that made intervention possible without apparent risk of failure and fractionalization. The situation pointed strongly to a coup that would try to implant an entirely different system, rather than attempt to repair the existing one. This tendency was reinforced by the fact that all the major political parties in Argentina had already been given a chance and had failed, and thus "had" to be ousted by the military.

General elections were scheduled for 1967, and it was evident that the legalista military (as well as many other sectors in Argentine society) were as divided as ever on the question of Peronista electoral participation. Given the social conditions, the organizational evolution of the military, and the fact that all the political parties with more than a minimum share of the vote had been given a chance, it is not an exaggeration to say that by the end of 1965 the major matter of speculation had become the timing of the coup, not its perpetration or its goals.[89] The timing was largely determined by the risk of military fractionalization around the old Peronismo issue: the coup had to occur late enough for many of the officers to perceive clearly the risk of organizational fractionalization, but it could not occur after the electoral campaigns had started. In this way the military leadership would simultaneously increase the probability of a high degree of military cohesion in support of the coup and a minimum of civilian opposition (particularly Peronista, if they were allowed to run in the 1967 elections) to their decision to intervene.[90] On 28 June 1966, the army chief of staff, General Pistarini, declared:

[The achievement] of efficiency, cohesion, and high professional capabilities [by the armed forces] has taken time and great sacrifice. . . . Any attempt to put the army at the service of secondary interests, or to identify it with political, economic, or social sectors, is an attempt against the [military] institution, because it seeks to create internal division and conflict. For this very reason it is also an attempt against the nation.[91]

Soon afterward the coup took place smoothly, and a new political system was inaugurated.

Well before June 1966, numerous civilian sectors had reached a "ceiling consensus," the legitimacy and efficacy of the regime were at a minimum, and almost every sector had been pleading for a military intervention that would drastically change the existing political system. However, for this to occur it was also necessary that the social situation pose new threats to highly valued military organizational achievements and that the process of military professionalization be substantially advanced. The gorila officers had intervened many times, but always for the purpose of pressing relatively limited demands and with the stated intention of returning power to civilians. When in 1962 these officers attempted to assume control for a long period, they were hindered by their precarious hold over a deeply fractionalized and scarcely professional military institution. The new professionalist military leaders—the somewhat ironically labeled legalista officers—intervened only when they were prepared to take government into their own hands for a long time with the aim of achieving very ambitious goals. For long-term intervention to be possible, two conditions lacking in 1962 had to be present in 1966: first, the social crisis necessary for a "ceiling consensus" and, second, the organizational-level variables (the degree of internal cohesion and the feeling of enhanced capabilities) that resulted from the process of professionalization and constitution of "apolitical" armed forces.

It seems ironic that those military leaders who epitomized professionalism and an anti-interventionist stand were those who led the coup that liquidated the existing political system.[92] But this apparent inconsistency must be seen in the light of the preceding circumstances. Mass praetorianism and a high degree of modernization induced the fractionalization of the military, who had collaborated in the extreme political instability that had characterized a good part of the period in which praetorianism prevailed. This situation adversely affected the military, leading to a period of withdrawal from direct political involvement and to concerted efforts at enhancing military organization. The continuation of mass praetorianism led many civilian sectors to reach a ceiling consensus, but the final systemic breakdown had to wait until the military felt that it could intervene again.[93] This discrepancy in the timing of the civilian and military decisions made the period that immediately preceded the final breakdown essentially a political vacuum, in which almost everything had been determined except the exact moment of military intervention.

In the period of withdrawal from direct political involvement, the military enhanced its capabilities—and enhanced even more its self-assessment of those capabilities. In addition, military personnel increased their personal contacts with the technocrats, who would participate in the coup coalition and occupy most of the high civilian government positions in the post-coup regime.

The continuation of mass praetorianism, and with it, the further deterioration of the social context, contrasted with the military's conviction of its enhanced capabilities. It also happens that whatever precautions are taken to isolate the armed forces from the social situation, sooner or later they create problems that threaten to reintroduce military fractionalization. The combination of these two factors led to goals for military intervention that were far more drastic than those envisioned by the military during its interventionist period.

Thus, the "apoliticism" and professionalism of the armed forces during a time of mass praetorianism in a society that had attained a high level of modernization significantly raised the threshold for military intervention; the hectic pattern of coups and planteos ended. Once that threshold had been reached, however, military intervention reoccurred—but it was more cohesive, much more ambitious, and aimed at a far more complete political domination than anything that had gone before. Contrary to what many analysts and policy-makers have expected since the 1950s, apoliticism and professionalism have not solved the endemic problems of militarism. They merely trade off a higher threshold for a far more comprehensive military invervention.

NOTES

1. See, e.g., *Washington Post,* 30 June 1966.
2. Survey (sample and methodology unknown) taken by *Primera Plana,* reported in Carlos Astiz, "The Argentine Armed Forces: Their Role and Political Involvement," *Western Political Quarterly* 22, no. 4 (1969). This article provides useful information and an analysis complementary to this chapter. In another survey, taken in July 1966 (N = 1,000 respondents of the Greater Buenos Aires area, methodology unknown), to the question "Do you think that the revolution of June 28th [1966] was necessary?" 77 percent answered "Yes" (*Correo de la Tarde,* 6–12 June 1967).
3. See, among others, the following official publications: "Mensaje de la Junta Revolucionaria al Pueblo Argentino" (1966); "Mensaje al País del Presidente de la Nación Teniente General Juan Carlos Onganía" (1966); "Mensaje del Teniente General Juan Carlos Onganía con motivo de asumir la Presidencia de la Nación" (1966); and "Mensaje del Presidente de la Nación en la reunión de camaradería de las Fuerzas Armadas" (1967). All were printed by Presidencia de la Nación, Argentina.
4. The best analyses of Argentine civil-military relations, although they do not cover all the main historical events, are Darío Cantón, *La política de los militares argentinos: 1900–1971* (México, D.F.: Siglo XXI, 1971), and Robert Potash, *The Army and Politics in Argentina* (Stanford, Ca.: Stanford University Press, 1969). See also Guillermo O'Donnell, "Modernización y golpes militares: Teoría, comparaciones y el caso argentino," *Desarrollo Económico* 17 (December 1972).
5. This question will be considered in more detail below.
6. For greater detail, the reader is referred to the various sources hereafter cited. An excellent general political history of Argentina is Carlos Alberto Floria and César García Belsunce, *Historia de los argentinos,* 2 vols. (Buenos Aires: Editorial Kapelusz, 1972).
7. It scarcely need be noted that this discrepancy has been repeatedly observed by students of Latin American history; see, for example, Stanley Stein and Barbara Stein, *The Colonial Heritage of Latin America* (New York: Oxford University Press, 1970). For an assessment of more recent evidence, see Federico Gil, *Instituciones y desarrollo político en América Latina* (Buenos Aires: INTAL, 1966).
8. On "political resources," see Robert A. Dahl, *Modern Political Analysis* (Englewood Cliffs, N.J.: Prentice-Hall, 1969).
9. "The Heritage of Latin America," in *The Founding of New Societies,* ed. Louis Hartz (New York, 1966).

10. Speech by José M. Gutiérrez to the constitutional convention (1862).

11. This temporal sequence of national unification is very different from that of earlier European modernizers. In those countries the harsh task of national unification had been largely completed before constitutionalism and democracy became an issue. Significantly, the only clear-cut South American exception to the sequence depicted in the text is Chile.

12. Other authors have observed this "constant" in Argentine society; see Carlos Alberto Floria, "Una explicación política de la Argentina" (Buenos Aires: Centro de Investigaciones y Acción Social, 1967), pp. 33–34; Robert A. Dahl, *Polyarchy: Participation and Opposition* (New Haven: Yale University Press, 1971), pp. 132–40; Eldon Kenworthy, "The Formation of the Peronist Coalition" (Ph.D. diss., Yale University, 1970).

13. An excellent theoretical analysis of legitimacy is Natalio Botana's *La légitimité: Problème politique* (Louvain: Université de Louvain, 1968). See also his "La crisis de legitimidad en la Argentina y el desarrollo de los partidos políticos," *Criterio,* no. 1604 (1970).

14. This has been labeled the "period of self-incrimination" by Albert O. Hirschman ("Introduction" to *Latin American Issues,* ed. Albert O. Hirschman [New York: Twentieth Century Fund, 1960]). But the incrimination was one-sided: it was directed by the ruling sectors at the majority of the population. Naturally, the response was bitter. The ruling sector's perception of the rest of the population was partly a process of selective borrowing; after a visit to Argentina, Lord Bryce noted: "The books most popular among those few who approach abstract subjects are those of Herbert Spencer. [Argentines] are unwilling to believe that he is not deemed in his own country to be a great philosopher" (cited in Arthur P. Whitaker, *Argentina* [Englewood Cliffs, N.J.: Prentice-Hall, 1964], p. 61).

15. On the great wave of European migration of this period, see Gino Germani, *Política y sociedad en una época de transición* (Buenos Aires: Editorial Paidós, 1962), pp. 179–216; Oscar Cornblit, "European Migrants in Argentine Industry and Politics," *The Politics of Conformity in Latin America,* ed. Claudio Veliz (Oxford: Oxford University Press, 1967); and Carl Solberg, *Immigration and Nationalism: Argentina and Chile, 1890–1914* (Austin: University of Texas Press, 1970).

16. For a description of this situation and an analysis of the factors that led to it, see Horacio Giberti, *El desarrollo agrario argentino* (Buenos Aires: Eudeba, 1964); James Scobie, *Revolution on the Pampas* (Austin: University of Texas Press, 1969); Roberto Cortés Conde and Ezequiel Gallo, *La formación de la Argentina moderna* (Buenos Aires: Editorial Paidós, 1967); and Roberto Cortés Conde, "Algunos aspectos de la expansión territorial en Argentina en la segunda mitad del siglo XIX," *Desarrollo Económico* 29 (1968).

17. Cited in Oscar Cornblit, E. Gallo, and Arturo O'Connell, "La generación del 80 y su proyecto: Antecedentes y consecuencias," in *Argentina: Sociedad de masas,* ed. Torcuato di Tella et al.(Buenos Aires: Eudeba, 1965), p. 54. This is an excellent monographic study of the period under consideration here.

18. See Scobie, *Revolution.* Only a small proportion of the industrialists were Argentine. A very small proportion of European migrants opted for Argentine citizenship, and most of them were politically inactive. See Cornblit, *European Migrants;* Germani, *Política*; and Carlos Díaz Alejandro, *Essays on the Economic History of the Argentine Republic* (New Haven: Yale University Press, 1970), chap. 1, for valuable data and good analyses.

19. On the socioeconomic background and policy preferences of this middle sector and its main political expression, the Radical party, see Cornblit *European Migrants;* E. Gallo and Silvia Sigal, "La formación de los partidos políticos contemporáneos: La Unión Cívica Radical (1800–1916)," in di Tella, *Argentina*; and Peter Smith, *Politics and Beef in Argentina: Patterns of Conflict and Change* (New York: Columbia University Press, 1969).

20. The expression is from Floria.

21. For expressions of this contempt, see Darío Cantón, *El parlamento argentino en épocas de cambio: 1880, 1910 y 1946* (Buenos Aires: Editorial del Instituto, 1966).

22. For an excellent analysis of these economic policies, see Díaz Alejandro, *Essays.* A review of the pertinent literature and an analysis of the sociopolitical implications of the policies can be found in Miguel Murmis and Juan Carlos Portantiero, "Crecimiento industrial y alianza de clases en Argentina, 1930–1940" (Instituto Torcuato di Tella, Centro de Investigaciones Sociales, *Documento de Trabajo,* 1968).

23. Using Karl Deutsch's concept, Peter Smith argues that "social mobilization" took place in

Argentina during this period (see his "Social Mobilization, Political Participation, and the Rise of Juan Perón," *Western Political Quarterly* 34, no. 1 [1969]).

24. This expression was coined by Manuel Fresco, a Conservador governor of Buenos Aires State, elected by fraud in the 1930s.

25. Whitaker, *Argentina*. For valuable information on Argentina from the 1930s until 1963, see Tulio Halperín Donghi, *Argentina en el callejón* (Montevideo: Editorial Arca, 1964).

26. The perception by the growing numbers of urban workers of the "democracy" they saw in operation could only reinforce their assessment of the political system and the ruling sectors.

27. The ruling sectors referred to the new migrants as "the shirtless," "the blackheads," "the zoological landslide," and other intentionally derogatory terms. Perón wisely responded by appropriating most of these terms to underline the popular character of his following. This was primarily the language of Conservadores and Radicales supporters, but the reactions of Socialists and Communists toward the new and increasingly active migrants were not noticeably better; see, among other discussions of the reactions of the "traditional" Argentine Left, Jorge Adelardo Ramos, *Revolución y contrarevolución en la Argentina* (La Reja, 1961), and Juan José Hernández Arregui, *La formación de la conciencia nacional* (Hachón, 1964). For a general analysis of this period, see Alberto Ciria, *Partidos y poder en la Argentina moderna (1930–1946)* (Jorge Alvarez Editor, 1964).

28. Kenworthy, "Formation," provides an interesting analysis of the formation of the populist Peronista coalition.

29. As an indication of the degree of misperception of the national mood by the "Democratic Union" (to say the very least), the Union allowed Spruille Braden, the U.S. ambassador, to campaign for them openly. Perón capitalized on this fact, presenting the election as a choice between "Braden or Perón."

30. A useful survey of interpretations of Peronismo is found in Carlos Fayt, ed., *La naturaleza del Peronismo* (Buenos Aires: Editorial Viracocha, 1967).

31. On the ideology of Peronismo during the period in which the movement was in power, see Alberto Ciria, *Perón y el justicialismo* (México, D.F.: Siglo XXI, 1971).

32. This concept is based on the work of Juan J. Linz, as developed in his introductory essay to *The Breakdown of Democratic Regimes*, ed. Juan J. Linz and Alfred Stepan (Baltimore: Johns Hopkins University Press, 1978). From the beginning the opposition tried to oust Perón illegally and engaged in very obstructionist parliamentary strategies.

33. Floria; "Una explicación política" (my translation).

34. The concept of polarization is discussed in Robert A. Dahl, "Some Explanations," in *Political Oppositions in Western Democracies*, ed. Robert A. Dahl (New Haven: Yale University Press, 1966), pp. 380ff.; it is further analyzed below. For a sense of the saliency of this cleavage, see (among many others) Dardo Cúneo, *El desencuentro argentino* (Buenos Aires: Pleamar, 1965); Floria, "Una explicación política"; Mariano Grondona, *Argentina en el tiempo y en el mundo* (Buenos Aires: Editorial Primera Plana, 1967); Augusto Morello and Antonio Tróccoli, *Argentina ahora y después* (La Plata: Editorial Platense, 1967); G. Merkx, "Politics and Economic Change in Argentina from 1870 to 1966" (Ph.D. diss., Yale University, 1968). For evidence from survey data, see José Luis de Imaz, *Motivación electoral* (Buenos Aires: Instituto de Desarrollo Económico, 1962), and Peter Snow, "Argentine Political Parties and the 1966 Revolution" (Laboratory of Political Research, University of Iowa, 1968).

35. For the relevant data on the economy, see tables 2–7.

36. For information concerning the high degree of domestic political violence in Argentina, as indicated by data from this period, see Bruce Russett et al., *World Handbook of Political and Social Indicators* (New Haven: Yale University Press, 1964).

37. This theme is examined in more detail in Guillermo A. O'Donnell, *Modernization and Bureaucratic-Authoritarianism: Studies in South American Politics* (Berkeley: Institute of International Studies, University of California, 1973), pp. 166–96.

38. University of California, *Statistical Abstract for Latin America* (Berkeley and Los Angeles: University of California, 1966).

39. Martin Needler, *Political Development in Latin America*, p. 96.

40. International Labour Organization, *Yearbook of Labour Statistics* (Geneva: ILO, 1967).

41. In my examination of economic aspects, I have relied heavily on the excellent *Essays* of Díaz

Alejandro. Other important sources are Carlos Díaz Alejandro, *Exchange Rate Devaluation in a Semi-Industrialized Country: The Experience of Argentina, 1955-1961* (Cambridge, Mass: MIT Press, 1965); Aldo Ferrer, *La económia argentina: Las etapas de su desarrollo y problemas actuales* (México, D.F., and Buenos Aires: Fondo de Cultura Económica, 1963); Guido di Tella and Miguel Zymelman, *Las etapas del desarrollo argentino* (Buenos Aires: Eudeba, 1967); J. Villanueva, "La inflación argentina," mimeographed (Instituto Torcuato di Tella, 1964); United Nations, Economic Commission for Latin America, "El desarrollo económico de la Argentina," 5 vols., mimeographed (New York: United Nations, 1959); United Nations, Economic Commission on Latin America and Consejo Nacional de Desarrollo (CONADE), *El desarrollo económico y la distribución del ingreso en la Argentina* (New York: United Nations, 1968).

42. Díaz Alejandro, *Essays,* p. 55.
43. Ibid., pp. 69-70.
44. Computed from Banco Central de la República Argentina, *Boletín Estadístico* several issues.
45. UN-ECLA and CONADE, *El desarrollo económico,* p. 193.
46. Diáz Alejandro, *Essays,* p. 75.
47. Computed from Dirección Nacional de Estadísticas y Censos, *Boletín Estadístico,* several issues, and Díaz Alejandro, *Essays,* Statistical Appendix.
48. Díaz Alejandro, *Essays,* p. 356.
49. Analysis of these and related aspects of economic policy can be found in Aldo Ferrer et al., *Los planes de estabilización en la Argentina* (Buenos Aires: Editorial Paidós, 1969).
50. UN-ECLA and CONADE, *El desarrollo económico,* p. 264 (my translation).
51. Jorge M. Katz, "Características estructurales del crecimiento industrial argentino," *Desarrollo Económico,* no. 26 (1967). An excellent exploration of the sociopolitical consequences of these changes is in Fernando Henrique Cardoso and Enzo Faletto, *Dependencia y desarrollo en América Latina* (México, D.F.: Siglo XXI, 1969), pp. 103 ff. For discussion of the urban unemployed, see UN-ECLA and CONADE, *El desarrollo económico,* pp. 123, 193 ff., and the Introductions to the "Planes de desarrollo" for 1965-69 and 1970-74 (Buenos Aires: Consejo Nacional de Desarrollo, 1965, 1970).
52. Consistent with this general point, many regions of the interior, also incapable of exerting effective pressure on the national government, were also heavy losers (see Consejo Nacional de Desarrollo, Introduction [1970]).
53. See Harold D. Lasswell and Daniel Lerner, ed., *Policy Sciences* (Stanford, Ca.: Stanford University Press, 1951).
54. Computed from Consejo Nacional de Desarrollo, *Plan Nacional de Desarrollo* (1965). For useful data on and analysis of this topic, see Oscar Ozlak, "Inflación y política fiscal en la Argentina: El impuesto a los réditos en el período 1956-1965" (Instituto Torcuato di Tella, Centro de Investigaciones en Administración Pública, *Documento de Trabajo,* 1970).
55. For data on this point, see Oficina de Estudios para la Cooperación Económica Internacional, *Argentina económica y financiera* (Buenos Aires: FIAT, 1966), p. 366.
56. See ibid., p. 351.
57. UN-ECLA and CONADE, *El desarrollo económico.*
58. See Eldon Kenworthy, "Coalitions in the Political Development of Latin America," in Sven Groennings et al., eds., *The Study of Coalition Behavior* (New York: Holt, Rinehart and Winston, 1970). For the decline in productivity, see Oficina de Estudios, *Argentina económica,* pp. 351 ff.
59. This situation could be described as one of "fluid scarcity." It is certainly very different from that in more traditional and more developed societies, where income shares (albeit by different mechanisms) are more stable in the short run. The political correlates of fluid scarcity are not likely to be similar to those of more stabilized allocations of economic goods. (An interesting examination of this aspect of Argentine politics can be found in Merkx, "Politics.")
60. Used here in the sense defined by Harold Lasswell and Abraham Kaplan in *Power and Society* (New Haven: Yale University Press, 1950)—i.e., the ability to impose severe deprivations.
61. Charles Anderson considers threat-capabilities a major asset in Latin American politics; see

his *Politics and Economic Change in Latin America* (New York: Van Nostrand, 1967), chap. 2. In a similar vein, see the interesting discussion of a "dual currency" (votes and control of means of violence) in Argentine politics in Kenworthy, "Coalitions," and idem, "Formation."

62. See Samuel Huntington, *Political Order in Changing Societies* (New Haven: Yale University Press, 1969), esp. pp. 192–237.

63. "Liderazgo político y debilidad institucional en la Argentina," *Desarrollo Económico*, no. 3 (1963). (Reprinted in idem, *The Conflict Society: Reaction and Revolution in Latin America* [American Universities Field Staff, 1966].)

64. Jeane Kirkpatrick, *Leader and Vanguard in Mass Society: A Study of Peronist Argentina* (Cambridge, Mass.: MIT Press, 1971); Gabriel Almond and Sidney Verba, *The Civic Culture* (Princeton, N.J.: Princeton University Press, 1963).

65. For other similar data, see Snow, "Argentine Political Parties."

66. Gallup survey, sample of the Greater Buenos Aires area (N = 1,000); reported in *Polls* (1967), pp. 21–31.

67. Snow reports a survey, taken in Buenos Aires before the 1966 coup, that showed 60 percent of the respondents in complete agreement with the statement "We have too many platforms and political programs; what we need is a strong man to lead us!" Another 23 percent agreed to some degree, and only 17 percent were in complete disagreement ("Argentine Political Parties," p. 42).

68. Kirkpatrick, *Leader and Vanguard in Mass Society.*

69. The best study of the Argentine elite—de Imaz, *Los que mandan*—has no interview data.

70. See Dardo Cúneo, *Comportamiento y crisis de la clase empresaria* (Buenos Aires: Editorial Pleamar, 1967); John Freels, *El sector industrial* (Buenos Aires: Eudeba, 1968); and Fernando Henrique Cardoso, *Ideologías* (México, D.F.: Siglo XXI, 1971).

71. See, e.g., the enthusiastic remarks about the coup by union and Peronista leaders in *La Prensa,* 29 and 30 June 1966. It soon became obvious to these leaders that these remarks expressed quite unrealistic hopes that they would have greater political access under the military government.

72. De Imaz, *Los que mandan,* p. 84.

73. The nickname *gorila* was a derogatory allusion to the strong anti-Peronista views of these military officers.

74. The prevailing trend in the study of civil-military relations in "developing" countries has been to endow the military with sets of attitudes and high decision-making capabilities based on taking at face value its organizational charts and public statements concerning its ethos. The military is then assigned a crucial developmental role, and assertions that the military is the only group able to exercise effective governmental power in "developing" societies are "explained." A good example of this approach, applied to Latin American countries, is in John Johnson, *The Military and Society in Latin America* (Stanford, Ca.: Stanford University Press, 1964). But, as Robert Price says, in a good critique of this literature, the empirical evidence does not support these analyses ("A Theoretical Approach to Military Rule in New States," *World Politics* 23, no. 3 [1971]). In contrast to this approach, several authors have argued (correctly, I think) that the political behavior of the military can only be understood in relation to the characteristics of the society in which it operates. They further argue (again correctly) that the middle class in modernizing societies may attempt either to increase or to diminish its participation in the political system, depending on whether it is still striving for its own political incorporation or has already achieved it. A link between these middle-class attitudes and military behavior is presumed to exist because of the predominantly middle-class origins of military officers. The most important statements of this interpretation are Jose Nun, "The Middle Class," in Veliz, *Politics of Conformity*; Huntington, *Political Order*; Needler, *Political Development*; and E. Nordlinger, "Soldiers in Mufti: The Impact of Military Rule upon Economic and Social Change in the Non-Western States," *American Political Science Review* 64, no. 4 (1970). But according to this line of interpretation, the political behavior of the military (in particular, the goals of their intervention) depends *entirely* on variables at the societal level. As I hope to show, though these variables are very important, they do not eliminate the need to consider *empirical* variations in organization (as contrasted with the organization the military attributes to itself). These "intervening" var-

iables mediate the effects of societal variables and the differences may lead to quite different patterns of political behavior in the military. Although the author does not explicitly discuss the issue in these terms, the two-level focus I am proposing has been fruitfully applied to the Brazilian case in Alfred Stepan, *The Military in Politics: Changing Patterns in Brazil*: (Princeton: Princeton University Press, 1971). For a detailed study of the theoretical and empirical questions raised by the behavior of the military in the Argentine case, see Guillermo O'Donnell, "Modernización y golpes militares: Teoría, comparaciones y el caso argentino," *Desarrollo Económico*, October–December 1972.

75. *La Prensa*, 7 April 1959.

76. For further analysis of this theme, see below.

77. Several authors have emphasized this factor; See Edwin Lieuwen, *Generals vs. Presidents: Neomilitarism in Latin America* (New York: Praeger, 1964), pp. 107 ff. An Argentine author, José M. Saravia, also argues that, in this case, organizational concerns—not democratic allegiance—were the major determinants of the actions of the legalista military officers. This interpretation is endorsed in a prologue to Saravia's book by General A. López Aufranc, one of the most influential military officers during these events; see *Hacia la salida* (Buenos Aires: Emecé, 1968).

78. The latter were given the denomination *legalistas,* a term with obvious positive connotations.

79. For further discussion of this election, see below.

80. The results I have described here are reasonably well-supported by the literature. The one exception is the reference to the changes in patterns of personal contacts; for this matter I have relied mainly on my own impressions as a participant-observer during the period.

81. For an interesting statement of the "orthodox" legalista position (and its manifold unresolved ambiguities), see General Benjamín R. Rattenbach, *El sector militar de la sociedad* (Buenos Aires: Círculo Militar Argentino, 1966).

82. *La Prensa*, 6 August 1964 (my translation).

83. This analysis was clearly the basis of the military's perception of its role, its appraisal of the social situation, and its justification for intervention, as is evident in the informal interviews and the military publications of the period. See, e.g., Colonel Mario Orsolini, *Ejército argentino y crecimiento nacional* (Buenos Aires: Editorial Arayú, 1965), and General Osiris Villegas, *Guerra revolucionaria comunista* (Buenos Aires: Pleamar, 1963). For a useful survey of the period, see Carlos Fayt, *El político armado: Dinámica del proceso político argentino, 1960–1971* (Buenos Aires: Ediciones Pannedille, 1971).

84. For a comprehensive statement of this position, see General Osiris Villegas, *Políticas y estrategias para el desarrollo y la seguridad nacional* (Buenos Aires: Pleamar, 1969). Villegas was the secretary of the National Security Council between 1966 and 1968.

85. For some of the many statements of this position, see the official publications cited in n.3.

86. The illogicality of this perception should have been clearly evident, considering that the military had means for solving its internal problems rarely available to civilian sectors (e.g., purges and open combat).

87. The discovery that the military's expectations were largely wrong, as well as of the resistance of social problems to military-style decision-making, are part of a study of the evolution of the political system inaugurated in 1966, which will not be undertaken here.

88. In this examination of military perceptions and motivations, I have limited myself to what seem to be the more important facets, as expressed in informal interviews and published sources. Using this type of information, I have not been able to determine to what extent these conceptions were sincerely held and to what extent they were "covers" for less apparent motivations. (It is my general impression that in most cases they were sincere.) As to the origins of these perceptions and motivations, in addition to the historical-contextual factors analyzed here, it seems very likely that other factors frequently suggested ("antisubversive doctrines," U.S. training missions, secondary socialization) also exerted an important influence. But with the type of information at hand, it is not possible to assess the actual relative contribution of each of these factors.

89. For references to the open discussion of these factors in the months prior to the coup, see Astiz, "Argentine Armed Forces."

90. In the pre- and post-coup interviews upon which I base these impressions, the opinion was

repeatedly expressed that the fate of the Radicales government had been decided long before the coup, but that it was convenient to postpone the decision until it became evident to most civilian sectors and military officers that a new coup was unavoidable. At the same time, there was concern that the coup not occur too close to the 1967 elections, for the reasons indicated in the text.

91. *La Prensa,* 29 June 1966 (my translation).

92. This observation and the others that follow apply to a large extent to the other two bureaucratic-authoritarian systems inaugurated in the 1960s in highly modernized countries: Brazil and Greece. With reference to the evolution of the military, they also apply to another highly "professionalist" coup—the one in Peru. However, the differences that result from a similar level of professionalization in the military but a lower level of social modernization generated, in the Peruvian case, important differences in the composition of the military coalition. This combination also resulted in variation in the politically incorporating and economically expanding goals of the resulting authoritarian system.

93. It should be recalled that for the inauguration of a bureaucratic-authoritarian system few economic and psychological payoffs are available, to most of the population, and that consequently coercion is indispensable for inaugurating and implementing the socioeconomic policies characteristic of that type of political system.

6.

A Structural-Historical Approach to the Breakdown of Democratic Institutions: Peru

Julio Cotler *

Many of the articles in this volume analyze the breakdown of democracy mainly at the superstructural level and concentrate to a large extent on the immediate events leading up to the final crisis. It is my contention that such an emphasis is not sufficient to explain the collapse of representative institutions. Rather, only through a historical analysis of the class structure in a society can one explain the nature of political institutions and therefore elucidate the fundamental reasons for their breakdown and change.

This distinction should not be taken as an example of economic determinism. Quite the contrary, the development of ideologies and the nature of specific events and personalities are of crucial importance in any political crisis. But these developments take place within the context of larger socioeconomic structures, and it is ultimately this larger framework that defines the alternatives open to political groups.

For these reasons, I have used a historical-structural approach in my analysis of the breakdown of democratic forms in Peru. The main argument advanced in this essay is that, given the nature of Peru's economic development and its continued dependence on the industrialized nations, democracy developed in form but not in content. Peru's role as a provider of raw materials to the industrialized world limited the development of an internal market and therefore blocked all possibilities for independent industrialization. Consequently, the country did not witness the rise of a national bourgeoisie that could partially incorporate the demands of the lower classes and establish a democratic political system.

Such an analysis suggests the hypothesis that the 1968 military coup in Peru

*I would like to thank both Florencia Mallon for her help in translating and editing this chapter and Alfred Stepan for his comments and suggestions. For a more detailed analysis of the Peruvian case see my *Clases, estado y nación en el Perú* (Lima: Instituto de Estudios Peruanos, 1978).

was not the breakdown of democracy at all, but rather the final collapse of an oligarchy that had used democratic forms to maintain control over the population. But one cannot assume that a similar situation obtained in every dependent country. While the history of all Latin American countries has been characterized by some degree of dependence on the world capitalist system, the effect of such a relationship on socioeconomic and political development was particularly pronounced in the Peruvian case. And it is only through a structural-historical analysis that the specific nature of this effect can be fully explained.

In an attempt to incorporate all the necessary levels of analysis, I have divided my essay into two parts. The first sets the historical-structural context for subsequent events. The second analyzes the actual crisis of the political superstructure.

More specifically, part one traces the historical development of the Peruvian oligarchy, its relations with foreign capital, and the mechanisms utilized to deal with popular mobilization. The first section examines the period from independence to the 1920s, when foreign investment was concentrated mainly in the primary sector of the economy. The second considers the 1950s and early 1960s, when foreign investment increased and was extended to both the secondary and tertiary sectors. The third focuses more particularly on the reaction of the lower sectors to the changes set in motion by the new influx of foreign capital, and the oligarchy's attempts to deal with this reaction. The fourth treats the effect of these transformations on attitudes within the church and the army, institutions which had previously provided important support for the regime.

In part two, I deal with the superstructural aspects of the political crisis, referring when necessary to the historical-structural background. The first section examines the changing nature of ideologies and political alliances from 1962 to 1965. The second narrates the events leading up to the October 1968 coup, focusing on the way in which structural and superstructural developments combined to close off all other alternatives.

Part I: The Historical-Structural Context

The Formation of the Dependent Oligarchy

Much of Latin America's history after independence has been characterized by the persistence of a "colonial heritage." In essence, this heritage is defined by the reestablishment of relations between the Latin American nations and the emerging metropolitan bourgeoisies in Europe, but without a reform of the socioeconomic and political structures that had existed in the former during the colonial period. Rather, the renewal of relationships was founded on an exchange of raw materials for manufactured products and on the provision of loans by the Europeans to facilitate the production and transport of these raw materials. But more important was the fact that the "unequal exchange" was based on the exploitation of American labor tied to a precapitalist system of social relations of production, resulting in the formation of extremely stratified societies.

Production and marketing were organized under a government which functioned as a *rentier,* subject to the authority of regional oligarchies and their *caudillos.* This government distributed privilege among the *caciques* and *gamonales,* hoping to reestablish the system of colonial domination. Such a pattern made the growth of a free labor market impossible; consequently, it blocked the rise of a national bourgeoisie and a proletariat, and doomed all attempts at national integration.

In some Latin American countries, it was possible for the national oligarchy, with the help of foreign capital and the local government, to establish some form of hegemony over the population. In these cases, the elite retained a part of the surplus extracted from the precapitalist labor force and used this capital in the development of an internal market and a system of state power. But in other countries, such as Peru, this did not happen. Instead, the renewal of relationships with the world capitalist system went through two stages. The first, characterized by the emergence of a sector within the dominant class which was able to accumulate capital during the guano boom and invest it in agriculture, served to strengthen the precapitalist nature of social relations of production. The second, distinguished by the massive and direct investment of foreign capital in the productive sector, resulted in the formation of a system of enclave economies.[1]

During the crisis of the colonial system, which began at the end of the eighteenth century and culminated in the Wars of Independence of the 1820s, Peru entered a process of political feudalization. During this period a number of regional oligarchies, working through caudillos, attempted to establish territorial hegemony but lacked the resources to succeed. Once relations were broken with the Spanish crown, the colonial aristocracy lost its economic and political basis for control, leaving the political arena open to these many nuclei of local power.

In the mid-nineteenth century, Peru renewed economic relations with Europe. This renewal was founded on the export of guano, a fertilizer rich in organic matter and destined to revolutionize European agricultural productivity. The guano trade gained such importance that, between 1850 and 1865, Peru led Latin America in volume of exports to Europe. For this reason, Peru was able to gain an excellent credit rating on the international financial market, indebting itself especially to the English banks.

The monopoly of income from the guano trade facilitated the rise of an oligarchical sector that invested in agriculture and mining. But this sector was unable to control the state by centralizing the political system and reducing the influence of the regional oligarchies. There were two reasons for this weakness. First, while the income generated by the export of guano increased internal demand, no expansion in internal production resulted, for under a system of free trade, the law of comparative advantage militated against such expansion. Secondly, investment in agriculture and mining occurred without a modification of the precapitalist and servile system of labor relations, thus reinforcing the colonial nature of Peruvian society.

Under such conditions, the development of a free labor market became impossible, thus stunting the growth of an internal market with capitalist nuclei. Traditional social relations remained intact, and no challenge was presented to the regional elites. Quite the contrary, the local power groups maintained control and blocked all measures taken by the new guano elite. The ongoing tension produced by such a conflict resulted in the persistence of *caudillismo* and civil war; consequently, the income from guano was spent in maintaining a military.[2]

In order to finance this continuing struggle and involve the population in a system of patronage and clientelism, the governments supported by the various regional oligarchies were forced to turn to the international banking system. They financed loans of ever-increasing proportions against future income from the guano trade. During the 1870s, this vicious cycle reached a climax, due both to a crisis in the European financial system and to a decline in the volume and quality of guano exports. Thus began the decline into bankruptcy of the Peruvian economy, which became inevitable after the War of the Pacific (1879–1884).

After this last debacle had left the country in a state of economic and political prostration, the foreign bondholders demanded that the government pay off the external debt accumulated over the previous thirty years. Pressure from the bondholders and the European nations forced the Peruvian government to sign the Grace Contract, transferring control of the railroads for ninety-nine years to the bondholders' representative, the Peruvian Corporation. These railroads had been built with foreign capital to facilitate exports. In addition, the Peruvian government gave up the rights to all customs revenue and to a million hectares in the jungle region.

From this point on, foreign capital began to gain control of all the country's main economic resources, initiating the second stage in Peru's renewal of relations with the world capitalist system. The railroad concession made possible the organization in the late 1890s of the Cerro de Pasco Corporation, financed by the Morgan group, in the central part of the country. English capital exploited petroleum, the wool industry, and shipping. All of the country's productive sectors—mining, foreign trade, banking, export agriculture, public services, and even the incipient industrial sector—fell into the hands, or under the influence, of foreign investors.[3]

The control of the national economy by foreign capital led to an abrupt concentration of property and rationalization of production, which in turn resulted in the displacement of small agricultural and industrial producers and petty merchants. Under these conditions, the Peruvian oligarchy was forced to assume a secondary role. Although its members were able to carry out their own consolidation of lands, mines, and industries, they had to accept financial, marketing, and transportation assistance from the foreign sector. Thanks to the increment in international demand, these native groups enriched themselves in the first two decades of this century, convinced that this was the correct road toward political dominance. But as soon became apparent, their role was merely to ensure and maintain imperialist domination, for their alternatives were limited by the enclave nature of the country's economy. The national elite came increasingly to accept these limitations.

The modes of production employed by foreign capital and its native associates continued to be based on the exploitation of dependent labor, limiting the development of a free labor market and therefore of the consumer market. In the same way as the traditional haciendas tied their peons and the Indian communities their members, the new companies involved in the commercialization of raw materials developed the *enganche* system and assured the survival of the *tambo*. Through *enganche,* the company's representatives would advance a sum of money to prospective workers, thus obligating them to work for the firm until the debt had been paid, and reviving the colonial practice of debt-bondage. The isolation of the plantation or mine forced the workers to buy all food, medicine, and tools in the tambo, which was, of course, controlled by the company. These items, like the machines, were imported by the enterprises which obtained a new source for the extraction of profits, impeding the propagation of the capitalist system. In this manner, "dualism" was introduced into Peruvian society: "modern" plantations and mines did not create economic linkages, thus insuring that the manual labor at their disposition remained cheap, because it originated in a basically precapitalist countryside.

In addition, these companies extended their landed property, incorporating some traditional haciendas; they then used the hacienda workers to produce the foodstuffs that would be sold, at market prices, in the tambos. In this way, the new firms were able to extract surplus at two levels: directly, from the workers; and indirectly, from the hacienda peons. Increased demand for foodstuffs, both in these developing productive centers and on the external market, also prompted the traditional *hacendados* to recapture their lands, demanding more work from the dependent labor force, in order to take advantage of new commercial opportunities.[4]

Possibilities for accumulation of capital within the country were, however, limited by the enclave nature of the imperialist firms. These companies had as their goal the export of raw materials, which would then be transformed into manufactured goods abroad. Moreover, the profits from exports were remitted to the countries of origin, leaving in Peru nothing but low wages and minimal taxes, the latter thanks to a policy of tax breaks that was passed to "contribute to national development."

But the implantation of enclave economies and reorganization of the traditional haciendas did send a tremor through Peru's traditional social structure. Thousands of tenant farmers and small proprietors were proletarianized by the expansion of plantations and mining areas. The dependent rural labor force was tied more firmly to the land by the hacendados. And both sectors forged new patron-client relationships with members of the Indian communities.[5] These changes combined to modify the status not only of peasant groups but also of the rural and urban middle classes and the regional oligarchies.

It was within this framework that Peru witnessed the rise of the first antioligarchical political groups, particularly APRA (Alianza Popular Revolucionaria Americana) and the Socialists.[6] The former, under the direction of Víctor Haya de la Torre, became the most important antioligarchic party in Peru until the mid-1950s. Its platform was based on a structural-dualist analysis of Peruvian society that saw the country as divided into a feudal sector and a capitalist-imperialist sector. Both sectors were united in common exploitation of the nation, blocking its development and oppressing both the middle and the lower classes. Political mobilization through an alliance of all the oppressed would allow for the creation of a strong anti-oligarchical and anti-imperialist state, which would then negotiate with foreign capital for the financing necessary to promote nationalist development.[7]

The Socialist movement, led by José Carlos Mariátegui, proposed the construction of a popular front that would bring together all the classes dominated by imperialist capital and its domestic allies with the goal of realizing a Socialist revolution which would carry out the democratic reforms. Mariátegui was firmly convinced that the creation of a native and autonomous capitalism in Latin America was impossible. He argued that the real consequence of the development of capitalism in Latin America would be to condemn the region to an intensified semicolonial dependence on the imperialist centers, therefore impeding both the liberation of the popular classes and the attainment of national development. Thus, owing to the dependent character of the local bourgeoisie, only socialism could resolve the problems of democratic construction in Latin America.[8]

The death of Mariátegui in 1930, the reputation of the Soviet revolution, and the control of the Communist party in Peru by the Comintern thwarted the chances that the movement, as envisioned by Mariátegui, could be realized. This made it possible for APRA to remain the standard-bearer of the anti-oligarchical and anti-imperialist struggles.

Faced with increasing Aprista pressure, particularly after the crisis of the 1930s, the dominant groups found that they did not possess the means to meet demands for social reform. This was true precisely because the profits from the enclave economies were not retained within national borders. It therefore became necessary to establish an alliance with the army and embark on a policy of violent repression. While in other Latin American countries the crisis produced by the intensification of class struggle was being averted through the development of a policy of import substitution based on the expansion of the internal market, Peru was enmeshed in a violent confrontation between APRA and the army. This confrontation was to define the political framework within which all subsequent national events were to unfold. Throughout the period between 1930 and 1945, APRA sought to penetrate the military, endeavoring to undermine this pillar of the oligarchical order. This effort caused the military hierarchy to redouble its opposition to APRA.

In 1945, popular pressures and a new democratic atmosphere stemming from the Fascist defeat prompted the political system to open itself to popular representation, and the first experiment in democracy in the history of the Peruvian republic was inaugurated. APRA managed to obtain significant representation in the legislative chambers. While APRA, in order to contribute to the solidification of electoral democracy, sought an understanding with the owners—their traditional enemies—the masses exercised pressure to increase economic and political benefits. These pressures, which threatened to destroy the oligarchical model of social domination, led to the resolute opposition of capital. Thus there emerged a political impasse whose only solution was violence. In 1948, the radicalized sectors of APRA began plans to carry out a popular revolution, and the bourgeoisie began to organize a military coup that would put an end to these dangers and politically consolidate their position. While the Aprista revolt miscarried, the military coup headed by General Odría triumphed, putting an end to the short and precarious experiment in democracy.

Once again the pattern of 1930 was repeated: the oligarchical bourgeoisie proved structurally incapable of attending to even the most modest popular demands and to make democratic development possible. For this reason General Odría dedicated himself with special fury to the destruction of the popular political organizations and to the persecution of political, union, and student leaders.

New Forms of Dependency

In 1950 Peru entered a period of substantial economic growth that lasted until 1965, averaging 6 percent a year or 3.5 percent annually per capita. This increase was based mainly on exports, which grew at 8.7 percent a year, as opposed to an average of 4.3 percent in Latin America as a whole. In addition, the terms of trade were favorable, since an increase in the prices of copper and fish meal meant an 8 percent yearly increase in the real value of exports. This growth resulted in a change in the composition of the national economy. While the relative contribution of agriculture dropped from 22 percent to 17 percent of the GNP, the fishing industry—a newcomer to the export sector in the mid-1950s—made up for this loss. Mining and industry, taken together, increased their contribution to GNP from 18 percent to 24 percent over this period, averaging an annual growth rate of 8 percent. The annual rate of growth for agriculture was much lower: it amounted to 2.7 percent a year for export agriculture and 0.8 percent a year for production consumed internally. Thus in 1960 Peru was forced to import 13 percent of the foodstuffs consumed within the country, and this proportion had risen to 24 percent by 1966. Politically, these changes meant the relative dislocation of the old agricultural exporters and their hacendado allies, and their replacement by the groups involved in mining, fishing, and industry.

The increase in exports, and the growth of the capitalist sector in general, was due largely to the participation of foreign capital. From the beginning of Odría's dictatorship in 1948 until the collapse of the experiment with democratic institutions in 1968, foreign investment was provided with special incentives, so that by 1964 foreign participation constituted 47 percent of the total amount invested in exports. In certain sectors, such as petroleum and iron, foreign investment was 100 percent; in copper, it was 88 percent; in zinc, 50 percent; in lead and silver, 50 percent; in fishing, 30 percent; in sugar, 23 percent; and in cotton, 8 percent. And between 1960 and 1966, due both to the 1959 and 1963 laws promoting industry and to special incentives provided in the automobile and chemical industries, U.S. investment in the industrial sector rose from $35 million to $92 million. In fact, three-fourths of the 9 percent annual rate of industrial growth was due to foreign investment.

A similar increase in foreign investment occurred in the financial sector. Between 1960 and 1966, the proportion of foreign capital in the banking system rose from 36 to 62 percent of the total. Thus, while the national banks were growing at a rate of 1 percent a year from 1962 to 1969, the foreign banks grew at an annual rate of 4 percent. This assault of foreign capital on the financial sector seems to have been connected with the rise in direct foreign participation in the dynamic sectors of the economy, especially in industry. The establishment of new industrial firms was increasingly financed by national savings: in 1966, national loans to foreign companies rose by 36 percent in relation to the previous year, while foreign loans fell by 6 percent. And finally, 34 percent of all bank loans were given to industry in 1966, in comparison with 27 percent in 1960.[9]

As had been true of the first two decades of the twentieth century, the period between 1950 and 1968 was characterized by the further concentration of property in foreign hands. Unlike the earlier period, however, this new phase of concentration occurred in both the primary sector and the industrial and banking sectors. Thus from 1950 on, the structure of the Peruvian economy began to lose its enclave nature. Not only did import substitution proceed at a fairly rapid pace, but raw materials also began to be at least partially processed before export.

Yet in contrast to what had occurred in other Latin American countries after the crisis of the 1930s, participation of foreign capital increased both relatively and absolutely, resulting in a further loss of wealth and autonomy by the national bourgeoisie. And while this process had been going on since the beginning of the twentieth century, its intensification during the 1950s sharpened the contradictions between the capitalist mode of production and the precapitalist forms which had been associated with it. Indeed, if until 1950 capitalist development had been closely connected to the survival of precapitalist relations of production, especially in the sierra, industrialization and urban growth began increasingly to transform this relationship into a historical anachronism.

This new phase of dependent-capitalist development led to a substantial modification in the Peruvian occupational and demographic structures. The penetration of new forms of social and labor relations into areas previously dominated by the traditional hacienda meant the relative erosion of the hacendado's power base. In association with these and other factors, migration from rural to urban areas and from the sierra to the coast increased markedly. Between 1940 and 1961, for example, Lima's population grew five-fold. And in the last decade of this period, the annual rate of growth in Lima reached 8 percent, due mainly to the influx of rural migrants.

Over the same intercensus period, the proportion of the population employed in the primary sector fell from 63 percent to 52 percent, while the proportion employed in the tertiary sector rose from 17 percent to 27 percent. The percentage of workers in the secondary sector held steady at 17 percent of the population, which is surprising, given the fact that the 1950s was a decade of industrial growth. Although a part of this discrepancy can be explained through faulty collection of data, most of it had to do with the structural transformation of the industrial sector. Many of the small and medium-sized industries closed down, to be replaced by larger, more capital intensive firms with a reduced capacity to absorb labor.

The rapid changes in the structure of production, property, and employment resulted both in a split within the elite and in the strengthening of popular political mobilization. Odría's government had been brought to power by the Alianza Nacional (National Alliance), which was made up predominantly of exporters. In its first years, therefore, this regime functioned in a typically oligarchical fashion. But socioeconomic diversification soon brought Odría under increasing pressure, both from new groups seeking admission into the oligarchy and from the growing lower- and middle-class movement still being led by APRA.

Odría responded to this pressure by using state revenues—which had expanded due to the growth in exports—in a bid for political autonomy, establishing programs of state aid for the lower classes. During the first six years of the 1950s, government spending, most of which was directed toward public works, rose. This strategy provided the masses with a share in the benefits of economic growth, in the form of employment, hospitals, and schools. But it also allowed Odría to forge important alliances with rising political groups through the careful allocation of construction contracts.

Odría also attempted to attack APRA's political base in a more direct fashion. He organized the Partido Restaurador (Party of Restoration), using the urban masses, and more particularly recent rural migrants, in an effort to forge a populist coalition. He further strengthened this coalition by increasing the scope of social security and workers' benefits and giving women the vote. Odría's combined policy of providing assistance to the lower sectors while allying himself with new groups in the bourgeoisie prompted a number of political observers to compare him with Perón.

But the oligarchical nature of Peru's economy and society put definite limits on Odría's bid for autonomy, since it was impossible to obtain access to the resources necessary for a long-term populist experiment. Even the timid populist pretensions demonstrated by Odría brought down on him the opposition of the oligarchy. Speaking through *La Prensa,* the oligarchy labeled the regime excessive and "arbitrary," and called for a return to duly elected government. In a sense, the nineteenth-century pattern of confrontation between the *civilistas* (civilian politicians of the oligarchy) and the military was reemerging. Within this pattern, the army was useful in the repression of popular discontent and of the divisions produced within the oligarchy. But once the intrinsic weakness of the elite led the military caudillos to use public funds in an attempt to create their own power base, the military regime came to be seen as a threat by the groups that had originally supported it.

A successful urban middle-class mobilization, set into motion by *La Prensa* in alliance with the APRA underground, forced Odría to call a high-level meeting at the convent of Santo Domingo. This meeting was essentially a conference with the oligarchy on the presentation of a common candidate for the forthcoming elections. At the conference it became clear that the winning candidate in any election needed to be able to count on the Aprista vote. Thus, instead of unification, the conference had an unusual outcome: the two factions of the oligarchy attempted to negotiate with APRA to obtain its support. Hernando de Lavalle, Odría's designated successor, offered to legalize APRA after a victory at the polls. Manuel Prado, leader of the opposing faction and a zealous persecutor of APRA during his previous presidential term (1939–45), offered this party cogovernment. This political alliance came to be known as *convivencia* (coexistence).

The New Nature of the Class Struggle

Prado's electoral triumph in 1956, with the support of APRA, marked the beginning of a new political era in Peru. As a basis for this new alliance, Prado's oligarchical faction promised to share political power with the Apristas as long as the latter continued to constitute a "loyal opposition." This meant that APRA relinquished all claim to a radical stance, favoring instead the expansion of existing channels for change, which would permit the modernization of the country without endangering the power structure.

Both groups had become convinced that in order to continue to exist and to further their particular political goals, it was necessary to reach a modus vivendi with the opposition. For the Pradista faction, this was the only way to ensure the existence of the stable political institutions necessary for the creation of a "climate of confidence for investment." In exchange for their quota of political participation, the Pradistas hoped, APRA would check popular unrest and keep the specter of communism under control. If APRA failed in its mission, the army could always be called in once more.

As for the Apristas, they had grown tired of the virulent military repression they had suffered because of their insistence that "Only APRA can save Peru." Moreover, Haya de la Torre had modified his position on the United States, insisting that the latter had changed, since its capital was now contributing to the abolition of Peru's feudal-capitalist dualism. It was now necessary to "popularize" the expanding capitalist system by making it more redistributive or risk the spread of international communism. Not only did APRA agree with the Pradista oligarchy on the dangers of communism, but it also hoped to "democratize" this oligarchical faction to the point that it would support APRA's bid for electoral power.

As soon as this "democratic coexistence" was established, however, it was called into question by new political groups wishing to appropriate APRA's old position on the Left. Structural changes in the socioeconomic system had created important new middle sectors, both technical and professional, as well as a new working-class generation, and these groups were eager to take up the anti-oligarchical banner dropped by APRA. Moreover, APRA's new "sellout" policy (*entreguismo*) generated the first wave of deserters among its youthful members, who hastened to join the ranks of the new movement. In a very short time, therefore, Peru witnessed not only the resurgence of the Communist party but also the creation of three new anti-oligarchical groups: the Christian Democrat party, the Movimiento Social Progresista (Progressive Social Movement), and Acción Popular (the Popular Action party). The last of these proved to be the most important, for in the space of a few weeks it managed to join together all the progressive forces previously sympathetic to APRA and to record an impressive one-third of the 1956 popular vote for its candidate, Fernando Belaúnde.[10]

In addition to this new anti-oligarchical struggle—which was a great deal less radical than APRA's initial mobilization in the thirties—two essentially new forces entered the political arena during this period: the peasantry and the urban shantytown dwellers.[11] The development of capitalism and its penetration into rural areas weakened the traditional hacendados' hold over the peasants, creating favorable conditions for the latter to initiate a sustained struggle to regain the land. The poorer urban sectors organized on two fronts: those faced with chronic underemployment and poor living conditions invaded empty urban lands to dramatize the housing problem; and those belonging to the labor force reorganized their unions and intensified their fight for participation in the national income. Thus land, housing, and employment became the central issues in the contest between pro- and anti-oligarchical forces.

It was within the context of this intense mobilization by both lower and middle sectors that Peru underwent a new process of profound politicization (i.e., the definition of particular interests within, and the struggle between, the different sectors and classes of society). With these new political tensions came the rise of "developmentalist" ideology, which emphasized the need for "structural" changes in Peruvian society in order to bring it out of its "underdeveloped" state. And within the dominant class, pressure from below combined with the rise of developmentalism to cause a split over the definition of a correct government policy.

The essence of the struggle between the two main factions of the elite was well captured in the polemic that arose between *La Prensa* and *El Comercio*, newspapers supported by different sectors of the oligarchy. Both publications agreed that the basic problem was communism, defined as the attempt of the lower sector to gain political power. They also agreed that the only solution to the problem was "development," seen as the expansion of national income and greater participation in this income by the lower classes. But they disagreed radically over the best way to stimulate economic growth and over the optimal mechanisms for income redistribution.

La Prensa, backed by the oligarchical group involved in exports and directly linked to international capital, espoused a policy best defined as laissez faire. The role of the state was seen exclusively as the provision of the necessary infrastructure and the lifting of all economic controls. In this way, the national bourgeoisie and the foreign capitalists could join in bringing new dynamism to the Peruvian economy. The problem of land could be solved by providing the necessary incentives for colonization of the jungle. The problems of housing and employment could be solved by lifting all fiscal restraints on rent and sale of housing and by creating organizations capable of channeling national savings into the construction industry. The increase in construction would not only take care of the housing shortage but would also provide employment for the urban population.

El Comercio, on the other hand, emphasized the need for structural reforms that would do away with the two basic contradictions in Peruvian society: the persistence of "feudalism" within the context of capitalist development and the increasing subordination of national to foreign capital. The most urgent priorities, therefore, were an agrarian, urban, and fiscal reform, and the creation of a powerful state that could control the economic sectors most important for nationalist development. A centralized state could organize production along modern lines and redistribute income to the masses so that their share of profits was in line with their participation in the productive process. It was hoped that this policy would favor the rise of a nationalist industrial bourgeoisie which, in alliance with the state, would lead the country forward to the realization of its economic potential.

These different economic policies implied extremely diverse political positions. *La Prensa* argued that only the institutionalization of "democracy" could provide the necessary base for its economic program. Without "democratic" institutions, military repression would lead to the rise of extremist movements. Furthermore, foreign capital, faced with uncertain long-term conditions, would not invest in Peru under a dictatorship. It was for these reasons that *La Prensa* favored the APRA-Prado coalition and its new policy of coexistence.

In contrast, *El Comercio* combined a reformist and anti-oligarchical economic stance with an extremely traditional political orientation. Economic reform by a centralized state was supported not for its own sake, but as the only way to maintain internal and external security. Peru was seen as threatened on two fronts: international communism on the one hand and Chile's "inveterate expansionist tendencies" on the other. Popular unrest, generated by poverty and exploitation, not only led to the diffusion of extremist ideologies but also prevented the creation of a national consciousness. And without a state to plan the economy, redistribute income, and solve the conflict between capital and labor, Peru would never develop a national identity to protect itself from Communist expansionism and Chilean "threats."

El Comercio's line of reasoning became increasingly attractive to certain sectors of the army. This sympathy was strengthened by the fact that the army and the *Comercio* group shared a profound hatred for APRA, both because of the type of popular participation this party had advanced in its early years and because of APRA's past attacks on the army and the church. Therefore, as time went on, *El Comercio* began to speak more and more directly to the army in its attacks on the APRA-Prado "democratic" experiment, calling for "structural changes" but always emphasizing the importance of maintaining the proper hierarchy of authority.

Then in 1957–58, a rapid fall in exports spawned a new political and economic crisis. President Prado offered the prime ministry to Pedro Beltrán, editor of *La Prensa*. In keeping with his liberal economic policies, Beltrán freed the exchange rate—which led to the devaluation of the currency—and lifted all controls on the movement of capital. In addition, he attempted to gain official approval for a hike in the price of gasoline, which was produced by the International Petroleum Company. This attempt initiated a violent debate in the legislature, not over the price itself but over the legality of IPC's operations in Peru. The controversy quickly spread to the pages of *La Prensa* and *El Comercio*, with the former defending the company and the latter attacking it on a daily basis. A growing nationalist trend emerged in support of *El Comercio*'s position, and this movement was joined by a large number of army officers.

Thus the socioeconomic diversification of Peruvian society facilitated the rise of new political sectors who openly questioned the hegemony of the dependent oligarchy. This polarization of class interests extended itself into the army and the church, permeating all sectors of society. In the 1950s, therefore, the dependent oligarchy found its privileged position under attack, a position it had been able to maintain exclusively because of the aid it had been receiving from the army.

The Roles of Army and Church in the Oligarchical Crisis

The Catholic church in Peru had traditionally been associated with the elite and had constituted one of the institutions through which the oligarchical state legitimized its power. With the mobilization of the 1950s the church responded by importing clergy and capital from other countries—especially from France and the United States—and initiated a strong anti-Communist campaign.[12]

Within the context of this campaign, elements of the clergy nonetheless began to perceive the dominant class as the true anti-Christian force, for they saw the continued exploitation of the masses as the underlying source of the country's discontent. This analysis was strengthened at the international level in the 1960s by the declarations of Vatican II and by the pope's explicit and emphatic censure of imperialism. Within Latin America, the conferences of bishops lent further support to this new trend.[13]

The church's progressive orientation soon gained the support of a majority of the clergy, not only in Peru but in other countries as well. The acceptance of progressivism led to an emphasis on new theological interpretations which helped to modify the image of the church and facilitate communication with the poor. And as a complement to the new ideology, a number of ecclesiastical groups became involved with the ongoing movements among peasants, urban squatters, urban unions, and student organizations.

In addition to participating in the mobilization of the lower sectors, the church organized a series of *cursillos de cristiandad* for members of the armed forces and for urban professionals. These courses were apparently designed to develop a militant Christian conscience within the new technocratic elements in the military and economic elites. In this way, the church hoped to initiate a reform from above by changing the ideas of people in positions of authority and influence. The final goal was the extension of a communitarian orientation throughout Peruvian society, which would help to quiet class struggle without major changes in class structure. This general plan meshed perfectly with the aspirations of the Christian Democrat party, whose members also hoped to eliminate social conflict by integrating all class interests into a single and organic body politic.

In a similar fashion and over the same period, the army underwent a series of ideological and institutional changes that helped to free it from oligarchical control and predispose it toward political intervention in order to insure national development. Up until the moment that a sector of the Peruvian elite, with the help of foreign investment, had managed to gain political control of the country, the Peruvian army had been little more than an armed group whose leaders were divided in their loyalties to different caudillos and the oligarchical factions they represented. But once the newly dominant dependent oligarchy controlled the state, the army united around an identification with this group and began to professionalize.

From the beginning, the function of the military was defined as the provision of support for the dependent oligarchical system. This meant not only political intervention whenever it became necessary to arbitrate conflicts within the oligarchy, but also the repression of political mobilization by the lower classes. Thus from the very moment of its establishment as a professional group, the army identified with the elite and developed a strong anti-Aprista policy.

Yet at the same time and throughout its history, the army found itself infiltrated by Apristas and by the anti-oligarchical ideology being formulated by APRA. As long as it was possible for most army officers to see their principal interests served by an alliance with the elite, the pro-oligarchical tendency continued to dominate. But the tension produced by this difference generated a technocratic-nationalist tendency within the ranks that later became responsible for the creation of the Centro de Altos Estudios Militares (CAEM).[14]

After World War II, the Peruvian army established strong connections with the United States army, purchasing military supplies and receiving extensive technical assistance. Accompanying this modernization was the development of a strong anti-Communist spirit, which combined easily with existing anti-Aprista feeling. And as a result of the introduction of new techniques, the Peruvian army initiated studies in military strategy based on actual conditions within the country, not on outmoded French manuals.

Within this framework, CAEM began a study of Peru's potential for national defense against a possible Communist or Chilean attack, paying special attention to the country's economic structure and the development of its educational, health, and communications facilities. When the results of this study were compared with the known potential of other Latin American countries, particularly those with which Peru shared borders, CAEM concluded that Peru was profoundly underdeveloped in terms of the resources it could mobilize in its own defense. CAEM therefore began immediately to investigate the causes for this state of affairs and to consider policies that would spur improvement of national defense. The developmentalist tone arising from this investigation was similar to the orientation of the new political parties created in 1950 but meshed especially well with the line being advanced by *El Comercio*. CAEM's findings can be summarized in the following sentence: "The sad and desperate reality is that, in Peru, real power is not Executive, Legislative, Judicial or Electoral power, but that which is held by landowners, exporters, bankers, and North American companies."[15]

A series of events then conspired to strengthen this analysis of Peru's dependency on foreign interests. The first of these was the support openly provided to the International Petroleum Company by the U.S. government, to the detriment of Peru's national interests. The second was the refusal by the United States to sell the country supersonic jets and its general reluctance to provide modern arms to Peru while giving them freely to other Latin American countries. Last was the U.S. refusal to give Belaúnde's government economic aid at a time of desperate need while continuing to provide it to Frei in Chile. These three events, along with a few less publicized occurrences, forced the military to conclude that national development was being limited by U.S. political and economic interests who were in association with the national oligarchy. As a result, many Peruvian officers reacted favorably to the theories of dependency being elaborated by Peruvian and other Latin American intellectuals.

While anti-imperialist sentiment developed in CAEM, the army as a whole carried out a reorganization of its institutional structure at the end of the 1950s. This reform had as one of its goals the strengthening of the army's section for military intelligence, prompted by the intensification of social conflict within the country. Careful observation of the Algerian and Vietnam wars, the Cuban Revolution, and popular movements within Latin America convinced military intelligence that the problem of national defense could no longer be seen solely as an external problem but was now also a question of internal security. This analysis was clearly based on anti-Communist considerations. The Soviet Union and China were thought to be creating subversive *focos* within the lower classes and intellectual groups of the Western nations in an attempt to destroy their institutions. And while the United States could be expected to counter any conventional attack these countries might attempt, it was up to Peru and to its army to insure social peace within national borders.

Studies carried out not only by CAEM but also by the army's intelligence service then led to the conclusion that the extreme poverty and exploitation characteristic of the countryside were the main causes for peasant movements. It was the traditional system of dominance, exemplified in the traditional haciendas, that generated agrarian movements, and through these, possible guerrilla focos. The conclusion was clear: it was necessary to ameliorate the conditions of life of the lower sectors in order to prevent the spread of the conflict that was threatening order in Peru.

For these reasons, therefore, an increasing section of the army came to support joint civil and military action for development, particularly the program of community development advanced by Acción Popular, and programs of jungle colonization and agrarian reform. The engineering divisions of the armed forces dedicated themselves to opening roads into the jungle in order to expand the agricultural frontier. The 1962 military junta, established to deal with the political crisis of that year, decreed an agrarian reform law for La Convención (in Cuzco), a center of peasant mobilization since the late 1950s.

But it was not until the outbreak of guerrilla activity all over the country in 1964 and 1965 that the army became truly alarmed about the potential danger the guerrillas could represent. Despite the fact that the guerrilla activity was quickly eliminated, the armed forces were left with the fear that these focos could reappear at any time and present an even more powerful challenge to institutionalized government. As a publication from the Ministry of War explained:

Although it is true that the guerrillas have been defeated, this does not mean that the "revolutionary" war in Peru has ended; the virus of subversion is latent in the universities and schools, unions and offices, clubs and homes. . . . The enemy is everywhere and the citizens should understand as much, and should therefore take an active part in the struggle, each within his own sphere of action and according to his own possibilities.[16]

From this time on the ideology developed by CAEM and the intelligence unit gained increasing acceptance within the army as a whole. Peru's status as a dependent nation was seen as the major cause for underdevelopment, for the impossibility of forming a national consciousness, and consequently for the rise of revolutionary movements. Thus national development became an urgent priority for the army, since it was intimately connected with national defense and internal security. Unless the army took an active and leading role in the elimination of Peru's oligarchical-dependent structures, the result would be a state of profound political disorganization and would lead, as it had done during the War of the Pacific, to a Chilean invasion. Thus the new military orientation came to agree closely with new tendencies in the church, and especially with the policies that had been formulated by *El Comercio* since the middle of 1950.

PART II: The Crisis of the Political Superstructure

The Political Crisis

Class conflict, and the polemic around its nature and solution, intensified greatly as the 1962 elections approached. One of the main reasons for this intensification was the rise of a peasant movement in the south of the country, led by Hugo Blanco. Centered in La Convención, Cuzco, this movement was widely perceived as an example of what could happen on a much larger scale if "traditional structures" were not quickly and completely reformed.

The three main candidates presenting themselves for the elections were Haya de la Torre, representing APRA; Fernando Belaúnde Terry, for Acción Popular; and General Manuel Odría, who represented the oligarchy's most traditional faction—including exporters and traditional landowners—but also had his own following among the poorer urban sectors to whom he had provided services during his last term in power. *La Prensa* backed both Odría and Haya de la Torre, while maintaining a clear preference for the latter. *El Comercio,* on the other hand, given its strong anti-Aprista stand, supported both Odría and Belaúnde but declared its preference for the Acción Popular candidate.

The electoral campaign was fierce, and the results promised to be close. Anticipating the possibility of an Aprista triumph, *El Comercio* began a strong campaign directed at the army, emphasizing the fraudulent nature of the electoral process. As was feared, the returns gave Haya de la Torre the victory by a close margin. The army, assured of support from *El Comercio* and repulsed by the thought of surrendering its autonomy to a mass party government, prepared a coup. A few days before the end of his term, Manuel Prado was exiled.

In 1962, therefore, the first institutional military government in Latin America was installed in Peru. A triumvirate of generals assumed control of the country and attempted to put into practice the new policies being formulated at the Centro de Altos Estudios Militares. The first measures taken included the organization of a national economic planning agency (Instituto Nacional de Planificación), the agrarian reform in La Convención, and the incarceration of several hundred workers, peasants, political leaders, and students. But the lack of political cohesion and ideological maturity among the officers combined with an increase in political unrest to force the junta to seek new elections in 1963. For the new elections, however, it was necessary to support a candidate who would be willing to carry out sweeping reforms without stirring up class conflict in such a way as to cause institutional chaos. For this reason the army, along with the church, supported Belaúnde in 1963.

The new electoral campaign was as heated as that of the year before. Because of popular pressure, all candidates were forced to present anti-oligarchical platforms, promising agrarian and industrial reform and a restructuring of the state. In addition, Belaúnde stated publicly that he would solve the ongoing conflict over the International Petroleum Company within ninety days of being elected, a promise which prompted the American ambassador to state his support for Haya de la Torre; this prompted the military government to request a replacement from Washington.

A close victory by Belaúnde launched the country into a state of uncontrolled euphoria. A university professor and architect who had personally campaigned throughout the country was now to become president and bring about the ''conquest of Peru by Peruvians.'' In keeping with this general tone, the peasant masses anticipated the coming agrarian reform by invading haciendas and taking land for themselves. Thousands of students flocked to the Cooperación Popular (Popular Cooperation) movement to help the peasants ''develop their communities,'' and professional and intellectual groups urged Peruvians to participate in the task of national development.

Six months into his term, Belaúnde called for municipal elections, which had been outlawed for almost fifty years. His party scored an impressive victory, raising their percentage of the vote from the 34 percent received in the presidential elections to 47 percent. Despite this popular support, however, the new government had inherited an unmanageable political system. Before stepping down, the junta had passed a new electoral law which, while neglecting to change the literacy requirement, established the principle of proportional representation. This meant that future presidents would not have a majority in Congress and would therefore have to look for support among opposing groups, because proportional representation would almost invariably mean a pluralistic government.[17]

Congress had been split in such a way that the largest group was formed by APRA, followed by the Acción Popular–Christian Democrat coalition (AP-DC), which supported the president, and the Unión Nacional Odriísta (UNO), which was led by Odría. Under these conditions, the main political problem was establishment of a coalition to facilitate relations between the executive and legislative branches. From the very beginning Manuel Seoane, APRA's second-in-command, along with a number of the Acción Popular leaders, began negotiations to establish a coalition between these two parties. Despite tactical conflicts within APRA, an important group of leaders continued to uphold its original position and could count on the support of its popular base. An equally reformist position was held by the majority of Acción Popular leaders.

But ideological affinities proved to be outweighed by other considerations. If the AP-DC alliance joined forces with APRA, it stood to lose its main basis of support in the army and the backing of *El Comercio*. Furthermore, a section of Acción Popular which would later be called the *termocéfalos* felt that APRA had "sold out" to the oligarchy, since it had supported Prado and Beltrán, director of *La Prensa*; therefore they felt that any alliance with them would mean giving up the reformist goals of Acción Popular. Within APRA there existed a feeling that AP was a treacherous competitor, since it had attempted to rob APRA of its reformist banners and appropriate the militancy which "naturally" belonged to the latter. Belaúnde was also perceived as siding with the Communists because of the radical tone of his proposals. And finally, Haya de la Torre felt a deep resentment for Belaúnde, for he saw the new president as having stolen from him the position of popular leader, a position Haya had held for thirty years.

Faced with the impossibility of conciliating the two main reformist forces, and the consequent loss of an alliance which would have brought them nearly 70 percent of the popular vote, APRA once again committed the unforgivable: it allied with the Odriístas. If the previous coalition with Prado had meant the loss of a large group of reformists who then swelled the ranks of new political parties, APRA's new "sell out" policy proved even more expensive. Numerous Apristas now entered the Movimiento de Izquierda Revolucionaria (MIR), an alliance of members from APRA Rebelde and other leftist groups who were attempting to follow the Cuban model in Peru.

The APRA-UNO coalition resulted, predictably enough, in a parliamentary block of all the reformist proposals being advanced by the executive. Prompted by the rash of land invasions occurring simultaneously with the discussions of the Agrarian Reform Law, APRA-UNO and *La Prensa* accused the government of promoting these "illegal" actions through Cooperación Popular. They demanded immediate repression of the peasants and cut the Cooperación Popular budget. These events caused the fall of Belaúnde's first cabinet.

Moreover, the Agrarian Reform Law presented by Acción Popular was sufficiently modified during the discussion in Parliament that it became completely ineffective. The three main points of contention were the type and size of property to which the law would apply, the mechanisms through which the law would be implemented, and the way in which the project would be financed. As to the first point, the coalition managed to exclude all property producing rice, sugar, and cotton, thus maintaining intact the nucleus of all important and powerful agricultural interests. Parliament then gained control of the financing, channeling it through a bureaucratic procedure so extended and complicated as to make rapid action on affected lands virtually impossible. And finally, although the coalition accepted payment for expropriation through government bonds, it also reduced the budget for the Office of Agrarian Reform, thus cutting off the funds necessary for the issue of these bonds.

In this way, APRA-UNO managed to block both of Belaúnde's main reformist programs from the beginning: Cooperación Popular, a movement designed to promote community development through public works and the joint action of the lower classes and the student population, and agrarian reform. This was not surprising, since the political structure allowed the legislature to control the executive:

The strength of the Congress derives from powers granted in the 1933 Constitution. First in importance is the power to *interpellate* (question) *and remove* ministers. With this power, Congress can censure ministers at will, but the president does not have the reciprocal power of most parliamentary systems, namely the ability to call new elections when his ministers receive a vote of no confidence. Second, the Congress must approve all taxes or changes in tax rates. In practice, this has allowed the Congress to get the credit for approving new programs but to block their implementation by refusing to finance them. Third, there is no presidential veto; the president may only "promulgate and implement" laws sent to him. In 1939 President Benavides called a plebiscite which approved a veto and limitations on the Congressional control over taxation, but these adjustments were voted out by an *Aprista*-dominated Congress in 1945. There remained a residual veto by compromise: the president could "observe" a law within ten days after receiving it, but no extraordinary majority was required to reinstate the law. Apra's support of Congressional prerogatives during Belaúnde's presidency is not surprising.[18]

The repression of the peasant movement demanded by the coalition provoked within the ranks of Acción Popular a movement to close down the Congress and call a national plebiscite, a move which would certainly have received the support of the military. Belaúnde rejected such an illegal measure and preferred to search out other political alternatives for solving the crisis. This incident marks the moment that APRA began to turn the Parliament into the "first power within the country," hoping to force the executive to surrender. Meanwhile, the coalition attempted to take all the credit for the government's successes and blame all the mistakes on Belaúnde.

Belaúnde proved to be unable to handle this situation, for he neither looked for a confrontation with the opposition parties nor tried to reach a modus vivendi. In addition to rejecting the possibility for a coup with popular and military support, Belaúnde did nothing to counter Parliament's attempts to dismantle his programs by cutting off funds. In fact, he totally dismissed the possibility of organizing popular support around the party system. Instead, he seemed to want to separate himself both from popular pressure and from that of his party, searching secretly for his own solution to the political crisis.

In addition to Belaúnde's personal inadequacies, the alternatives available for action were limited by other factors. One was the previously mentioned problems involved in a possible alliance with APRA. A further complication proved to be Belaúnde's campaign promise to resolve the conflict surrounding the International Petroleum Company, which led to the U.S. government's decision to cut off funds to Peru.[19]

By the end of Belaúnde's first year in power, it had already become clear that there was little hope for the elimination of traditional and oligarchical social structures in Peru. In 1964, this hopelessness manifested itself in the decision of certain sectors of the Left to adopt the guerrilla foco technique. Luis de la Puente, an old Aprista leader, led the MIR in the constitution of four focos of insurgency which were rapidly destroyed. A similar experiment by the Ejército de Liberación Nacional (National Liberation Army) suffered the same fate the next year.[20]

Despite the tactical failure of the guerrillas, the movement as a whole provided Belaúnde's opposition with new ammunition in the political struggle. In 1964, *La Prensa* initiated a campaign designed to discredit the president by branding him an agent, ally, and "comrade in arms" of the Communists. Belaúnde's first reaction to the guerrillas had been to underestimate their importance, and *La Prensa* did not allow him to forget it, going as far as to direct an appeal to the army in the hopes of breaking down the alliance existing between the officers and Acción Popular. In this way, *La Prensa* hoped to force the government to call in Beltrán as economic adviser and bring the period of reformism to an end. The final move in this campaign was a collaboration between Congress and *La Prensa* in raising a national loan based on "bonds for the defense of national sovereignty," of which Beltrán himself bought the first million.

Faced with the combined influence of this campaign and pressure from the military, Belaúnde had no choice but to institute an openly repressive policy. The guerrilla focos were located and destroyed, and the peasant movement liquidated. Simultaneously, the government struck against the growing union movement that was trying to separate itself from the influence of the Aprista Confederación de Trabajadores del Perú. The overall result of this policy was the breakdown of all unity on the left. Belaúnde's government quickly lost all support from the radicalized popular sectors and was reduced to seeking temporary alliances with political and military leaders.

But the guerrilla movement marked an important turning point in the attitudes within the military. From this point on, CAEM's warnings about the possibility of revolutionary war took on a new immediacy, and heated discussions began on the need to take drastic measures to avoid political disintegration. The military had hoped for structural reform, but Belaúnde's regime had done nothing but cause a continual political crisis that made reform impossible. Increasingly, therefore, the officers of the armed forces began to argue that it was not feasible to rely on political parties and the parliamentary system to carry out such reforms.

A further problem for Belaúnde was the progressive worsening of Peru's economic situation. Public expenditures rose noticeably during the Acción Popular government. This increase was caused in part by the APRA-UNO coalition's attempts to create an independent power base. The coalition had initiated a policy of patronage and clientelism, through which they hoped to maintain the support of their allies and also court the backing of new groups. One of the mechanisms of implementation for this plan was a system of "parliamentary initiatives," which consisted in presenting a set sum of money to each parliamentary member to spend as he saw fit. But part of the increase in public expenditures was also due to Belaúnde's policies. Seeing his attempts at structural reform blocked by Congress, the president began to promote the development of the country's infrastructure and educational system as a substitute for socioeconomic transformation.

Yet Congress refused to finance increased public spending through a reform in the tax system, forcing the government to rely on deficit financing. During the first fiscal year of the regime the budgetary deficit reached 1,618 million *soles*, which increased to 2,535 million in 1965 and 3,012 million in 1966, an annual rate of 96 percent.

Given the continued intransigence of the APRA-UNO coalition, Belaúnde was unable to finance the deficit internally and was forced to rely on international loans. But the United States was maintaining a financial blockade on Peru until the resolution of the problem with the International Petroleum Company. Consequently, the only loans available were short-term, high-interest loans. This led to an increase in the country's external debt from $120 million in 1963 to $670 million in 1967. Expressed in other terms, this debt constituted 8 percent of exports in 1965 but 18 percent in 1968.

To compound these problems, exports and foreign investment began to fall off in 1965. As investment decreased, all productive sectors of the economy—raw materials, manufacturing, and banking—were hard hit. Combined with the problems of budgetary deficit, this decrease in production contributed to an increase in inflation, which reached 14 percent per year between 1963 and 1967. Then in 1966, as exports continued to decrease and the external debt continued to increase, Peru was faced with a problem in the balance of payments. From then on, the Acción Popular government, and with it the oligarchical regime, would begin to see its very existence come into question.

The Denouement

Beginning in 1966, therefore, the economic crisis reached such proportions that it demanded immediate and energetic action.[21] Four aspects of the crisis needed special attention: the balance of payments, the budgetary deficit, financing of the external debt, and the revitalization of the export sector. In all cases, the alternatives were limited. The balance of payments problem could be solved in one of two ways: through a devaluation of the currency, which would put the burden on the consumer, or through exchange rate and import controls, which would generate strong opposition from the oligarchy and foreign interests. In the case of the budget deficit, the choices were similar. The burden of balancing the budget could be placed on the lower and middle sectors through a reduction in expenditures, thus lowering employment, consumption, and investment, or it could be placed on the foreign capital and oligarchy through new direct taxes on income.

The financing of the external debt and the provision of funds for the export sector were dependent on the ability of the government to reach a new agreement with sources of foreign capital. This ability depended, in turn, on working out the continuing problem with IPC, since, without a solution to this impasse, the United States would not provide assistance to Peru. Yet despite new incentives for agreement, which consisted of $350 million for the exploitation of new copper deposits, a solution did not seem imminent.

The best course of action, therefore, was to attack those problems that could be solved internally: balancing the budget, increasing direct taxes, and controlling the movement of stock. But Congress continued its policy of intransigent opposition, causing several cabinets to fall. Almost through default, a 50 percent official devaluation of the *sol* was announced in August 1967.

A month later, elections were called in the department of Lima to replace a deceased AP representative. These elections had the character of a plebscite, for the department of Lima contained nearly half of the national electorate. The APRA-UNO candidate, who ran on the slogan "No More Taxes," won the election, but a candidate for the unified Left also managed to obtain 18 percent of the vote. Not only did this election demonstrate the AP's loss of its popular base, therefore, but it also pointed to the existence of an important sector capable of uniting the Left around a series of common goals.

Faced with these results, the political forces decided to regroup. Acción Popular, controlled by the termocéfalos, separated itself from the president and reaffirmed the AP's original platform, calling for tax reform, administrative reform of government, careful economic planning, and—most important of all—agrarian and industrial reform. Belaúnde, cut off from his political base, began negotiations with Haya de la Torre and Odría. And the Christian Democrats not only dissolved their alliance with the Acción Popular but also broke off from their own conservative wing.

Faced with a worsening economic and political crisis, Belaúnde invited an "independent" to be his minister of economics and to attempt a solution. When this move failed, the minister accused APRA of manipulating the situation to bring about a second monetary devaluation, thus discrediting the president even further and strengthening their own position in the upcoming elections. This accusation was widely believed, and APRA, seeing tensions rise, especially within the ranks of the military, reconsidered its strategy.

Then in February 1968, a high-level smuggling ring was exposed, implicating important members of the Ministry of Economics and the armed forces. Scandal spread throughout the country, discrediting all national institutions and bringing the military directly into the fray. The ensuing investigation was carried out by an Aprista congressional representative, which presented an immediate threat to the image and prestige of the army. At the same time Belaúnde, hoping to maintain the support of the military and force the congressional opposition to solve the economic crisis, requested the appointment of an army officer as minister of economics. But the measures proposed by the new minister turned out to be the same as those presented by the two previous ministers, for they were based on the recommendations of the Alliance for Progress, which advocated the strengthening and piecemeal reform of existing structures.

Within this framework, *La Prensa* redoubled its attack on the regime, this time generalizing its criticism to include the technocrats, the United States government and the Alliance for Progress. In this way, the newspaper hoped to present its stance as a nationalist one. The new minister of economics then resigned rather than risk an open confrontation with Parliament. The rest of the cabinet followed suit almost immediately.

In June 1968, Belaúnde made one last attempt to salvage the situation by installing a cabinet that was headed by another "independent," Oswaldo Hercelles, and a new minister of hacienda, Manuel Ulloa. Several of the ministers in this cabinet were marginal Apristas, and others belonged to the faction of Acción Popular that had recommended alliance with APRA from the very beginning. This cabinet therefore began its activities by "conversing" with the opposition and became known in the political folklore as the "conversed" cabinet.

The new conformation of alliances, along with the growing Aprista fear that the military might intervene in the 1969 elections if things got much worse, contributed to the decision to grant Hercelles extraordinary powers. This allowed the cabinet to govern without parliamentary regulation for sixty days. Ulloa was therefore able to initiate a strong policy of stabilization, signing more than three hundred decrees in two months.

Over this period, Ulloa put into practice a series of measures that Parliament had systematically blocked for over five years. He taxed inheritance and personal income. He reformed the laws on ownership of stock, facilitating the circulation of shares and making it more difficult to avoid paying taxes on them. He limited participation by foreign capital in Peruvian banks to 33 percent and prohibited foreign banks from opening branches that could take over internal savings. Not only was this last measure a nationalist one, but it also helped open up sources of credit to the national bourgeoisie. In addition, Ulloa increased state participation in the Central Reserve Bank and gave representation on its board of directors to the Confederación de Trabajadores del Perú (Union of Peruvian Workers) and the Federación de Campesinos del Perú (Federation of Peruvian Peasants), both controlled by APRA, and to the Sociedad de Minería (Mining Society), controlled by the oligarchy and foreign capital. Finally, Ulloa ruled that industries strategic to the development of the country should be owned only by the state, or at least that two-thirds of their stock must be in the hands of Peruvians.

Complementing these domestic measures was an agreement on the refinancing of the external debt and a successful bid for more foreign investment. Moreover, the imminent arrival of North American funds for the exploitation of the Cuajone deposits was announced. Ulloa's supporters maintained that these successes were due to his energetic domestic measures. His detractors, especially the termocéfalos, argued that he had received such favorable terms because he had once been an executive in a company financed by U.S. capital. Either way, however, the solution of Peru's economic crisis seemed assured. The only missing step was the working out of an agreement with IPC.

Ulloa's rapid success was a result of his alliance with APRA. This alliance also led to a new regrouping of the country's political groups, with Acción Popular and the radical wing of the Christian Democrats uniting behind Edgardo Seoane as a presidential candidate for 1969. APRA had, in the meantime, also separated from UNO, which itself had split into two groups.

The interesting question then becomes: why did APRA change its position again, and why so rapidly? The most plausible answer seems to lie in the proximity of the presidential elections. APRA needed a new ally with which it could govern the country, an ally acceptable to the national and foreign capitalists and capable of neutralizing the army. Moreover, Ulloa knew that without APRA he would only be acceptable to the personal supporters of Belaúnde. The termocéfalos, Odriístas, and La Prensa would be opposed in any case, and the army and El Comercio could be appeased with a nationalist stance; thus APRA was Ulloa's best ally, and Ulloa was APRA's best candidate for the coming election.

Starting in July, however, all hopes for new political alliances were dashed by a crisis over an agreement with IPC. At that point IPC decided to negotiate, and indicated that it was willing to accept the terms that had been presented by the Peruvian government five years earlier. Under these terms, IPC agreed to turn over to the government a number of semidepleted oil wells but demanded that in return the government retract all other claims. In addition, the much-disputed refinery at Talara would stay in the hands of IPC, and their concession on the distribution of gasoline would be extended for forty years, with an option to renew at the end of this period for another forty. Finally, IPC wanted exploration rights to a million hectares in the jungle.

On 28 July 1968, Belaúnde addressed the nation, promising that the country's problems with IPC were over. He invited parliamentary leaders and high-ranking military officers to assist in the signing of the agreement. In this way, Belaúnde hoped to make this "triumph" a national occasion, not a partisan one, and to regain favor with the nationalist forces.

Temporarily, Belaúnde's attempt at national unity seemed a success. Even *El Comercio,* which in principle objected to the terms of the agreement, toned down its criticism when faced with the government's first triumph in the midst of failure. But it did not take long for a new scandal to emerge, this time over the definition of the ongoing relationship between the state, new owner of the national oil wells, and the foreign-owned refinery.

In September, the director of the Empresa Petrolera Fiscal (the state oil company) announced over national television that someone had stolen the last page of the Act of Talara, as the agreement had come to be called. This was the page that defined the price that IPC would pay EPF for the petroleum the latter was forced to sell. Once again, scandal spread rapidly. Seoane and Acción Popular publicly denied any connection with the president, and Belaúnde attempted to regain control of AP headquarters through the use of police and hired gunmen. APRA also denied any connection with the agreement and the scandal, and left Ulloa and the cabinet to their own devices. *El Comercio* attacked the government vehemently in its editorials and the army felt the shock of public immorality and political disorder.

By the end of September, the whole cabinet was forced to resign. After several unsuccessful attempts, the president managed to organize a new one on 2 October. But this last cabinet did not survive for more than twenty-four hours. The army had been planning a coup since February, and it now took place ahead of schedule. An armored division on maneuvers forty kilometers from the capital cut short its practice and marched on the presidential palace.

Conclusion

To sum up, then, my main points are the following. Because of the dependent relationship forged between the Peruvian oligarchy and foreign capital, there developed in Peru a system of enclave economies. This prevented the rise of an independent national bourgeoisie which could have developed the economy and controlled enough resources to give in to some of the demands of the popular sectors. Consequently, when faced with popular mobilization in the 1930s, the oligarchy was forced to rely on the army and follow a policy of intense repression.

When foreign investment extended to the industrial and banking sectors in the 1950s, Peru's economy began to lose its enclave nature. Yet it was precisely this expansion of international capital which reaffirmed the extreme precariousness of the Peruvian bourgeoisie and state, sealing the fate of both. The ensuing changes in the country's demographic and occupational structures intensified and extended the class struggle, and new lower-class groups entered the political arena. In an attempt to maintain control in this situation of social-structural transformation, the Peruvian oligarchy began an experiment with democratic institutions in 1956. This experiment was carried on between 1963 and 1968 with the Acción Popular regime of Fernando Belaúnde. But the two mass parties—APRA and Acción Popular—were unable to agree on a coalition because of their differing historical backgrounds and their differing bases of political support. In effect, the fact that the modern section of the bourgeoisie, together with the army and the church, supported Acción Popular and its program of reforms and not APRA stemmed from their fear that APRA would modernize the country by means of a popular mobilization. They saw such mobilization as a threat, because it might set into motion a process which would end up destroying their autonomy and special interests. Thus APRA allied itself with the traditional UNO group in Congress, and through continual blockage of Belaúnde's reformist proposals brought Acción Popular to its knees. The army, fearful of the threat to internal security presented by the political crisis, and convinced that the only road to stabilization was through structural reform, stepped in to institute the reformist policies that the Acción Popular government had been unable to put into practice. As carried out by the army, however, these reforms had a clear technocratic and administrative character designed to obviate any possibility that the masses might take the initiative and develop politically in an autonomous manner. Thus the revolutionary government of the armed forces realized a good part of the program of the Acción Popular and of the original plans of APRA, but without direct participation of the political parties or of the popular classes.

NOTES

1. Fernando Henrique Cardoso and Enzo Faletto, *Dependencia y desarrollo en América Latina* (Mexico City: Ed. Siglo XXI, 1969).
2. Shane Hunt, "Growth and Guano in Nineteenth Century Peru," Discussion Paper no. 34, Research Program in Economic Development (Princeton, N.J.: Woodrow Wilson School of Public and International Affairs, February 1973).
3. William Bollinger, "The Rise of U.S. Influence in the Peruvian Economy, 1869–1921," (M.A. thesis, University of California, 1972); James C. Carey, *Peru and the United States, 1900–1962* (Notre Dame, Ind.: University of Notre Dame Press, 1964); Rosemary Thorpe and Geoff Bertram, "Industrialization in an Open Economy, 1870–1940," manuscript (Oxford University, 1974).

4. Aníbal Quijano, "El Perú en la crisis de los años treinta," in *La crisis de los años treinta en América Latina,* ed. Pablo Gonzáles Casanova (Mexico City: UNAM, forthcoming); De-Wind Adrian, "De campesinos a mineros," *Estudios Andinos,* no. 2, 1974–76, pp. 1–32.

5. Julio Cotler, "The Mechanics of Internal Domination and Social Change in Peru," in *Masses in Latin America,* ed. Irving L. Horowitz, (New York: Oxford University Press, 1970), pp. 407–44.

6. Peter F. Klarén, *Modernization, Dislocation and Aprismo: Origins of the Peruvian Aprista Party, 1870–1932,* Latin American Monographs no. 2, Institute of Latin American Studies (Austin: University of Texas Press, 1973).

7. Víctor Raúl Haya de la Torre, *El Antimperialismo y el APRA,* Cuarta Edición (Lima: Editorial-Imprenta Amauta, 1972).

8. For Mariátegui's thought see his *Siete ensayos de interpretación de la realidad peruana* (Lima: Biblioteca Amauta, 1971), and his *Ideología y política* (Lima: Biblioteca Amauta, 1971.)

9. Rosemary Thorpe, "The Expansion of Foreign Ownership in Peru in the 1960's: A Perspective on the Military's Economic Policy," manuscript (Oxford University, 1976).

10. See François Bourricaud, *Power and Society in Contemporary Peru* (New York: Praeger Publishers, 1970), pt. 2, chap. 4; pt. 3, chap. 1.

11. Hugo Blanco, *Tierra o muerte* (Mexico City: Ed. Siglo XXI, 1973); Julio Cotler and Felipe Portocarrero, "Peru: Peasant Organizations," in *Latin American Peasant Movements,* ed. Henry A. Landsberger (Ithaca, N.Y.: Cornell University Press, 1969), pp. 297–322; Wesley Craig, "From Hacienda to Community: An Analysis of Solidarity and Social Change in Peru," Latin American Studies Program, Cornell University (Dissertation Series no. 6, 1967); David Collier, *Squatters and Oligarchs: Authoritarian Rule and Policy Change in Peru* (Baltimore, Md.: Johns Hopkins University Press, 1976).

12. Luigi R. Einaudi et al., "Latin American Institutional Development: The Changing Catholic Church" (Santa Monica, Ca.: Rand Corporation, 1969).

13. Primera semana social del Perú, *Exigencias sociales del catolicismo en el Perú* (Lima: agosto, 1959).

14. Víctor Villanueva, *El CAEM y la revolución peruana* (Lima: Instituto de Estudios Peruanos, 1972).

15. CAEM, *El Estado y la política general* (Chorrillos: CAEM, 1963), p. 92.

16. Ministerio de Guerra, "Los guerrillas en el Perú y su represión" (Lima: Ministerio de Guerra, 1966).

17. Guillermo Hoyos Osores, "Crisis de la democracia en el Perú," *Cuadernos Americanos* (México: enero-febrero, 1969), pp. 7–31.

18. Jane Jaquette, "The Politics of Development in Peru" (Ph.D. diss., Cornell University, 1971), pp. 139–40.

19. Richard Goodwin, "Letter from Peru," *The New Yorker,* 17 May 1969.

20. Richard Gott, *Guerrilla Movements in Latin America* (New York: Doubleday and Co., 1971), pp. 307–94; Hector Béjar, *Peru 1965: Notes on a Guerrilla Experience* (New York: Monthly Review Press, 1969).

21. For a detailed discussion of this and other aspects of the development, see Julio Cotler, "Political Crisis and Military Populism in Peru," *Studies in Comparative International Development* 6 no. 5 (1970–71): 95–113; and Jaquette, "Politics of Development."

Biographical Notes

JULIO COTLER is Senior Researcher at the Instituto de Estudios Peruanos, in Lima, and has been a Professor at the University of San Marcos and at the Universidad Nacional Autónoma de México. He received his doctorate in sociology from the University of Bordeaux in 1960. He has just completed *Clases, estado, y nación en el Perú*, is co-editor, with Richard Fagen, of *Latin America and the United States: The Changing Political Realities*, and has published extensively on peasant movements, corporatism, military populism, internal domination, and dependency.

DANIEL LEVINE is Associate Professor of Political Science at the University of Michigan and, during 1978–79, Visiting Fulbright Professor at the National University of Guatemala. He received his doctorate from Yale University in 1970. He is the author of *Conflict and Political Change in Venezuela* and has published widely on Venezuelan politics, the Catholic Church, Latin American social change, and political culture.

JUAN J. LINZ is Pelatiah Perit Professor of Political and Social Science at Yale University. He received his doctorate from Columbia University in 1959 and has taught at Columbia University, Stanford University, the University of Madrid, and the Universidad Autónoma of Madrid. He is Chairman of the Committee on Political Sociology of the International Sociological and Political Science Associations. His publications include "Totalitarian and Authoritarian Regimes," in *Handbook of Political Science*, ed. F. Greenstein and N. Polsby; "Some Notes toward a Comparative Study of Fascism in Comparative Sociological Perspective," in *Fascism*, ed. W. Laquer; and numerous monographs and essays on Spanish elites and entrepreneurs, quantitative history, and parties and elections in Spain and Germany.

GUILLERMO O'DONNELL is Director and founder of CEDES (Centro de Estudios de Estado y Sociedad) in Buenos Aires. He did advanced studies in law and political science at the National University of Buenos Aires and Yale University and has been a Visiting Professor at the University of Michigan and a Fellow of the Institute for Advanced Study, Princeton. His publications include *Modernization and Bureaucratic-Authoritarianism: Studies in South American Politics*, and, with Delfina Linck, *Dependencia y Autonomía*. He is currently completing a book on the "bureaucratic-authoritarian" period in Argentina between 1966 and 1973.

PETER H. SMITH is Chairman of the Department of History, University of Wisconsin at Madison. He received his doctorate from Columbia University in 1966. Among his many publications are *Politics and Beef in Argentina: Patterns of Conflict and Change; Argentina and the Failure of Democracy: Conflict Among Political Elites, 1904–1955;* and *Labyrinths of Power: Political Recruitment in Twentieth-Century Mexico.*

ALFRED STEPAN is Professor of Political Science at Yale University and frequently serves as Chairman of Yale's Council on Latin American Studies. He received his doctorate from Columbia University in 1969 and has taught at Yale since then. He has been a Guggenheim Fellow and, from 1978 to 1979, will be a Visiting Fellow at St. Antony's College, Oxford University. He has published *The Military in Politics: Changing Patterns in Brazil* and *The State and Society: Peru in Comparative Perspective*. He is the editor of *Authoritarian Brazil: Origins, Policies, and Future,* and co-editor, with Bruce Russett, of *Military Force and American Society.*

ALEXANDER WILDE is a Research Associate in the Woodrow Wilson International Center for Scholars in Washington, D.C. He received his doctorate in political science from Columbia University in 1972 and has taught at the University of Wisconsin at Madison and at Haverford College. He is the author of various articles on politics and religion, as well as the book, *Politics and the Church in Colombia*. With Arturo Valenzuela he has written studies on budgetary politics in Chile. He has just completed a monograph, *Conversaciones de caballeros: La democracia oligárquica en Colombia*.

Index